~~~~~~~~~~~~~~~~~~~~~~~~~~~~~

Hug Abroad

~~~~~~~~~~~~~~~~~~~~~~~~~~~~~

Simple

Service

Overseas

By Kimi Cassia

Table of Contents

Chapter 1
March to a Different Drummer

So, what would you do if you really did get on a plane and fly overseas? How would you bless the people? Well, what is your natural talent or passion? Fishing you say? OK. This is one dream I have if you were to come visit me abroad; let me paint it for you.

"Stand in line!" The translation echoed in Spanish across the front yard. We were the house at the end of a country gravel road in the middle of a mountain range somewhere in Latin America. Acres filled with tall, slim pine trees interspersed with an occasional tropical bush surrounded the home.

Small fisher boys and girls from the country neighborhood stood in a line, gently shoving and pushing a little, making the line straighter. A group of native adults smiled, watching from a distance under the shade of the tall plantain trees lining the fence.

In a friendly voice you yelled out "How many of you don't have fishing poles?"

Hands shot in the air, some empty, but most in a tightly clenched fist filled with their homemade do-jiggers. The temptation to raise their hand was greater than their ability to wait.

Two-inch hand-carved H-shaped poles seemed to be the most popular. A few others had carved branches looped with a wad of fishing line tied on to the very ends.

"Please share your poles with those who have none after you have caught your fish. How many need fishing line?"

Hands went up in the air, many with the other one hiding their pole wrapped in fishing line.

"Go over to the volunteers to get your line, if you need some."

Everyone moved toward the volunteers. It wasn't every day one could get free fishing line.

The adults were called over and asked to help with the hooks. Each child had to fish with one adult, each adult with two children.

The rules were easy. If you caught a fish, you had to stop fishing, give away your pole to someone who didn't have one, and got to keep your fish.

All fish must be pulled out if they are on the line. No throwbacks.

"Adults who refrain from grabbing poles out of the hands of kids will be allowed to fish afterward."

The adults chuckled and elbowed each other.

The huge water basin behind the house had been stocked with seventy-two medium-sized Talapia bought from the fisheries down the hill.

What would the fish eat? It was BYOW (bring your own worm). Handfuls of worms squirmed about in open palms, jars, cups, or caps.

Little Juanito had a handful of dead flies to offer his fish.

We were almost ready.

Excitement filled the air.

First prize for the largest fish was ten dollars and a new kid-sized fishing pole brought from the US. Second prize for the first fish caught was five dollars and a packet of fancy lures—an unseen, unknown item here. Third prize for the smallest fish was three dollars and a plastic worm bucket.

All children would get to pick from a bag of Jesus stickers and a bag of erasers.

On Sunday at a local church, caps emblazoned with "Jesus, Fisher of Men" in Spanish and English would be handed out by you and the volunteers, to the first thirty regular church-attending children who could recite Matthew 4:19–20. Just to be safe, you brought fifty caps. There would be a lot of kids at church this coming Sunday, maybe close to two hundred.

You also received an invitation from the church to give your testimony during the service. The children would listen and remember the stories of their special US friend recounting what you said, looked like, did, why you came, and wonder if you'll return to visit again. As a guest you will be long remembered and spoken of by name by the children in this community.

"Who is the most famous fisher of all men?"

"Jesus," a few answered quickly.

"How does he catch us?"

A native leader from the church asked more questions, taught for about ten minutes, repeated Sunday's verse to be memorized, and then led in prayer, "May we all be fishers of men".

After that, it was fishing fun time.

This dream includes you, needs you to visit and bless us in a real way, and do what you can to love your neighbor in this nation. Your small fishing activity would invite neighborhood children to our house, require them to invent their own poles, recognize talent, award three top winners, make each child a winner, provide a fish for the family dinner, share your faith, have a Bible verse memorized, gather children to church, and gift a piece of clothing. Your time and talent would be greatly appreciated. We're just waiting to be loved.

Your gift of friendship, fun and encouragement will bury itself in the hearts of your overseas loved ones. For a moment you may fill the place of a sister, brother, mother, father, grandpa, grandma, or best friend, by giving advice, recognition and encouragement, or sometimes just a simple hug.

This is the gift of Dorcas, to love our neighbors. Dorcas, from the bible, was a woman doing what she could to serve her neighbors. She sewed garments for the widows. Like Dorcas, your simple talents are valuable, dare I say purposeful, in this life. These simple talents can be guided to serve others in a big way.

~I am just one, but the power of one doubles with just one more.~

Sharing your talent not only blesses your overseas neighbors but also empowers them to become the teachers. Your influence will continue in the lives of those you touch as your passion is passed on by them. Any teaching done in a school setting for students will be absorbed by the instructors also, who may utilize parts of your teaching for years.

Our Father ordered us to love him first, and said secondly, "*Thou shalt love thy neighbor as thyself*" (Mark 12:31). We need to be told, reminded, that this is a commandment. He meant for your neighbors to love you too, brothers and sisters united, exchanging talents, passions and life. This exchange was meant to be double-sided. There is a unique purpose we fulfill together that can only happen when we share the same moment in time. Your hidden talents can bless many and, counted all together, can bless a nation. Get prepared, get on the plane, and team up with our talented overseas leaders to be a part of the solution. Then when you return home, continue to bless others with your hidden talents; be confident, get involved, and keep moving in any neighborhood you find yourself in.

I'm writing this to you or for someone you know and love who has a heart like mine. This story is for those chosen few, who yearn to live even if it means giving up a comfortable lifestyle for a time. It is for those willing to love more, maybe to be loved less—for those who know there is more to each day, although the days may be fewer. My hope is to inspire in you the courage to do what you were meant to complete in this life, as incomplete as you may feel. If God could use only perfect people, he would have an army of one.

This I do also for my beloveds—those who are waiting for you to come into their lives to befriend them, encourage and work alongside them, maybe even feed and bless them with the love of belonging because they have no one to belong to. And for the mothers that were praying before their deaths that you would come and be there for their children in some small way—to hug them, hold them, have fun with them, and show that they are loveable and of value, in her place. God has chosen you to be the connection just for this moment, to fulfill His promise to them that He will provide His love. Just being yourself and doing what you are capable of doing is all that God asks of you. He is not seeking perfection, only faithful action. We are patiently waiting to meet you.

~Your experience may be short, or maybe it will stretch into years, but your service will be valued and appreciated and will become a positive part of the eternal value of life.~

As you read my words, imagine yourself making decisions different from mine. Imagine working with those here who have come before you. Feel the reality of living life free to daily serve. God has a plan for your life. He needs you to be open in order to be in the right place at the right time. Embrace loss as it becomes gain. Educate yourself and be prepared; the door will open in a way and when you least expect it. Your time to become His hands extended is intentional. Believe He will guide you and then go.

"Could I come visit you in Latin America?"
"Sure, come on down."
"What will I be doing?"
"Let's see when you get here."

A new kind of traveler is making the headlines: A hiker helps build a school, a college student helps dig a well, a hairdresser provides a library, a retired couple found an orphanage. Regular folk are doing irregular works all over the globe. These new travelers develop their vision while on their trips offering what they can to the neighbors they have met. Off the beaten path these travelers discover their purpose and fulfill it to the best of their abilities.

Most people travel overseas with groups if they are not visiting family or friends. These trips are organized and overseen by people who know about the important pitfalls, pleasures, laws, and culture of the new country. They provide classes or guides with tours set up to help a new guest travel safely, joyfully, and supervised. As the world has opened up to the casual traveler, more and more people are deciding to travel on their own. They make their own airline reservations, learn about travel laws, get shots, find hotels, exchange money, take taxis or buses, and buy food, sometimes in various countries, each one with a different language and possibly very different cultures. These travelers have grown from being primarily young and single to include older retired visitors, and now embrace families with children. Gender has become less of an issue; men or women of any age can be seen travelling alone. They choose to become a part of a new country for a time, just being themselves, visiting another part of their world, letting the unknown lead.

While living overseas, I have met many of these people. They are not part of a group, not with a company and they are not international students. Their hearts led them to come and share life for a time with their brothers and sisters of a different nation. Their presence affects the lives of the people they meet—other travelers and natives alike. The small things they do, the encouraging things they say and the investment they make in the friendships formed empower the people they eventually leave behind. Each act of kindness, each morsel shared, each smile or laugh, each small gift lightens the heart of the receiver who needs to be filled in order to support others who are needier. These travelers individually do make a difference in the lives of the people they meet; each drop in the bucket gets it closer to overflowing. This unspoken mission field has been silently active for centuries although formally unrecognized by the church community. Like Dorcas, these regular men and women have always been around, active wherever they are.

If today Dorcas were a hairdresser she would pamper ladies with a new cut. If she were a construction worker she would oversee a simple but correctly done roof repair, a gardener to supervise the planting of a few home gardens, a dog lover to teach a non-abusive dog-training class, a basketball player to organize a fun neighborhood playoff, or a photographer to organize a "prettiest yard" competition. She surely would visit and chat with students who are studying conversational English in public and private schools or offer conversation and her testimony freely in any church or neighborhood. She would hug and serve wherever she could touch a life. The list of what one can do is as varied as the passions God gave you. Your simple service was given to you to share.

Dorcas multiplied would have an effect. This effect would be like a spark, bringing a flash of life into daily living; spreading your talent, your passion, and joy to those like yourself, those ready and eager to receive it throughout the world. With your service you can also choose to model your faith, touching individuals by supporting those who are already leading or by challenging others to a higher standard. We need you now to share your talent and passion in service, the one you've been dreaming of sharing. A talent unused is worthless; a talent shared brings life.

Let's see if you are one of those called to offer a simple service overseas. Get ready to take a break from your world so we can join forces for a short time to see what our sparks ignite—it could be fun.

Somewhere in Latin America

The coconut trees were at least fifty feet high, taller than most I had seen in a private setting. They graced us with a little shade that was in slight movement, swaying gently in the cooling breeze. This detention center was in the middle of expansive tropical beauty—perfectly picturesque nature surrounded us on all sides. Tangala was blessed with being the agriculture production farm for all the other national detention centers. They provided vegetables, fruit, chicken, pork, and cattle products for everyone else. The boys here did farm work, a healthy work that provided a free-feeling kind of mental release from their reality while exercising the whole body.

Three boys hung around Sister Rose, not really paying attention to her but curious of our conversational exchange in English nonetheless.

"When I planted those coconut trees thirty years ago, I never imagined I would still be here today to see them," she remarked, a little amazed.

Sister Rose was a Catholic nun from the States. Dressed in a blue and white uniform dress, she was as round as she was tall. Her blue eyes pierced through her glasses.

"Thirty years is a long time."

"Yes, I was thirty-nine when I first came." She focused in on me. "So, what is it you want to do?"

"Well, I can visit on weekends, if that's OK."

She paused. "What activities would you like to do with the boys?"

"I don't know. What do you think?"

"How about basketball? They play but they don't know the rules, looks like a mess."

Basketball is a sissy sport here, dominated by girls playing in every schoolyard in the country. Being female, it was assumed I played, but at five foot one had never really taken the sport seriously.

"I don't know anything about basketball."

"OK. Do you sing?"

I blushed at the thought of leading 112 boys in song. "No."

Then it hit me—but I presented the idea slowly. "I can visit the boys who never have visitors."

Every Saturday was visitor's day at the center. Family and friends could enter inside the grounds and freely visit their loved one. They brought food, clothes, pictures, and news from home. They smiled and laughed, and when it was time to depart cried. And every Saturday, sometimes for years, there were some boys who no one ever visited. Yet every Saturday they waited, a bit distanced from the arrivals, inconspicuous, wondering silently if maybe this would be the Saturday someone, anyone, would come to visit them.

"Perfect," she said, then whirled around and started walking away, turning her head only slightly to continue the conversation. "I'll let you know which ones they are."

Suddenly my talent was clear; I would be a family visitor. Like Dorcas, my service began where there was a simple need.

This new position in life made me a server. The people would refer to me as an independent missionary. Yet, my actions were simply what a common person overseas could do to reach out to their brothers and sisters. No church had sent me. I was not specially trained. Those of us from the branch of Dorcas do have our place; we are good neighbors. We commonly belong to a church in our new community and are active with them. This gives us an opportunity to be effective where others aren't, to touch where others have missed, to be there when others have gone. We may not be evangelists or teachers or preachers. We're just Christians visiting or living our lives in a neighborhood far from the United States. As situations come up, we realize that something can be done. We pray about it with our church, get informed, and then we get into action, together. We learn from the ground up. Maybe our talents do not create great waves of excitement, but they do fill in the holes by recognizing each life to be valuable.

God has called more of us than are here, but like the one-talent slave, too many have buried their talent, waiting for an unknown sign or undefined time. Each one of us has at least one seemingly insignificant, somewhat unprofessional talent. Hopefully, yours will be put to work, not buried awaiting our Lord's return. If you are sitting on your God-given purpose, you can feel it. There is a deep desire in you to jump into action and do what you can. In these last times before Christ's victorious return, we really must make the effort to get moving. Who do you think is supposed to invite the "last soul" to become a believer?

In the US churches we sing, with our hearts in our throats, "Lord, send me." Watching the notices on TV of children walking miles to drink contaminated, infectious drinking water, we insist, "This must be fixed." Learning that every minute a baby dies from malaria, we shout, "Where is the protection?!" Prepare to be led. You are His hands extended.

Independent overseas servers do get up and go. This I know because there are many of us here already, often times working alongside the long-term and short-term missionaries sent by their churches and the native missionaries already in action; we're united. Today's short-term missionary teams are a powerful addition to the service of the long-term missionaries. Serving in astounding numbers, they gift us with small miracles that can touch an entire community. They are incredibly effective in many ways while visiting for no longer than a week or two. These same people, independently returning to serve on their own, can be counted as from the branch of Dorcas. Together, long-term, short-term, and independent missionaries can complete His will for these end times. He is equipping us, the common saints, to touch our brother and sister saints in all of the world. We need just a bit of your time. Step out of your parade and march to a different drummer.

Chapter 2

Leaving All Behind

"WHERE are you going?"
"You can't help ALL the poor of the world!"
"Tell me you didn't sell your house."
"Can I come visit you? I need a vacation."
"Isn't there a war going on there?"
"You'll be back before you know it."
"Why would you want to go THERE?"
"Hasta la vista, baby."

I had heard it all. My decision to get on a plane and visit a new nation for a time had not been easy.

My first glimpse out the plane window was just as we were landing. Looking out over miles and miles as far as one could see were rolling hills backed by a huge cascade of mountain peaks surrounding us on all sides. Tiny houses roofed in clay shingles cooking in the heat of day covered the landscape. Straining, I tried to imagine the life going on below, a new life foreign to me, different yet similar in many ways. With fear grabbing at me I tried to act calm. I was in shock but tried to look cool. I was alone but full of purpose. As the wheels of the plane touched the runway, the strain of the motors and the brakes vibrated throughout the plane. We lurched forward, back and then quickly came to a stop. Suddenly, all the passengers on the plane erupted in applause. We had landed and we were safe. Evidently, this was a great accomplishment.

Leaving the open door of the plane, we were greeted by a gush of hot air. It felt toasty but good compared to the cold of the North. My first reactions were overwhelming. It felt as if I had just returned home, as if I had been gone a long time but was finally back. We walked a short distance, entering the immigration area of the airport. Standing in the tourist line I felt a strong desire to be in the resident line. As my visa was stamped and temporary residency papers stapled, my country contact arrived alongside me. It was my distant cousin, Greg, who was a little older than me. Looking tall at five foot ten with dark brown hair, he blended into the Hispanic crowd, given away only by his baby-blue eyes. He had been living in this country for the last eight years, staying after finishing his Peace Corps service, and had agreed to help me during my arrival time.

~It's always best to have a country contact waiting for you at the airport but every day many tourists worldwide go it alone so you could too.~

Our greeting was pleasant as he ushered me through the crowd to the carousel displaying my two suitcases. He picked them up with a heave; they were heavy. I felt grateful for his help. These two suitcases held all I had brought with me of my previous thirty-six years of existence. When you answer the call to follow God's purpose in your life, sometimes He asks for it all or almost all. There I was with nothing but two suitcases and an undamaged belief that the best was yet to come.

Latin America may seem like a far-off, distant part of the world to most, but to me it held an image full of life, revealing a precious yet unknown future, permitting me to become a complete version of my real self, something I could never experience by knowing only the United States. It teased me with a view of life and love from another side of reality, the side to where you must go if you want to experience it, must stay to become intimate, must stretch yourself to become all that you can be and less of what you were. To be honest, shock set in. Boy, I had really done it now; here I was. A thought terrified me; how can I survive *here*? Then my heart beat ecstatically; life was beginning anew. And I shouldn't admit this, but homesickness had hit me, even before landing. All these emotions meshed together. Yet, this seemed to be the right place, this new place that held a mysterious future for me that was beyond what I could imagine.

Greg helped me exchange a few dollars for the national currency, nick named pesos, after the Mexican dollar. The exchange rate was seven to one, so I got a pile of "pesos" for my dollars.

~You can usually find a very good currency exchange at any overseas airport—just make sure you know the rate and figure out how much you should be receiving beforehand.~

We then flagged down an old, rickety yellow taxi. Greg negotiated with the driver in Spanish.

"The Little Pico is very far," said the driver to no one in particular.

And it is where the rich live.

"Yes, I live there." Greg spoke with highly correct Spanish grammar and a nearly native accent.

"Two hundred pesos."

"I could take a taxi to Valley of the Angels for that amount."

A planned pause followed then Greg continued, "I usually pay no more than forty-five."

"Forty-five is not a price; it's a gift," challenged the taxi driver.

"All right, I'll pay you too much, sixty pesos. That's my final offer."

"It's a deal, but my family will be hungry tonight. I will make no money on this."

~It's necessary to negotiate the price of your trip before entering the taxi or it could cost you double. Clearly repeat or write down the agreed-upon price.~

It would be a thirty-minute ride for a cost of eight dollars. As the taxi wound up the hillside road sounds trailed behind us: dogs barking, horns honking, roosters crowing, Latin music blaring. Sounds of everyday life hummed together, rising above the city. Trying to imagine what everyday life was like; my mind absorbed the reality around me. It felt good, it felt peaceful, it felt a little bit known. Farther and farther up the winding potholed road we maneuvered, passing great mansions on either side almost completely hidden by high stone walls covered with giant-leafed tropical trees and huge flowering plants. There definitely was great wealth here. Mile after mile we passed mansions that were huge, exotic, and beautiful, almost a surreal sight in this struggling country. Small shacks called homes filled the spaces between the mansions, mixing extreme poverty with what could be seen as abhorrent riches.

We finally arrived at the bumpy dirt road that led us to Greg and his wife's humble home. Their yard was large and sparsely filled with towering pine trees. This country is very proud of its great amount of pine that covers much of the nation. It smelled like the North gone tropical. Banana trees, plantain, and all types of citrus fruit trees mixed in with the pines, creating a new tropical vegetation collage.

Located right next to the parking area outside the home was a human-sized metal cage where their pet, Mapache—a raccoon—lived. Mapache was known for looking friendly just before snatching whatever you held right out of your hand, running to the middle of his cage, and throwing it down a tube, where it was extremely hard to retrieve. He was excited to see us.

From the front door of their white brick home, Sonia, Greg's wife appeared, her shoulder-length black hair shining in the sun. Smiling beautifully, she gave me a pleasant welcome in Spanish, which warmed me to her. I had met her briefly three years previously during my first trip to this country with my mom, dad, and sister for their wedding. She had been a beautiful bride and now was opening her home to me and didn't show her nervousness.

Greg had met Sonia in a small, hot, dusty town—San Jose—far from the capital. Hidden in a valley surrounded by majestic mountain ranges reaching high into the sky on all sides and divided by a smooth, flat, lazily winding river, San Jose was located in one of the most picturesque locations of this nation. Crossing over the top of the mountains into the valley, you had a bird's-eye view looking down on San Jose, much like the view from a plane. Because of this huge mountainous divide, the townspeople considered themselves country folk and the rest of us on the other side of the mountains as city dwellers.

The sunrise in this small village is greeted each morning by a gigantic chorus of animal sounds: cows mooing, oxen bellowing, horses neighing, donkeys hee-hawing, chickens clucking, roosters crowing, birds chirping, goats bleating, dogs barking, cats meowing, pigs oinking, and frogs croaking—all at the same time. The sound is fantastically loud and dominates the air for about half an hour. No need for alarm clocks in San Jose; no one could miss the blast of morning music cheering on the new day. Greg was serving in the Peace Corps, and Sonia was doing her internship for her medical studies when they met. She was his perfect vision of Latina beauty and quick as a whip. He fell for her immediately and had to invent an illness excuse in order to meet her. Knowing he couldn't play sick forever, he finally asked her for a date. Pretending to be bothered by the request, she agreed. After finishing his service of two years in the Peace Corps, Greg asked Sonia to marry him. He then was fortunate enough to get a job in the capital helping to develop nationally made school texts, while Sonia continued her studies for her doctoral exams to become a pediatrician. They were very protective of me and had offered to have me stay with them until I found my own apartment. It couldn't have been a better place to unpack.

My reasons for coming to this country were varied. Divorce was one. The other important reason I will share with you too. A car accident had left me in vulnerable health. My heart and immune system were damaged. The doctors advised me to live close to a hospital, yet to try stay out of the hospital because of deadly viruses one could catch there. The loss of my spleen in the accident combined with a low white-blood-cell count meant any flu or cold could be fatal. Antibiotics would be my salvation if I didn't pick up the habit of using them too much.

But the cold weather of the North had gotten to me. For nearly a year my lungs had battled walking pneumonia; my immune system had finally given up the fight. There was an infection in my hair, ears, nose, throat, chest, and on the bottom of my feet, as well as eyes that were blood-streaked. Peaceful breathing eluded me; continuous coughing had left me exhausted. It seemed good health would never be restored. God had saved me from death, so I made the decision to choose life over just living. For thirteen years I had begged God to allow me to serve in another nation and now was the time to make the move. My calling to serve overseas had been answered. As soon as my house sold I said good-bye to my family and church, packed up two suitcases, and left, arriving at the only place on earth where I could live with my very own family doctor in a tropical paradise. My goal was to get well, however long that would take. Strangely, it felt like this was exactly where I was supposed to be for this moment in time.

~Try to be wise in your decisions if you suffer from health problems, some problems maybe too severe and not worth the risk you will find in overseas travel.~

Daily life meant beginning from scratch. A schedule had to be created. Weekdays I woke up to an empty house, as Greg and Sonia had to leave early for work. In order to get down the hill before traffic, they drove together in their only car, a seventeen-year-old, mostly white, tiny Honda Civic that looked pretty beat up but proved to be unusually reliable.

The sun rose brightly every morning at around six a.m., filling the silent house with light. The sun became my tropical alarm clock. Jumping out of bed barefoot, I would patter across the tepid tiles, shower in cool water, and go outside to soak in nature and read my Bible, drinking coffee made from fresh coffee beans. There's nothing like drinking fresh coffee every morning in the country where it is grown.

These moments with God were used to pray for everyone and everything, reflect on years past or just on yesterday, recheck and review major decisions to assure myself I was indeed in His will for my life at this time. Knowing His will comes from spending time with Him, believing not in a religion but a true relationship. Being alone in a new country urges the soul to rely purely on God and His promises. It feels like a need that can't be pushed aside. Feeling vulnerable, as I truly was, it forced me to look toward Him. It was my time to be still and listen to God, so I did.

Later it would be time to go inside to practice my horrid Spanish on the live-in maid. Her name was Maria, just like so many other women I was to meet over the years. In Latin America it is an honor to name your daughter after the Virgin Mary, so you will meet a lot of Marias. Jesus is equally popular and is followed by many other biblical names like Gamaliel, Osni, Israel. This custom of naming surely touches the tender side of our Lord.

~Maids are commonplace in this country and in only a few other Latin nations. Many live-in while others go home each night.~

Maids do help a lot in the home. They help hand wash and line dry the clothes. It is heavy work to hand wash loads of clothes. And daily, most of the year around noon, clouds would start to form so that by two p.m. rain would begin to fall. That meant all your clothes must be washed, dried, and taken in before two. This can be tricky, even on a weekend day. Or if you leave the house while the clothes are still hanging to dry they may be stolen right off the lines, all of them. Sometimes this can happen even while you're home. Imagine working eight to five all week and trying to fit in hand washing and line drying all your family's clothing on the weekends. You can pay someone to wash at about 8 cents per item if you don't have a maid. This service works wonderfully and helps an unemployed or underemployed woman work. She can wash at your house or at her house any day you need her.

~Having another wash your clothes usually results in a few things being stretched, scrubbed too strongly, looking faded, or simply missing. Keep the most expensive and fragile to wash yourself.~

A maid can buy fresh fruits and vegetables midweek at the open-air market, and of course, again early Saturday morning when it's the best but most crowded time to buy fresh foods. Some people get up as early as five thirty to get the best food choices in the outdoor markets on Saturdays as the crowds begin around six thirty. I got up at five thirty only once. The market was filled with smells, some not too nice—maybe from the open-air stalls of hanging meat, or buckets of cheese, or bits of yesterday's smashed vegetables and fruits underfoot. The air was crisp, as the sun had just appeared over the rooftops of the buildings. The fruits and vegetables were bright and beautiful. But my talent is not in negotiating a price; whatever they tell me, I accept. OK is the only word that leaves my mouth. Since I didn't know the prices well it would be easy to be overcharged without even knowing it. If you like to bargain, the open-air markets can be quite fun but maids usually get the best prices.

~If you love to bargain remember not to get too excited. Go ahead and pay the nickel or fifty cents more they're asking.~

The maid does all the household cleaning and cooks the meals. This is really nice. Your home is always well swept, picked up, and the food is waiting for you—plus, there are no after-meal dishes to clean. For a working couple, having a maid frees you up because all these daily chores take more time to get done here than in the US. Maids at this time were usually paid around $130 per month. Greg and Sonia always tried to pay more than the average wage even though in their house there wasn't as much to do. They both left regularly at five thirty for work and, after a long day, would stop by to eat dinner at Sonia's parents' house in town, then returned home around seven to wind down and sleep. Sonia had become an only child after losing both her sisters to untimely childhood deaths, so Greg protected this time she had with her parents and does so even today. Sonia's mother loved cooking for her daughter and son-in-law every evening, enjoying the time to visit too. Greg's accurate Spanish allowed him to chat easily with his parents-in-law, offering him the opportunity to perfect real native Spanish. I have met many visitors that end up spending their days surrounded by English speakers and in all their years spent living overseas they never really learn to speak the language. To become bilingual you must arrange your daily schedule carefully and decide to speak the language as much as possible.

~Taking language classes overseas creates a superb learning opportunity and classes are usually inexpensive. Make the effort to speak the native language each day.~

A true breakfast in Latin countries is hearty—no cereal and milk. Maria would usually serve me an egg, beans, cheese, and tortillas, along with superb coffee. We would attempt a short conversation. Maria was always pleasant, polite, friendly, and worked while we talked. She shared little of her life but joined my attempt at small talk. After years of Spanish classes and a teaching certificate to teach language, you would think my Spanish would be pretty fluent. Well, it wasn't. My university at that time offered degrees only in Spanish literature, not the language. This meant most of the classes I took were in reading and writing Spanish with no amount of time for speaking, albeit for our ten-minute reports at the end of the term. My strength in Spanish was not conversation. I was able teach phrases, grammar, or vocabulary, but speaking was a different and more difficult talent.

Maria became my victim. Each morning I would try to expand my knowledge of Spanish on her. "Good Morning. How did you sleep?" As I became bolder, I attempted to ask more difficult questions that had easily understood answers, a trick most new speakers use. She was very nice to me. Our conversations would last only a minute or two until we were ready to end it only to try again the next day. Every new speaker has to find their Maria.

~It is not proper manners to become friends with the hired help in order to respect the employer/employee relationship inside the home. Be polite but not too friendly.~

As I was too cautious to try travelling alone by bus or taxi, the habit of taking small walks along the road to pass the time satisfied me. Getting to know your neighborhood on foot is the best way to ensure you won't get lost. At each fenced property was a guard or vigilante whom I greeted. This made me feel safer, believing that maybe one of them would help me out if I ever needed it.

~Make casual acquaintances as you explore your neighborhood; they might protect you more than you may ever know.~

The vigilante next to Greg's house was Don Amado, Mr. Beloved. He lived on his own very small piece of land close to the street. His tiny wooden shack was barely three hundred square feet divided into two rooms. Out back was an open-air adobe stove and a wooden latrine. The donkey was often tied up in the shade close to a banana tree, and there were chickens running around, occasionally chased by small half-naked children—the bottom half. Usually the sight was accompanied by a familiar TV jingle echoing in the air. Inside the home I could see a well-swept hard dirt floor and one old wooden chair normally occupied by a young teenage boy. No paint cheered up the room; just a single brilliant light bulb hanging by a cord shone, lighting up the darkness. On the roof was a twisted menagerie of wire on a pole suggesting a homemade antenna that connected itself to very old black-and-white TV that provided an almost clear image. One day a hamburger commercial was blaring, painfully reminding me of the world I had left behind but not forgotten.

The commercial reminded me of what was now my recent past, lurking in the shadows of my present. My new country would offer me a unique blend of the old and new joined into one. Leaving all behind, including my support systems and comforts, offered me a chance to mature in myself. It would be a time to set aside preconceived ideas of life, choose anew, struggle with what was perceived as just or unjust, true or untrue and leap into the unknown to do the best I could at finding the new me to present to the world.

Chapter 3
Seeing with New Eyes

Mr. Beloved's family had a home where they lived more like temporary campers than city dwellers. They watched the TV with wonder of a life gifted to others but denied them. But the truth is, just seeing such a lively, succulent commercial was fun in and of itself, better than not seeing it at all, better than nothing they say. The TV was considered a necessary item, even for the extremely poor. It filled the silence, overwhelmed the mind, brightened the heart with music and movement and was their connection to the rest of the world, to life, love and fantasy, especially for those who could not even read their own name. You can see the conflict TV produces in our overseas lives as a totally unnecessary daily necessity.

"Hmmph," I thought listening to the jingle—only a day's wages for a hamburger combo. I hurt for them and was confused.

"Dear Lord Jesus, give this family one really fun dinner at a hamburger joint."

No, that was from the heart but not right.

"Dear Lord, give these people a good job so they can buy a good house, a car and go to a hamburger joint."

Was that it? Things? Did I just want things for them?

"Jesus, what is it that I want you to do for these people that I have chosen to care about?"

OK, I knew.

"Dear Jesus, bless the authorities and leaders of this nation so they may follow you and bless their people greatly."

That was good; it didn't touch everything but it was OK for now.

It is very easy to want to save and help people with things, giving all our time responding to their needs and not really serving the eternal issues in life—serving the kingdom of God. Jesus comes first always; serving to the poverty is an easy trap to fall into. He wants his children saved spiritually, blessed for eternity, and provided for in this eternal life. So praying for material goods wasn't the answer; it had to be something bigger.

~In fulfilling your purpose your prayers better unite with God's will for you and His people.~

Some will say, "*But the poor will always be with us*" (Mark 4:17). This verse is true but greatly misunderstood. Jesus said that Mary must not choose to serve the poor *over* serving Him. We need to do more than respond to the ailment; we can cure the ailment by encouraging others to choose Jesus, and that must not be lost in our service. Jesus had chosen me to carry this burden of bringing hope and joy. And carrying hope and joy is a wonderful burden. I wondered how to help my neighbors in my new nation, but could think of nothing. It was hard enough trying to take care of myself.

~ Personal reflection in a completely new part of the world is one of the many hidden gifts we get when we choose to serve.~

My walks became full. Every day I would stroll by the same homes, greeting, "Hi, Don Amado," "Good day, Don Fernando," "How is it going, Juan?" Occasionally, a guard would approach and we would attempt a small conversation, usually about the weather or about the United States. I always left them assured that their country was a beautiful, wonderful place, and I was very happy to be here—confessions that surprised but pleased them. They were accustomed to viewing their country as inconsequential. Yet, this country is anything but that. Nature and beauty abound. It is a nation overlooked and thereby blessed by its pristine condition, a precious stone still undiscovered.

~Be sure to share your love for their country often; say what is true for you and refrain from criticizing, especially with casual acquaintances. Help them see and understand your appreciation.~

Absorbed by every detail of the homes and gardens, I would squint through the small breaks in the great gates straining to see inside the yards of the mansions separated from the world as much as they could be. Peering into the small shacks I tried to see and understand what life was like for them, to feel and comprehend what was real. On occasion, children would curiously approach, smiling, giggling, oblivious to their lack of clothing, chattering something to me. This exchange always gave me a sense of acceptance. Maybe this foreign lady did not look too scary or dangerous.

~Most children ask for money, some for candy. It is incredibly wise not to give anything or within seconds you will have a stadium full of children following you, all crying out for a gift.~

Each day I ventured farther and farther away from Greg's house. My hope was to become a bigger part of my new surroundings. It was necessary to conquer the nearby landscapes in order to shake the feelings of loss that could overwhelm me if I let them. Everything from my former life was gone. Well, not gone, but so far away that it felt as if everything had disappeared forever, as if this change was so permanent I would never be able to visit the US again, even though reason assured me it was possible to jump on a plane and return any day. I felt so new and alone, so very sure of my bright yet unknown future, even while filled with anxiousness for today. Expanding the walks made me feel more confident in my new environment while helping me lose weight too. It became a great pleasure, enjoying the discovery of each new home, its trees and flowers. Each corner opened up its secrets, making me feel at home.

One day it was time to decide if I was going to cross the main road or not. A little hesitant to risk expanding my walks along the busier, dustier main road, a corner house caught my eye and curiosity. It was a dirty white color with a small garden in front, each row labeled with a small piece of paper. Lines of sprouts were just peeking up, displaying the straight lines that led to the small post at each end. I wondered what types of tropical vegetables were planted, but I was too timid to approach. The days passed, my walks ending at the road. At home I would scribble out possible conversation bits for my approach thus trying to perfect my spoken Spanish. Seeing three or four young teenage boys working in the garden with an adult I finally got up the courage to cross and begin a conversation. The adult saw me first.

"Hi there."

A look of surprise crossed his face. "Hi."

All three boys froze in motion, poised but silent.

"I'm Kimi. My cousin lives down the street."

"Nice to meet you; I'm Miguel."

"What're you planting?"

"The boys have two rows of carrots, three tomatoes, and one of onions."

"Are these your sons?"

He smiled and glanced back. They grinned almost giggling. "No, this is a government-run detention center."

My eyebrows lifted, giving way to my feelings. Looking around I saw no sign anywhere.

"I am a teacher here," he said.

"Nice to meet you. I'm a teacher too. Maybe someday I can come to visit."

"Yes, we'd be happy to have you," he said, almost as if he believed it would never happen.

They waved me off and got back to work pampering their tiny plants. Maybe Miguel thought I would never come back, but he didn't realize how desperate I was to be busy doing something and learning the language with the people. My goal was to be a part of this country. I wasn't just a lost sissy visitor looking for a nice way to spend my vacation. I was permanently lost. Maybe the boys needed me as much as I needed them; we could help each other carry our weights.

These boys had been accused of illegal actions or found living on the streets. They were temporarily placed in this home for thirty days until family could be contacted or the court could decide sentencing. At this time it was illegal to live on the streets. If allowed, street life would quickly lead to more committed crimes and it was dangerous way of life for anyone, especially children. This meant street children had all committed a crime according to the law, even if it was only to be found hanging around a lot on the streets. They would be arrested and brought directly to the center. If someone from their family did not come to get them within the thirty days, they would become wards of the court and held until they turned eighteen. The boys who were not reunited or had actually committed crimes were then sent to a permanent facility in the country—a two-hour bus ride from the capital which ensured little chance of family contact.

One day a tall, slender, blond "gringo" (white foreign male) was entering the house with a small entourage of teenage boys. His name was Johnnie; he was a regular volunteer in the center. Walking over I immediately introduced myself and asked if he needed help. He invited me in to show me around. The house was sprinkled with a few old wood furnishings. The boys were very sparsely dressed and it was cold and dark inside. The walls could have used new paint. It was a little depressing but well swept and in order.

Johnnie's ministry was an independent missionary service. He was living in this country with his wife and five children, not sent by his church but receiving independent US support to serve. Johnnie and his family attended an Evangelical church in town, and on their way there would round up willing teens to go to church with them every weekend ending the day by taking them out for cheap tacos and a coke. This quickly worked into weekday visits, assisting with employment, encouraging studies, giving personal support, and creating a Christian soccer team. His service also included the boys in the center. Johnnie would visit the boys each week, bringing them treats, presenting a biblical teaching, praying, then showing a movie or playing a game or sport. He was the light of their lives. He was serving boys by showing them Christ's love, teaching from the Bible, and encouraging them as a father. We called them "Johnnie's Boys."

~It is best to join the ministry or work for someone already successfully serving. Your talent or passion may branch out of that experience or eventually you may be left on your own.~

One project he had going with the boys was making friendship bracelets and ankle bands to sell. With the money they would buy extra food from the neighborhood *pulperia* store, junk food like chips or a Coke. The boys were motivated as they loved to eat. Johnnie bought the embroidery thread (which was a little expensive) and the boys sold their goods for one dollar each, considered quite a bargain for them.

Becoming shy about approaching the boys, I held up a short story.

"Anyone want to read me a book?"

No one volunteered.

"I'll buy a friendship bracelet from whoever will read to me."

Alonso, one of the taller boys, was the first to volunteer.

We went aside so the other boys could not hear him read and maybe laugh.

"I don't read so well."

"That's OK. I don't speak Spanish that well."

He read the book—which was about keeping your faith during difficult times—with only a little struggle. Then I read the book to him, struggling the whole time. When we finished he asked me which colors would be best for my bracelet. Barefoot he sat on top of the large dining room table, put his foot up near him, tied the embroidery string on his toes and began weaving my bracelet. A bracelet would take about an hour to weave if you were good. Rodrigo came up to me and offered to read next. He said he could read better than Alonso. The reading and weaving were a success. My visits included bringing plenty of money to buy bracelets and ankle bands. And, of course, these items made excellent gifts for my friends and family at home for only a dollar each!

~ Reading with young people is a great way to learn Spanish and a solid help for them in their reading abilities.~

Every visit I observed Johnnie showing his love through fun and games and learned from him. The time was enjoyable but seemed to always be weighted down by the news that one or two of the boys had gone—either home to be with his family or shipped to the detention center. They just disappeared; I never even got to say good-bye.

And saying good-bye was an emotional requirement for me at this time. Missing my family in the US horribly; culture shock was taking hold. Any emotional need not satisfied at the moment would unleash these feelings. Depression would overcome me in an instant. Sometimes it felt as if I had just been told someone I loved had died. Keeping these feelings at bay was necessary. Burying these momentary shock waves became normal, but at home I would relive the decisions made that culminated in my move. Crying over missed celebrations I would then worry about health issues. Beans, rice, tortillas and so much Spanish tired me. It felt as if everything had been lost, even though so much had been gained. Sadness hung over like a cloud ready to burst. I tried to hide it and pretend it wasn't there, but in secret it was always with me.

Culture shock is a necessary passage of rite when you change countries. You cannot physically be separated from everything you have known and loved and not be affected, regardless of how positive the new experience is. It really cannot be avoided; it's just that each person is different in their intensity and responses. When a couple arrives it will usually hit one and then the other later. Perhaps you will suffer within the first thirty days or at the end of two years. Maybe you'll scream and cry or maybe you'll be silent. For a family, the emotional chaos may hit them one at a time, lasting for most of the year, so being aware of this helps tremendously.

~Culture shock does go away; it is a feeling.~

Once you get through it, you will return home with new eyes; you will claim two countries as yours. Culture shock helps us become more sensitive to newcomers to the US, returning soldiers or children in transition like foster children. With culture shock you will realize that just because you are in this country, it does not mean you become native; you are still American. Time will let you know you will never be exactly like one born here. You will think like an American, discuss like an American, and laugh at jokes like an American living in another country. Your Spanish may grow to be quite fluent or it may not.

Yet, you will change and blend in to your new culture in small ways. Maybe you won't get so upset when your hair gets rained on. Maybe you will tear a paper towel in half to clean up a little spill. Maybe you will wait a long time for the bus and not even notice the delay. Immigrants coming to the US have been told by a few they must become Americans, whatever that means. Now, you will better understand their plight. Once home again, you will begin to be the bridge for US newcomers, realizing it is you that must speak up to ignorant comments—nicely, of course. And your native friends will be doing the same for you during your time with them.

Chapter 4
Serving with Those Who Lead

Joyous times were found most Saturdays with Greg and Sonia, who liked to take long rides discovering the countryside beauty. We went to Rosalia, where Greg had trained in the Peace Corps. It was an adorably quaint village on a steep hillside looking over the capital in the far-off distance. Walking around, we stopped in various wooden-shack shops selling intricately designed carved wood chests, rustic clay pots and figurines, or colorful hand woven hammocks. Outside donkeys were tied to posts, goats precariously stood on ledges to soak in the sun, tropical flowers overflowed in the tiny gardens and the old Catholic church stood gracefully overlooking the valley. Life from ancient times was cemented here, giving a look into the past despite the encroachment of the future. It was a tourist's dream.

Another Saturday they took me to Lake Oja, renowned as our only lake. We lunched at an open-air lakeside restaurant/hotel. It was almost empty except for a few US Air Force soldiers from the base located in Aguasales who were there with their bargain priced prostitutes. They were drinking beer, playing pool and in turn disappearing down the stairs to a cabaña. As an American female, it felt quite uncomfortable and embarrassing to see this side of our Air Force, but it is the side that the nationals always see.

It was a wonderful lakeside lunch, whole fire-baked fish (complete with eyeballs) and green plantains fried like Jo-Jos. We ate, talked, laughed, and relaxed, absorbing the great feeling of nature and water. Then, curiously, we saw rain beginning to fall on the other side of the lake while we were seated in pure sunshine. A great cumbersome dark cloud moved across the lake, pelting down rain. Then, like a wall it approached us, descending upon the restaurant, blowing the tablecloths in fury and raining on the outer tables. We all moved into the center as the cloud storm passed. It was marvelous. Nature is grand in this country. Nature wins.

Some weekends we would go shopping in the downtown area of the capital, picking up odds and ends and shopping for foodstuffs. Some stores were just like at home except smaller in size. You could find anything you craved, but you had to pay the high price for luxury. Clothing stores were stocked full of small-sized clothing, Americans are a bigger group of people. These outings with Greg and his wife helped me learn enough about my new home that it was time to begin venturing out more on my own.

~Bring lots of clothes and comfortable shoes with you, even though on occasion you can find something here the cost may be high and the choices limited.~

Five weeks had passed since my arrival. The highlight of my weeks was my volunteer time at the detention center. My daily walks expanded to cover the opposite side of the main road as well, extending these jaunts to one hour and fifteen minutes. While walking, I would read the signs posted around, practicing my Spanish. One sign said “El Sembrador Misiones” (the Seed Planter Missions) and listed a phone number with English names: Peter and Carol. It seemed a good idea to call and ask which church they attended so maybe I could go with them. Peter was the director of Seed Planter Missions. He was a short, almost bald, gruff type with glasses who bordered on angry most of the time. He had taken an early retirement and with his family was trying to do God's will. God had given him much in his life. Carol, his wife, was slightly taller, thin, with shoulder length brown hair and wore glasses. She was a pretty fifty-year-old who had a great sense of humor and was a genuine friend to all. They lived in one of the grandest mansions I had ever seen loaned to serve Christ's missionaries; it rests on a huge ledge overlooking the capital above the Coca-Cola sign. The view is magnificent. Their ministry received medical and dental volunteer groups from the United States most every week of the year, providing brigades to many very needy people in poor neighborhoods. Their labor was effective; people were truly helped. A brigade was made up of ten to twenty volunteers from the States, including doctors, dentists, nurses, assistants, students, and lay people. These teams were joined by national doctors and dental students who gave up time and earnings to volunteer. Together they made a great team.

~Doctors earned about $300 a month at this time. Their service and dedication was honorable.~

Carol quickly invited me to their church. "You wanna go with us Sunday to service?"

A sense of relief fell over me. I was in a new country and a Christian without a congregation. Church would provide me the opportunity to know the native people, my brothers and sisters in Christ—superb. "Where do you go?"

"It's a little community church clear across town, a few miles out on the other side."

"Can't let your toes show," offered their thirteen-year-old daughter, Tara, glancing down at my walking sandals.

"I'm not going to church," stated twelve-year-old Beth. Both girls were pretty, half black, and adopted from the US.

"Yes you are, Beth! Don't even go there."

Turning to me, Carol said, "The women here don't wear open-toed sandals to church. Occasionally we do, if they're nice sandals."

"No problem. Thanks for telling me. Should I wear a dress?"

"Yes, or a skirt."

"Does that mean me too?" joked Thomas, their youngest child, full black, adopted from the island of Tonga.

Tara gave him a slight swipe of a slap across his curly-haired head. "You're so hilarious."

They were cute kids who were homeschooled by Carol. They spoke some Spanish and seemed to enjoy the adventurous life that their new country offered them.

I walked to their house Sunday for church. We all piled into their van and began the great descent down the hill. After crossing the capital, we arrived at a quiet suburb in the country. The church looked like it would be fun. There were no doors or walls except for one small back wall—just a concrete floor with benches shaded by a large metal roof. It was open air, and the lively music flowed from the front, drifting across the nearby neighborhood. The praise music was modern Christian; some of the songs I recognized from my US church, except the words were in Spanish. Hearing music I recognized made me feel wonderful. It lifted the cloud of sadness for the moment. I felt alive with the music.

~Music is a great way to learn a language. Memorize all the songs you can.~

Few people had come as early as we did, so we sat down and watched the arrivals. The ladies wore their hair up, wore high heels, and were dressed in lovely cotton dresses—some solid colors, some matching prints, some in elegant colors and lace, some in vibrant tropical colors. As the native people dress up out of respect to God, all of us females were wearing skirts or dresses. Women here rarely wore pants at all and surely did not do so at church. Our real goal was to praise God, honor their standards, and not create controversy over differences in culture or clothing. It was our responsibility to blend in. We were in their country and we wanted to show respect.

~Please be sensitive also. It will feel like you are being forced to change, but really you are just joining them.~

The men wore long-sleeved shirts with slacks and shiny shoes, their hair shining with gel; most wore ties. The children were well dressed, smiling and running around, laughing and chattering. We sat near the back. This helped a lot when the whole church stood up together, as we weren't blocking the view of too many people. We were a tall group. Feeling comfortable as the shortest in our group at five foot one, I was seen as a medium/tall woman here. Probably true as I could see clear to the front of the church even when everyone was standing. Small blessings.

We had a nice service. After enjoying the music so close that the vibrations could be felt, I concentrated on listening to the Spanish. Yet, it is difficult to listen for more than five minutes in a language you can't understand, let alone two hours. But it was also important to look attentive in church, not bored or ready to fall asleep and that was harder to do than you might imagine. I adopted the habit of repeating in my head every word that was said for as long as possible. This helped greatly to improve my spoken Spanish and comprehension. Church on Sundays filled a void in my life; I had a spiritual home.

My new friends, too, were a wonderful addition to my world. They invited me to tag along with them whenever I wanted, which, of course, I did. They helped me shake off the feelings of sadness and aloneness that occasionally wanted overwhelmed me. They opened my eyes to the reality of everyday life in our new country by way of serving with their medical brigades.

~ Service is one way to touch another eternally, you both share the moment. Jump at the chance to volunteer for a medical brigade anytime.~

Joining Peter and Carol's medical brigades for part of each week as a volunteer translator was my second step into volunteerism. It felt great to be needed. There were many stateside people who were excited and happy to be serving along with many dedicated and professional national volunteers providing an invaluable service to the people who could least afford it. My Spanish got a great fine tuning doing this volunteer work. Catching the most common phrases and vocabulary used to attend to the people, I soon could say just enough to serve. Normally, my service would be for one or two days out of a week.

The team would meet in the mansion above the Coca-Cola sign and we would begin by introducing ourselves, then sing songs, pray, eat breakfast, and head off in a long caravan of bright and sparkling air-conditioned minibuses for a distant hilltop. Most often we worked in modest churches or well-used school buildings, but always were greeted by a small crowd of people already waiting in line, guided by some members of that community's church who had organized the brigade. The church connection was important so that the whole person could be attended to—the body and the soul. We unloaded the cars, prayed again—this time with a face-to-face deep sense of the urgent need of the people surrounding us—and divided up the work.

With some ability to speak and understand Spanish, I usually took names of the patients at the door. This included taking a small summary of their medical needs. The patients would then wait until they were guided to the medical, dental, or optometry areas. US volunteers, who came to serve but who knew nothing about medicine, were trained to use simple equipment or were asked to help in the pharmacy filling prescriptions to help with mostly common ailments. Others were asked to hold heads while the dentists pulled out teeth. This was a heavy and tiring job and much needed by the dentists who were usually small, thin, but ferocious female dental students from the university. Truly, pulling out teeth is a lot harder than one would think, and these small women dentists did a fearsome service.

Most of the doctors on the brigades were nationals but US doctors also volunteered their time assisted by a translator. While the majority of patients came for common and treatable ailments or infections usually cured with antibiotics, the most vital job that brigades provided was informing critically ill patients that they needed to go to the hospital immediately. Health, lives and limbs were saved. It was a great honor to work alongside these people, American and National. Their dedication truly touched me.

~You really don't know what your gifting is until you serve; then you'll find out what you're talented at.~

Once helping in the pharmacy, which was located in a back classroom, and assisted by two US lay people and a US veterinarian I had the job of translating prescriptions for them to fill and then reading the instructions as clearly as possible to the patients. The veterinarian helped with the more difficult prescriptions of antibiotics, double-checking the drugs and the amount prescribed for each patient while the two lay people filled the rest of the orders: bagging vitamins, eye drops, cough medicine, ibuprofen, antibiotics or head lice shampoo as instructed. My job was to explain carefully and simply to each patient which medicine they were receiving and the instructions for the dose. It was important to give the instructions for antibiotics with very clear wording as many people can't read or need glasses to read such fine print.

"These are your pills. Take one each time you eat a meal but only three in one day, only three." Holding up three fingers as I spoke, "No more than three. Take one before breakfast, one before lunch, and one before dinner."

"Yes, thank you."

"Even though you feel better, continue taking the pills, three a day, until they are gone. Leave the bottle empty."

"Yes, I will."

"These pills are not for anyone else; they can make others sick, even if they have the same problem. These pills are just for you."

"Yes, I see."

"You must keep these pills up high; they can hurt a baby or a small child."

"Yes, thank you."

"If you are still sick when the bottle is empty or you get sicker, go to a doctor that same day. Don't wait for tomorrow; go right away. OK?"

"I understand."

"To get well you must follow these instructions. If you forget them, have someone read them to you again. See, they are here on the bottle."

Again I would repeat these instructions to a family member or friend. Most of our patients would possibly not see a doctor again for many years. Our doctor-patient ratio is one to seventeen hundred in this country. Plus, the patients were always worried about hidden or extra costs in seeking medical treatment, which did always seem to appear, so they would stay home instead and wait it out.

Out of nowhere three middle-aged women scuttled in carrying an old, very heavy overstuffed chair. In the middle silently sat one thin, very wrinkled little lady surrounded by the flurry of attention. She moved only her eyes, slowly. The women who brought her in were telling the female doctor that she was a neighbor left abandoned by all her children. She had been a good mother to her children, but they were very bad sons and daughters, ungrateful, leaving her alone like this. These neighbor ladies had helped as much as they could, but she continued to be very sick. They explained that they could do no more for her; she looked to them as if she was dying. That's when I noticed that this tiny frail lady seemed to be listening.

Bending down I asked, "Do you know what day it is?"

She slowly answered, "Friday." It was Saturday, but her answer was good enough for me; I knew she was coherent.

"We are going to send you to the hospital." She looked straight into my eyes. "The doctors will try to fix your problem. They have very good doctors there."

I paused. "But if they can't fix you, are you ready to meet Jesus?"

She said quietly, "Yes."

"Sometimes the doctors can't help people even though they do their best. But Jesus will be waiting for you if that happens, so don't worry. You won't be alone; He will be there with you."

"Yes," she whispered.

That was all I could say before I got choked up and turned away to hide my tears. The women together picked up the heavy overstuffed chair with the tiny lady and shuffled out to the street where they had contacted a taxi to take her to the hospital. Then the taxi sped away and her chair sat empty.

At the next brigade, one of the doctors asked me to be her assistant, to help translate for her with the other volunteers. She had a wonderful way with her patients. A young girl who was eight months pregnant came asking for medicine for her baby.

"Have you been to a doctor about your pregnancy?"

"No," answered the girl, who couldn't have been more than sixteen years old.

"You don't want your baby, do you?"

She winced. "Yes, I do. I want medicine for my baby."

The doctor pressed on. "But a mother who loves her baby doesn't wait. You've waited too many months to ask a doctor if your baby is okay. Your baby needs a mother who will take care of him. He needs a mother who will go to the doctor early and get him medicine."

"I can take care of my baby." She lifted her chin, convincing herself.

"Then you must do exactly as I say. I will give you these pills to take for seven days. When you finish, you must go to a doctor and have a test done to see if your baby is okay. You must go to a doctor when you finish taking these pills. Do you promise me you will see a doctor?"

"I will. I will take care of my baby."

"If you love your baby, you will make sure you visit a doctor."

"Thank you, Doctor."

~It is not wise to advise anyone about any medical condition. Do not share any of your medications. If people ask you for medicine send them to a pastor, he will know how to help.~

The doctor was also brought a little eight-year-old girl who had an arm twisted backward because it had been broken and healed without being set.

"You should have brought me your daughter the day she broke her arm."

"She's not my daughter."

"They are all our children."

"She's my best friend's daughter."

"Why didn't you bring her that same day then?"

"I was too busy. My husband said he needed me at home."

"So you let this little girl's arm heal backward?" She paused, not really expecting a response. "You know we'll have to break her arm again in order to reset it."

The little girl glanced at the lady, fixing her gaze, understanding the pain she would again have to go through.

The doctor worried about re-breaking a poorly healed bone. "Next time make sure you bring in a child, anyone's child, right away. Don't wait. Tell your husband I said so."

As independent servers we may be asked to be available to drive someone to the doctor in an emergency. And we gladly agree to be called upon. It can be night or day; it can be a light or a serious injury.

Our neighbors rarely do call on us though as they rely on their own emergency system first. But when we are needed, transporting can be quite serious if the person is dying or has an open wound. We may be held responsible for what we do or do not do. It is an honor to be called to serve in these moments, and a time to call upon God to protect and guide us. Yet in all my years, I have never heard of someone being accused or threatened because of seemingly faulty assistance.

You may also be the only person to say something at a family burial. If needed, be prepared to pray or speak the final farewell and release the family member into the hands of our Savior, joining all present in spirit. In these moments faith in God covers us all, bringing calmness to a devastating situation, providing a support that will unite while watching our Father at work, touching lives. It humbles me to be able to serve in these ways.

Sometimes culture differences appear within the volunteers. A doctor once defended me when I was faced with a comment made by a Christian man while working at a brigade.

"Are you single, divorced, or widowed?"

"Divorced."

"You know the Bible that says that men can remarry after divorce but women can only remarry if their husband has died."

I was silent.

The doctor quickly defended me.

"The only one who can remarry in purity is the one who has not been abusive, unfaithful, or left the home. That's why most remarried women are pure in God's eyes."

Never had I prepared myself to defend my marital status from public attack, and certainly not in a land where I was the stranger and fighting to speak their language. It was my first taste of a new truth, a woman must be ready to defend herself, especially here in this country. The cards are stacked against women in cumbersome and ever so slight ways. Just because I was a foreigner did not mean I would not be treated or thought of as just another woman. My learning had just begun.

~My best defense in countering the demeaning authority against women in my own home or mission was to simply quote, "Joe Everyman[he] said so before he left," claiming a male who was no longer there had made the decision. It worked wonderfully.~

A Baptist brigade in the countryside took us to the town of Buendia (Good Day). There I met a big person, Luis Yoro, who stood five foot three. He was helping with the brigade and seemed to be directing things. After a full day's work and a nice dinner, the team met later that night for a celebration with the townsfolk. The people politely listened to all the speakers but ended the presentation with a chorus, chanting, "Luisito, Luisito" (Little Luis, Little Luis). Luis got on stage, took the microphone, and began belting out Christian songs with his outstandingly huge country voice. He had grown up in Buendia and they knew he had a great voice. He was their Luisito. We clapped and sang and enjoyed the music immensely. Luis's talents didn't stop at singing. He also had a popular Christian program called *Frontiers Without Borders* that played on one of our TV channels. He was a fearless man, truly a bigger-than-life character. As he was from the branch of Dorcas, no church funded his ministries and activities. He earned and received support privately.

Luis greeted and translated for teams and brigades from the US often. He was great fun, as his joking around was as great as his singing talent. His English became perfected by his one-hundred-joke ensemble that was repeated joke by joke to each new unsuspecting group of listeners. His wonderful wife—smart and efficient—put up with his giant self-esteem and grandiose visions of himself.

"If I had not been married, I would have had a hundred American wives." His wife and daughters were sitting nearby.

"And a hundred divorces," I quickly responded.

"If he lets in any more air, he will float away," commented his wife.

Luis begins his ensemble like this:

"You Americans really want to put us Latinos in harm's way."

"How is that, Luis?"

"Well, let me tell you. When there is danger in the air, you yell out the name of a bird so we will all look up and not take cover."

"Duck."

"What'd I say?"

An astute language learner, Luis listened to stories told by others too.

"And then we noticed that very old lady was buck naked," said the visitor, and everyone laughed.

"What is buck?" asked Luis.

"It means totally; she was totally naked."

Later when they asked Luis how he liked the food, he commented, "It was buck good."

Luis was also kind-hearted. Hearing me complain that I couldn't find Internet access, he offered to let me visit his home once a month to use his computer—a serious offer. This greatly increased good contact with my family and church at home. Unknown to us, Luis's gifting opened up the channel for God to complete his will for me and my many loved ones.

~Expect to have occasional difficulty connecting to the Internet. Don't worry, it'll be back in a few minutes or hours or days.~

Chapter 5
The Gifting of Talents

Every person has a talent. If you are ready to give it, God will use you. This is how I met others like myself. Meeting my cousin on occasion for lunch at his workplace near the US Embassy was enjoyable. It was a comfortable bus ride now that I had been here almost four months. Walking alone from the taxi stop to meet Greg at the embassy, I noticed it was still a little early so I sat down in front of a huge closed-down movie theater to watch the traffic. A blue and black Suburban van drove passed and headed up the hill toward Greg's neighborhood. What surprised me was that it was the exact same model, year, and color of the car I had left in the US. Which, by the way, was also the same car the current president drove; only, his was red and black.

That Sunday there was a new missionary family presented to the church. This family was blond and blue-eyed, except for their pretty dark-haired, slim mother. Pam was an honest and direct yet polite Southern beauty—intelligent too. Brett charmed people with his strong but playful energy for life and his uplifting talk. They had come with their three young daughters—Chastity: six, Charity: four and Hope: two—in order to serve in an orphanage. Leaving their beloved Georgia behind after selling their part of a family peanut farm and getting support from local churches, they had come to serve as a missionary family. In their blue and black Suburban van full of their belongings they had arrived just the day before. They were Southern and brought the South with them.

"Yes, Ma'am."

"Yes, Sir."

"Ya fixin ta eat with us, Miss Kimi?"

"Look over thar."

"How y'all doin'?"

"Come back, hear now?"

They found a huge brick mansion to rent near Greg's house for only five hundred dollars a month. It was a beautiful home outside and in. Dark wood lined the ceilings, doorways, and stairs. High ceilings, tiled floors, and large windows graced the rooms. Numerous bedrooms, all large with walk-in bathrooms and balconies, took over the upstairs. The living room had a brick wall fireplace built-in for chilly winter nights, and the dining room was huge with a modest chandelier and a table that could seat twenty. The kitchen was large and old-fashioned, inviting lots of the home cooking that took place there. Southern cooking triumphed in this small corner of the country. A large outdoor patio curled around the side of the house on the second floor. These patio corners were decorated with statues of cherubs, hanging plants, and columned divisions wide enough to sit on. One side of the house was joined by a small public park like area. It was a dream house in paradise.

This home was truly a blessing, and they used it well as the mission house while they got their ministry legalized with the government. They believed the Lord wanted them working only with girls. Girls who had become homeless were at great risk of becoming abused—sexually and physically, if that had not already happened. Girls could be thrown out of their homes for many different reasons: having boyfriends, looking sexy in front of their stepfathers, moving provocatively, wanting to party or go dancing, and of course for trying to avoid abuse inside their homes. Brett and Pam felt these girls had the greatest need to be protected. They also wanted to work in the poorest part of the country to serve the families who could least afford it. They named their ministry “Tabitha Arise.”

While waiting to be legally licensed, they were very active in the medical brigades, inviting teams to stay in their home most every week of each month. Their Southern accents and hospitality were cherished by me as well as everyone they met. It was great fun to visit and tag along with them, especially because Pam and I happened to be almost the same age and, of course, they had a car. Pam and Brett’s Spanish was very limited so they asked me to give them language classes—I think they paid me five dollars an hour. Both were sharp students, playfully competitive with each other, learned quickly, and they Southern-slurred all over the Spanish. Humor is always a good thing to have while learning a new language.

~It seems that completing the second year level of language studies in the US before travelling and then continuing with classes in your new country is the key to maximizing fluency in the shortest period of time.~

One day Pam and Brett had just come back from an invitation to pray for an elderly man who was dying in his home. This had made them both very pensive. It is a great challenge to be there for someone who is passing on. There isn’t time for returning tomorrow to say what you wanted to say or help in the way he might have wanted. You must rely on the Lord, be His words and His Life in that very important moment.

Pam mentioned, “You know, it was so sad being there, but I was honored to help this man. When we left it began to rain and I said, ‘Look, the Lord’s praying with us.’ And the family just looked at me strangely.” She gave me a sideways smirk.

"Then in the car, Brett couldn't hold it in any longer. He told me, 'You know what you said? You said *orinando* instead of *orando*. Look, the Lord's peeing with us.' And you know," she continued, "that family just looked solemn and nodded their heads at me. Didn't say a thing."

We broke out laughing, she with embarrassment and I wondering if I wanted her to tell people I was her Spanish teacher. They became my very good friends, even family.

Six months had gone by when my life was graced with a message from a single female independent server-type from my church in the US who wanted to come visit and volunteer for a few months. She had met me before at our home church and wanted to join me. Although I did not remember her I joyfully invited her down. Tammy was fifteen years my junior, and I prayed that we would be able to enjoy each other despite our age differences. At the airport I was a little apprehensive, hoping she would find me, as I had no idea what she looked liked. A tall, plump, big-breasted, smiling blonde with dimples and glasses approached me wearing a long gathered skirt and carrying her two suitcases. She looked a little delicate for life here with her hair blow-dried back and soft makeup. But God knew she was ready for service and just needed a transition home before heading out on her own. Pam and Brett prayed together and offered to let her stay with them for a while in their home, which gave us all time to find out what Tammy's vision was.

She sat on the bottom bunk bed in one of the bedrooms of the mission's mansion slowly unpacking in front of ten curious eyes. Pam, Chastity, Charity, Hope, and I all looked on.

"I just thought it would be awesome to come down and live life for a while serving. I've graduated from college and would like to practice my Spanish. I want Jesus to pick my future. My money should last me maybe three or four months."

She was an independent missionary, from the branch of Dorcas for sure. That is when we noticed that it was great fun to ask people *why* they had chosen to come to this country, because it seemed that no one really had a good answer. We expected firm answers supported by enthralling stories of sacrifice and pleading with God, but heard more pliable reasons.

"We knew a couple who worked here."

"We had planned on going to Asia but an opportunity opened up here."

"I had travelled as far as Mexico and decided to keep going south."

"My company sent me here once many years ago. I decided to visit again."

"My parents were missionaries and we visited here once."

"I wasn't really sure where this country was and that intrigued me."

My answer seemed to be the most logical since I knew someone who was living here now. "My cousin lives in that house over there."

None of us had spent years or even months begging the Lord to let us move to this country and only this country; it just seemed like a good option at the time. And curiously enough, it was. Tammy and I began our escapades tromping into the unknown. Now accustomed to walking hours a day with Tammy I could venture out and go anywhere. Everything was new for her, so we spent most of our time getting to know the capital.

Each day became an adventure. Our first bus ride down the hill should have been uneventful, and it would have been if the first bus to stop hadn't have been a military bus. The bus stopped right in front of us and opened the door. A man got off and we got in. Once inside we noticed everyone was male and in uniform. We placed ourselves near the front, ready to jump out. Once moving, we peeked over our shoulders. Yes, they were soldiers, all of them, in camouflage army fatigues.

"Where does this bus go?" Tammy asked me in almost a whisper.

"I don't know. I'll ask."

Leaning forward I spoke loudly enough to be heard over the rumbling motor.

"To the center?"

"Yes."

"He said we're going downtown. We'll get off as soon as we can."

We sat in silence, trying to look out the windows casually, calmly. As each soldier got off the bus they would pay the driver. The bus wound and curved all the way down the three-mile hill, stopping every so often, making the ride a long one.

Arriving at the city center the bus stopped at a park. We both jumped up and were off that bus in a flash. A few chuckles and "Good-bye, American girls" could be heard from the back of the bus.

"I forgot to pay." Returning to the driver I asked, "How much do I owe?"

He mumbled something but I couldn't understand him.

Quickly I pulled out some coins and a few pesos and pushed them toward him in an opened palm. He picked out forty cents.

Buses were cheap! That was twenty centavos each or about three US cents. Our joy at finding super cheap transportation evaporated as we realized we were alone in the center of town and did not know exactly where or how to get back. We chose a seat on a concrete bench in the park to look inconspicuous while we composed ourselves and prayed for Jesus to help. That's when we noticed that all around the park were small minivans used as buses. They were parked and waiting to fill up with riders before taking off. A new minivan arrived in the place of our bus and the attendant yelled, "Little Pico." This was the bus stop central. Now we knew how to get home, so we were relieved. We gathered up our courage and began walking, somewhere. But not too far—just a block down, then we'd return to the park to make sure we weren't lost, and set out down the other block. The next day we took the bus again and began expanding our conquests.

~Buses are great inexpensive ways to travel. You must always take all precautions to be safe. Thieves have been known to get on the buses to rob everyone.~

We got to know the city quite well by walking. Once we were looking for a specific pharmacy to request a refill. Prescriptions from a doctor are not necessary to buy medicines, as most people can't afford go to a doctor and pay for drugs. Each pharmacy has a doctor on hand to help you pick the correct medicine. Most of the time this is quite helpful; no need to bother the doctors for small issues. You can get antibiotics and even an injection right there from the doctor in the pharmacy. Once here, if you have any questions about medicines, just go to a pharmacy and ask the doctor. They may even have an attendant who speaks English. Still, be cautious, you are your own best doctor anywhere you travel.

~Not all brands or fancy medicines are available. Check it out online. If you have any trouble once overseas get in contact with an embassy doctor.~

Pharmacies are found in most neighborhoods but are sometimes difficult to locate. Asking people on the street for directions draws unwanted attention, so step into an occasional *pulperia*, a tiny 7-11-type store, found absolutely everywhere, and ask. The directions one receives can be at best unreliable. This is because the kindhearted Latino way is to give you some kind of answer, even if they really don't know anything at all, in order to be kind and courteous. It would feel rude to turn you away without helping a little. This led us to the habit of asking directions every block or so to clarify which information was correct and which was false and to assure we were getting closer to our goal little by little.

The pharmacy we needed ended up being clear across the city a couple miles from the bus stop. We walked and walked until Tammy finally tuckered out. The distance, heat, and the newness of the country had won. After a short rest, I encouraged her to keep up with me sure that we were very close to the pharmacy. Twelve blocks later we found it. Within minutes it was then time to turn around and walk miles back to the bus stop. Her joke became, "Only twelve more blocks."

Safety is an issue for anyone walking in a large metropolitan city. Being a foreigner makes you more of a target, but at least we know that and can take extra precautions. When walking, you must remember to leave all your jewelry at home—even your watch, rings, and earrings. Thieves assume you're wearing real gold even if you are not. A good habit is to always carry a small cheap purse with a comb, some chapstick, a copy of your passport and a little money in it for them to steal. You do need a photocopy of your passport on you at all times.

It is safer to put your money in many different pockets (or your bra) and keep only a little in your purse so they think they've gotten it all. Wearing a fanny pack or backpack invite unwanted attention. If I had to carry something valuable, I would put it in a small black plastic shopping bag and carry it like a purchase. Leave all your makeup at the house you're staying in; it's very expensive and hard to get. A cheap bottle of foundation can cost near twenty dollars US. We protected our makeup with our lives. Two things happened because of our daily trips downtown. One, we got to know the city better than most who grew up there and two, we both got skinny. We had little trouble on the streets, even though we passed thousands of people daily, thousands who did not give us any reason for alarm. We soaked in the sights, smells, and sounds of Latin life. We went to the bank, got mailing addresses based in Florida, called home, exchanged money, looked for tennis shoes for women, got our hair cut and nails manicured, renewed our visas, found the church doctor, found a dentist, and bought gifts to take home. All was as it should be, although two more dangerous incidents that happened should be mentioned.

A drugged-out man tried to pull the sunglasses off Tammy's face as he passed her on the sidewalk. He found himself in a life-and-death grip with both of us, two "*gringas*", intent on not being robbed, so he gave in and let go. Another day two young teen boys were sitting by the side of an overgrown broken-down sidewalk path as we passed. One said, "Get the second one." Meaning me. As Tammy passed he rose up, and I softly said, "He's going to rob me." Tammy lashed around, I backed up, and the boy veered away from me. "Old woman," he yelled. But most of the time our walks were sprinkled with other kinds of comments.

Comments that were, well, positive. “Hey, little momma!” “Hi, Love,” “Daddy is looking,” “Beauty,” and “Adopt me.” The best one was thrown at Tammy, “I’m Tarzan; you must be Jane.” My favorite was from a taxi driver: “I want to have four children with you.” Obviously, he knew very little about American women, but he was cute and deliciously dark-skinned. It is never wise to look at the men who are yelling the comments since that is what prostitutes do. Tammy must have looked more than I did, as most of the comments were directed at her.

The Spanish we needed for daily life survival got easier too. We could understand numbers, say our simple phrases, and almost understand directions. We learned the names of many items, where they were sold and how much they should cost. We always calculated the prices in our mind into dollars. A Coke was forty cents, almost the same as in the US. A pound of cheese was about a dollar fifty, a loaf of bread one dollar, a bag of chips two dollars, and a pound of meat a dollar fifty. One whole uncooked chicken was three dollars. Most native families generally eat meat once or twice a week, replacing meat with cheese and eggs on the other days. Fruits and vegetables were cheap. A banana cost five cents, an orange seven cents, one mango thirty cents, a pineapple seventy cents, and an avocado forty cents. Corn, rice, and beans are the cheapest of foods, as they are used in all three meals. If you choose to eat like the nationals, you could get by on about a hundred and fifty US dollars a month for food, eating some meat each day. Adding Cokes or chips could bump it up to two hundred.

Clothes were cheaper but generally of poorer quality. A pair of jeans was twelve dollars, a shirt maybe six. We could find most anything we looked for but it just wasn’t always easy to find the quality, color, or brand we wanted. It was easy to get by on about four hundred dollars a month, living quite frugally and renting just a room.

Renting a room is quite common. Families often open up a back room or two to family members, students, or strangers. A room would rent for twenty-five to forty-five dollars a month, electricity and water included. The rooms are small, ten by ten or fifteen by fifteen and usually not in great condition or located near the toilet or garbage. These are the extra rooms no one wants. Better rooms run around a hundred dollars a month. Bathrooms are always shared. Living is not private and family rules must be obeyed, but you can always find a cheap place to live if you need to.

~Make sure you let others know where you are living and register your address with the US Embassy so they may find you in an emergency.~

We explored the city by taking buses to see where they would go, as their routes were roundtrip; they would go and return back to the same place. Once we took a bus as it crossed from one side of the city to the other. We just sat in the bus looking at the new sights, finding a burger joint, identifying the huge open-air market we had heard about, discovering new neighborhoods. We rode with innocent assurance that all was well until we noticed everyone else had gotten off our bus and we were the only passengers left. It was about four thirty and all buses stopped every day at five. The driver and his attendant just looked at us. We looked back. “This is the last stop,” the driver said. They both laughed.

Quickly we got off and ran to the last bus heading toward the city. Riding back in silence we looked out over the city lighting up its darkened sky, pinpoints of lights shining here and there. We felt a little nervous, as we had to get back before the last Little Pico bus left or we would really be stranded. We weren't even sure this bus would go near our bus station park, but it did and we caught the last bus up the hill. Praise Jesus.

Time passed. I had been in this country for nine months. Independence Day came, celebrated on September fifteenth. This day the city puts on a great parade through the main streets that ends up in the stadium. Everyone in all of the country is marching or watching the parade. The parade is made up of military marching teams or high school groups or bands. No floats or clowns—just marching. Tammy and I decided to be a part of the crowd in the stadium and took the bus downtown not realizing there might only be bus service half the day.

People were everywhere, celebrating in one way or another. Some were drinking too much alcohol; a shot only cost five cents. At the stadium we were herded into an entrance with many other people; there was no charge to see the parade. The seats were packed. Noise filled the air, with the smell of heat trapped in the bleachers. We tried go to the opposite side to sit in the shade, but we were unable to get there. There was too much commotion and too many people. As we tried to leave, the end of the parade came into view. Throughout the stadium people quickly stood up to go to avoid the crowd. Caught in a human mass from the front, sides, and back, we were compacted together and forced to move where it went. Panic set in. We could not get out. My foot slipped out of my sandal and I couldn't stop or bend down or pause. Shifting my bare foot I luckily found the sandal immediately. Shuffling along with the mass of people until we could see ahead and escape from the push we emerged blocks away from the stadium. We stood aside for a moment to catch our breath; that had been scary. Quietly we walked thirty minutes to the bus park to find the last bus waiting to go up the hill but returned home only to find the electricity was out.

Electricity was rationed at this time. This meant that every other week we had electricity from five p.m. to five a.m. and then the next week from five a.m. to five p.m. Our goal was to make it home from our daily trips downtown before the electricity had been cut off, or our walk from the bus would be in complete darkness. But today we were too late. Only the shadows of candles burning in the neighboring houses could be seen or the lights of an occasional car coming home. My preference was the five a.m. to five p.m. schedule, as we could wake up, bathe with hot water, blow-dry our hair, and eat a hot breakfast before the electricity was cut. But this schedule meant no lights at night, no TV, no computer. Either way we were inconvenienced. Life without electricity is quiet. Food is cold. Everyone goes to bed early.

Chapter 6
The Beauty of a New Country

My cousin mentioned that one could cheaply rent Sunny Cay, a small private, deserted island off the northern coast. He had stayed at Sunny Cay before. Tammy and I decided it was time to take advantage of a quick vacation opportunity and learn more of our new country.

"We want to rent two nights on Sunny Cay."

"This private island rents for a hundred dollars a night." Fifty each!

"Normally you need to book nine months ahead of time, but the last two dates during hurricane advisory season were cancelled and are open. Would you like to book those?"

"Of course."

"To stay on the island you need to bring all your own food and supplies."

"Not a problem."

"We'll book your flights and you can pick up your tickets in two days."

We were thrilled. Hurricane season wouldn't dampen our spirits. Our planned menu included little cooking. At the "*gringo*" grocery store—so called because they carried luxury foods from the US—we found our delicious supplies, goodies that we had not eaten much of—chips, cookies, bologna, hotdogs, sugared cereal, and Kool-Aid. Because our travelling would be done by taxi, bus, plane and then boat, we needed to plan carefully. We were limited to one suitcase each and one plastic food chest, but not to worry—we wouldn't need much clothing on the island. We got everything done in the two days.

At five a.m. we took the taxi to the bus, rode on the bus for five hours to the airport on the coast, then flew for twenty-five minutes to land on the bigger island. As the little plane lowered for a landing, we gasped for air once we could see the landing strip. It ran from one end of the peninsula to the other, all three hundred feet of it. George, a tanned, barefoot, windswept but strong-looking man in his late fifties came to greet us. Sunny Cay was George's island; maybe he would sell it to us for enough money he offered. George walked us to his boat and loaded us on, then puttered around the island to buy water and rent snorkeling gear.

Then off we went into the blue seas to find our tiny island. Tammy and I were two happy *gringas*. The deep blue sea reflected light from the shining hot sun as the cool spray from the boat bolting through the waves kept us comfortable. The air smelled of ocean freshness. We were in a tropical paradise. First, we passed the island of Paradise Cay, filled to the brim with homes precariously perched over the sea. It was a bustling island community shaded by tropical plants and tossed about by an ocean breeze.

George took advantage of the time on the boat to explain what life on the island would entail—if only we could understand his pirate English.

"Yus cun call me anytyme by usin the ham radio. Me wife un me wul answer yus right aways."

Great, who knew how to use a ham radio?

"If'n we call yus an yus don't answer wul be lookin fur yus quick sos call back right aways."

"OK." We both nodded our heads.

"If'n yus wanter go fish'n fur sharks I cun come in fur du day and fish wish yus fur a fee."

No, we shook our heads.

"Ur if'n yus wanna I cun bring outta native Garifuna ta cook yus a seafud sup lunch."

Garifuna are the black native island people who speak a mix of Garifuna, Spanish and English, all in one sentence. They are fascinating to listen to.

Yes, our heads bounced up and down.

"Tweni dollurs."

"OK."

We opted for the lunch and ordered sea snail seafood soup for the next day. He was available for one trip out if we needed anything, but any extra trips would come with an additional cost. We were told to feel free to call on the ham radio as often as we wished and to be sure to mention anything that seemed dangerous, scary, or strange.

Now so far out that we could not see land anywhere, we were lost in the open expanse of ocean. God seemed really huge at that moment, the moment when one realizes how powerful and overwhelming nature actually is and how small we really are. It was a little unsettling to be surrounded by just water with no land in sight. Soon we spotted the island trees far off in the distance: a fir tree, a small grove of coconut trees, and palm trees spattered about. The island was just big enough for the rambling wood house that could sleep eight and some room to walk—maybe an acre in size.

George helped us unload, showed us the ham radio, and took off. Awesome—we were alone on a deserted tropical island. Tammy and I checked out the island and decided to fix dinner, then go swimming and eat later—island life. The water hit us with a cool-warm sensation and was clear enough that we could observe the shoreline, steering clear of sharp rocks and deep drops. We woke up with the sun and spent the next day snorkeling morning, noon, and night. The views were astounding; the ample coral reefs were in pristine condition—large, colorful, and completely untouched. Fish abounded, competing with land flowers in vibrant color, shape, and patterns. Even a few nurse sharks swam away from us. Huge sea coral and sponges decorated the sand floor and helped hide creatures of all kinds. We were experiencing a day in the life of the ocean, like the rich and famous.

George's wife gave a quick check-up call and warned of a small storm heading our way. That evening started off with a distant storm approaching the island at a fast speed. We decided to sit on our beach chairs and experience the moment. As the storm was touching shore, the wind picked up and lightning flashed in the background. We were temporarily blinded by a photoflash picture of the palm tree figures blackened out by the piercing light behind. Suddenly, the storm was above us, flashing tree shadows onto the sand surrounding us, the rain pelting down and quickly filling the rain barrels. Seconds later it passed over us and was heading out to sea on the other side of the island. We had sat through a tropical storm on the beach—cool. We woke up ready to snorkel every minute until we had to leave at noon. Neither one of us was ready to leave, and we both vowed it would be the ideal place to bring a husband, especially for the honeymoon. That trip was a once-in-a-lifetime adventure.

~Missionary work is not all hard work and no play! Get to know your country.~

Tammy and I returned to the capital and looked forward to Sunday at church, the same church that Peter, Carol, Pam and Brett attended. We had made a few national friends at church too and were happy to see them at least once a week. The music was always great. I began videotaping our life and was thrilled with the filming. After taping the church service, Tammy and I stopped for lunch in a small restaurant located in the capital's only mall. It was a small mall void of popular fast-food restaurants but refreshing nevertheless. The restaurant was not very crowded, so we sat halfway toward the back. We both ordered a typical plate of rice, beans, egg, cheese, avocado, and tortillas with fried plantain strips for $2.35. I had the video camera hidden in a regular black shopping bag. Lunch was good and we enjoyed the break. Because my Spanish was better, I got up to pay the bill. A few seconds later Tammy came up too, to check her part of the bill. In that instant, someone grabbed the black bag containing my video camera. When we returned it was gone. The employees claimed maybe some kids had entered while we were paying and stole it, but we had seen no one enter the restaurant. There were no kids around. More than likely an employee had stolen it. There was nothing much I could legally do but file an accusation with the police, which I decided not to do. My camera was gone.

~There are mall policemen who can be called when personal safety is threatened or a crook is caught in the act. In most instances no complaint filed will ever be answered.~

Our daily adventures filled our lives with ups and downs, mostly unexpected, but life seemed full and exciting. Before we knew it Tammy had to decide how long her trip here was to last. Her money had stretched longer than she had first guessed it would but she was down to the last penny. Writing home for a loan to get by on she decided to try to get a job. We heard that there was a need for an assistant to live in our church's orphanage for six months in the town of Los Santos, a small dry, dusty village about an hour outside the capital. She decided to volunteer. She would get free room and board and every other weekend off. Now she could afford to stay a little longer and help children who were separated from their families. We went together to check out the orphanage.

~Volunteer opportunities do abound but they really are volunteer. You must be able to support yourself.~

The bus ride took about two hours, and the walk to the country town was about twenty minutes more. The area was a little hotter and drier than the capital. The town was very small, connected by dirt roads and dust-covered houses with laundry drying in the breeze, and an occasional cow or horse grazing nearby. Men rode around town on horseback. It reminded me of how the Wild West must have looked. The orphanage was made of simple, unpainted wooden rooms and had no electricity, but it did have running water. She would help care for twelve boys, and her Spanish would get even better! Because there was a "mother" hired to oversee the cooking and cleaning, Tammy would help out with duties. Her job was to help get everyone up and ready for school, clean up after breakfast, and help prepare lunch. Then she was pretty much done and available to do activities with the boys. She decided to open an English class for them and began teaching.

~Offering free English classes is a great gift for any community. Don't make regular attendance an issue and try to teach or re-teach in small, short lessons. Don't give homework or most won't come back.~

It is difficult to raise all the support needed for an orphanage. Our church was a small community church with little tithing options with which to assist the boys. Some days there was not enough food for all three meals. Maybe they would skip breakfast or lunch or even dinner. Tammy got skinnier, almost too thin. The funding that ran the orphanage came through gifting from here and abroad. US churches and teams sent their support to make this home blessing possible; even Tammy's mother collected funds and underclothing to send to the boys. It was help from many bighearted donors that made all the difference. Tammy loved each one, they became her boys. She felt the life of God around her, alive and within reach. She recognized the hand of the Father himself at work. She would return every other weekend and tell stories of each one of her boys—her eyes shining, her dimples showing—as she filled me in on the fun and sadness of their lives. Tammy was doing His will for her at that time.

Winter vacation began on the US Thanksgiving holiday on one of Tammy's weekends home. My plan was to cook a big dinner and take it to the center for Johnnie and the boys near my cousin's house. Tammy and I prepared a turkey and stuffing (that Greg and Sonia graciously offered to pay for), a chocolate pie, a pumpkin pie, mashed potatoes, three-bean salad, muffins, and Coke. It was a task to find everything we needed, but we did it. The only boys left at the center were those who had not received permission to go home; they were a little depressed. But even with the dark dining area and cold air, our spirits weren't to be dampened. The dinner was great. The boys were ecstatic. They had never eaten turkey or pie. They ate and asked for seconds. We prayed together afterward and thanked God for all He had given us and promised to take better care of His gifts in the future. Outside we took a group photo. The days were sweet.

Around that time Sonia took her doctor's exams and passed with the highest marks. She could now fight for one of the three positions open that year. But her position was stolen from her, underhandedly taken by another, and she did not get hired. She then applied for a scholarship to study emergency medicine in Michigan and won. Greg and Sonia would move to the US after Christmas. I would be on my own.

~A missionary life includes the reality that all relationships may be transient. Those you are with this year may not be in the country next year. It is a difficult adjustment.~

Christmas is a quieter celebration here than in the US. All wages are calculated on a fourteen-month scale. This means you receive a wage each month, and twice a year you get one month extra. December fifteenth is the fourteenth month payday. That's when the Christmas season begins, and by December twenty-fifth it's all over. If it wasn't for the fourteenth-month pay, we would have no Christmas celebration at all, since the monthly wage really doesn't cover the monthly basics, so saving is virtually impossible. Of course, some unscrupulous men spend their extra wage on alcohol and spend their free time passed out in the street, but for most families this extra pay brings real joy.

Santa doesn't really come here, even though the children talk about him as if he's real until they're around seven years old. Rarely does a child wake up to find something left by Santa under their beds. Sometimes it happens just once in their lives. Yet, many homes are decorated with plastic Christmas trees brought from the US or a leafless bush, no more than two feet high, that's been spray-painted with white fluff and stabilized with a wood block. Christmas cheer though, is present. Most children expect to receive clothes: maybe a pair of shoes, a pair of jeans, or a new dress from their parents. Toys are not really given. Songs are not really sung.

~Other countries not Christian based may show no signs of Christmas. Or they may celebrate other holidays you might not prefer to join. Feel blessed and joyful during these times and witness to others with your friendship.~

The churches celebrate with a special service but nothing more. Street decorations are sparse. The real celebration comes the night before Christmas. All dinners take place on the twenty-fourth: chicken and rice, *tamalitos* (corn roll-ups made with beans or meat inside), and *carne asada* (a mouthwatering mix of beef strips cooked in a special salsa with green pepper strips and onion). Great food of every kind is presented. The women cook all day with all the maids joining in. A lot of alcohol is ingested, and everyone stays up until midnight to light fireworks. So many fireworks are lit that the streets box in the deafening sound of continuous explosions for hours while the air fills up with smoke so thick you have a hard time seeing the neighbor's house. When all is quiet they exchange presents, if they have some.

Christmas dawns with a silence unheard of in a capital city. No one wakes up, no one cooks, no one talks until around three p.m. Christmas day had no church service, no bus service, no visiting, no shopping, and the TV people evidently didn't wake up because none of the channels were playing either. Merry Christmas. New Year's Eve is celebrated with special foods too. *Nacatamales* bring in the flavor of the New Year. *Nacatamales* are made of a pork or beef bone with meat chunk sided by rice cooked with vegetables and wrapped in a corn dough, which is then wrapped in a special banana leaf and cooked in boiling water until done. The recipe cooks one hundred at once, and this process takes about six hours. They are a national favorite and a great treat, but a lot of work. Fireworks explode every so often throughout the night until a fireworks grand finale dominates at midnight. The goal is to continue the noise until one a.m., for a whole hour. And they do. Alcoholic drinks are served beginning early in the night.

New Year's Day repeats the empty silence of Christmas Day, and then we're off on a new year. Tammy and I enjoyed the fun but missed the traditional celebrations of the States. Plus, we missed our families even more during this time. Phone calls and letters did not fill the gap enough to free us from homesickness during the holidays. Depression was encroaching. My prayer to Father God was that he would show me what I had to live for; to know what my purpose was. I prayed and prayed; the Lord had to answer me. During the night of the second week He gave me this dream. I was with teen boys in a two-story house in the woods. My husband loved me and worked volunteering at the church. We raised animals, planted gardens, and my husband helped the boys with their schoolwork but I had to leave to work every day at a profession. This was His promise to me. Writing this down I held firmly onto my belief that Jesus had given me this for a purpose.

Because this country is a Christian nation and historically Catholic, the life and death of Jesus is celebrated each day. It is public, and people casually talk about Him. If appropriate, he is even included in the news on TV. He is recognized as Lord of our life. Belief is normal, not hidden or almost outlawed as in the US. On TV in the US you can hear all kinds of cuss words, but faith statements are blocked, except of course if you're saying "Jesus Christ" in place of "crap" or "shit." Prostitutes, drug addicts, killers, rapists, wife beaters, and gay and lesbian people are all invited to talk about their lives and beliefs in detail, but no Christians, no stories of faith or answered prayer testimonies. Movies do not portray normal life showing people saying, "I'll pray for you" or "Jesus can heal" or "See you at church." We are a void group; we are ignored and lost in public. We don't exist; everyone else does. But in this country faith is normal. You have the right not to believe too, but everyone assumes you are normal if you do have a faith.

We pray for water when the water gets cut, we pray for electricity when the electricity gets cut, we pray for health when we get sick and to be able to afford medicine or a doctor's visit, we pray for our loved ones who suffer injustices not attended to by the police. We believe prayer changes things. We believe what the Bible says. That is just common fact.

Greg gave his notice at work, and he and Sonia packed up and moved to the US for a three-year stay. I had been here eleven months and needed to expand my wings, find a room to rent and one for Tammy for her weekend visits to the capital, which were especially important now that she had a boyfriend. Pam and Brett were moving because they had been blessed with the purchase of a twelve-acre farm in Maranila, one of the poorest and coldest areas. The government had approved their status and work permits, so they were ready to begin building a home for girls. Their land was majestic, hidden in a forest off from the main gravel country road and sided by a half mile-high cliff that allowed one to overlook a beautiful valley and take in the wonder of nature. Eventually, they built four homes and a mission's house for the teams.

In that part of the woods there was no electricity except by a gas-generated motor, only well water, and very few neighbors. The simple *campesino* life. They bought goats, cows, chickens, and made a pond. Every week teams arrived, providing a medical brigade to one fortunate lost community hidden in the picture-perfect hillsides. So Tammy and I were off on our own as our support systems had both moved.

We got the word out that we were interested in renting a room in a native family home. Tammy with one family and I with another, as two rooms were hard to come by. A lady from the church found me an English teacher to rent a room from. Their house was in Colony Kennedy, named after John F. Kennedy and built in the 1960s through US government funds. There was rumor that Joe Kennedy had visited in person once. The neighborhood had a reputation for being dangerous, but the tree-lined streets and narrow walkways separating the homes made it look warm and inviting. I decided to take the risk. My room was located at the back of the house, across from the outside water tank and the latrine. The ceiling had been covered with red plastic paper, hanging as if ready to fall. It felt to me like an old brothel room. Yes, there were *cucarachas* (cockroaches) and, yes, a few rats. It rented for fourteen dollars a month—my price. It was located almost within walking distance from the church, maybe one hour, but normally I would walk twenty minutes to the bus and then get to church in less than fifteen minutes.

The neighborhood was a little dangerous. You had to look both ways before approaching your gate to go home, as the time it took to get out your keys and unlock the gate was enough time for someone to assault you. Once someone passed by me and in English said, "Don't you know it's dangerous here?" I didn't look to see who it was; just kept on walking, passing by my gate to throw him off. I loved going to Bible study at a church family's house only a few blocks away but even that was a little dangerous returning after dark.

Returning home before five one afternoon, still in the daylight, I decided to cut through the Catholic churchyard in order to avoid walking three large blocks more. Besides, there was always a vigilante on duty guarding the place. Taking the last corner I ran right into two young men. They smiled. One quickly reached out and pulled me by the corner of my shirt; the other one raised a machete above his head. "Give me your purse." I screamed so loud I didn't recognize my own voice. At the same time I twisted away from the machete, they let go and took off running. Running as fast as I could after them, I suddenly realized what I was doing and turned around to run for the vigilante. We lost them.

The funny thing was, there was nothing in my purse but coins, a comb, chapstick, and a copy of my passport. My money was well hidden in my clothing. Sometimes intelligence escapes me. That was the last and most dangerous assault I have had, and it did scare me. Later, I realized that the machete had been raised in a manner to scare. To hit someone he would have had to raise it and swing in the opposite direction. They just wanted to intimidate me into giving them my purse. Little consolation, but some. Maybe life was no more dangerous in this country than in the US. After all, I won't die in a car accident because I'm never in a car or even on the freeway. Every day in the States I risked my life in my car. You just exchange one risk for another. To me things seemed pretty even, taken in all together. Tammy found a room with a family nearby; we were neighbors in Colony Kennedy.

Fortunately there was work to be found teaching English, tutoring four hours a week and teaching a class at church. These two jobs brought in about twelve dollars a week, not deducting bus fare. It was more a fun experience for me than an actual earning opportunity.

My class was taught without books, just a chalkboard. Everyone earned an A.

At church we learned that the new presidential candidate, Carlos Canales, was attending a Christian Businessmen's Breakfast with Latin America's "Billy Graham"—Luis Palau—who was Bible trained at Multnomah School of the Bible in Oregon. Years earlier I had traveled to Argentina with my US church to attend brigades lead by Ed Silvoso, Luis's brother-in-law. It was a Businessmen's Breakfast so I asked to attend with a young member of our church. I knew he would agree to take me because he preached a really good sermon about Adam and Eve without calling it the fall of Eve. There is hope in the new generation. It was super to be only a few feet from Luis Palau, a great, active man of God. These truly are blessed times to be a Christian. More than ever before we have the opportunity to meet our worldwide leaders. Carlos Canales would later win the presidency. His wife, Mary Snow—an American he met while she was in the Peace Corps—became our beloved First Lady. It was a great breakfast.

Life turned sweeter when Tammy and I stumbled upon a garage sale. A missionary family was returning to the States and had to get rid of all that could not be carried on the plane. This step in overseas work is a deep one. Returning to the States means we must leave most all behind, arriving to start life over yet another time from scratch. It is a difficult transition even if you are thrilled to be going back to the States.

~You need to have a returning plan, options for housing, furnishings, finances, job, and transportation. Moving back is a big deal and can be quite an emotionally damaging time. Take time to protect yourself with a viable plan. ~

We arrived late to the garage sale but didn't have much money to spend anyway. There wasn't a lot left except a big box of Christian books. I asked about the price of the books and he said if I took the whole box he'd just charge me for three. Small miracles! My reading life had been restored; I got to read like a crazy woman. I still have some of those books today. English reading material is like gold for us. You can bring only so much on the plane, and books in English are costly.

~Bring some books to read and exchange with others while you're overseas.~

The time finally came when my money was running out. I had been here for eleven months and had earned only a nominal amount. I prayed and was still waiting for a hint from Jesus. Deciding between returning home or remaining wasn't difficult for me; staying was my desire but there was no choice without funds to live on. With just enough money in the bank to fly home I continued to pray and dipped into the funds. My new goal was to try to earn more by teaching. At my age, teaching was the only job open to me. Teaching or owning your own business are the two options easily open to people over thirty-five. Even managers and supervisors are normally limited to those under forty. It's a tough reality that needs to be changed.

~Finding a good paying job is almost impossible overseas. If you do find work count on making just enough to buy a few necessities.~

Later that week God answered my plea. Arriving home the teacher told me I had a phone call and handed me a number, someone wanting an English teacher. Calling back, my thoughts were on trying to add this class to my schedule somehow. Unknown to me, this school was one of the best bilingual schools in the capital. Could I sub? Just for a day? They were short three teachers. Yes. It was always hard for me not to offer help in a time of need anyway. The next morning I grabbed my teaching certificate, diploma, and resume and left in a taxi for the school. They were more than happy to see me and led me directly to their second grade classroom full of twenty-eight short, little students. My experiences teaching had included university, high school, and middle school. No primary. I did briefly remember telling the Lord, "I can teach anything but primary." Remember not to say that to the Lord.

We began the day with introductions in order for me to learn how much they were capable of doing. Soon I realized they were ESL students! This I could do. I knew what would be hard for them, what they needed to learn next and it turned out to be OK. At the end of the day, the administration commented that they were surprised to see that I had not asked for any help all day and asked me to consider taking the class. At $325 a month it was one of the highest paying teaching positions in the nation. What a relief. My stay would be extended. Jesus had heard my pleas and blessed me beyond my hopes.

Chapter 7
The Fork in the Road

The benefits of teaching supported me in many ways. My contract included a house within walking distance from the school—about forty-five minutes away, a once-a-year return ticket to the US and health insurance. The school served hot lunches in the cafeteria, and had free Internet use available; e-mail was our link home. Tammy was completing her six months in the orphanage when a surprise opening came up at the school. They hired her for first grade. She shared the house with me. Within a few months we had bought beds, couches, a dining table, microwave, TV with cable, kitchen gadgets, plate sets, glass sets—everything you would need to be happy in a home. We seemed to spend about half our income on monthly living and invested the other half in furnishings. Even though we taught right across the hall from one another in school, it seems we may have only seen each other a few times at work. Teaching is like that; when you have twenty-eight little bodies that all need your attention, you attend. She was a natural for first grade, and trust me, teaching little guys to become bilingual when they're just learning to read and write is a challenge.

When summer came, Tammy and I pooled our airfare money together and decided to get back to the US by taking the bus to California, then flying the distance from LA to home for just ninety-nine dollars. It was a long, long trip. The Latin American countries we travelled through were interesting; some looked more advanced and modern. After days of travelling we arrived at the Mexican border at about three a.m. Two older Christian guys who had been travelling with us helped find us a room for the three remaining hours until the bus left for Mexico City. Mexico was a marathon; the bus ran day and night. They would omit announcing if or when we would be stopping to eat, so eating was sporadic. We would eat, then they would stop thirty minutes later for a dinner hour. We didn't eat because it was too early; then they wouldn't stop until eleven p.m. when everything was closed anyway. Mexico had many drug police officers who would enter the bus and glare at the people to see who winced or not. A really cute thirty-year-old policeman got on the bus and Tammy took a second glance.

"Can I see your documents?" he said in slightly accented English, which was just cute enough.

"Sure, anything else I can offer you?" Tammy smiled, her dimples beckoning.

"Yes." He called for another police officer, who was female.

"Please follow this officer into the bathroom at the back of the bus so she can check you."

Tammy turned a million shades of red and reluctantly started toward the back of the bus following the police lady.

The others in the bus were silent. We all awaited the outcome.

Tammy emerged still beet red and flung herself down into the seat. Everyone else heaved a sigh of relief—no hidden drugs.

"You'll never guess where she had to look."

Wrong timing for flirting.

~Stay far away from anything that may resemble drug trafficking or any other illegal activity.~

Mexico was a wonderful country but the trip was long. Three days and nights, soaking in the sights from the bus windows, took us to the most dangerous part of the trip—the border crossing from Tijuana into California. We had pushed through each and every day by bus, trying to assure ourselves that we would arrive in time for the ninety-nine-dollar flight out of LA. At two a.m. Friday, we were crossing the border, closed in on both sides by drunk, drugged, or rowdy Californian youths, some jokingly insulting each other. It was tense, for us anyway. We could understand every word of the threats; they were in English. Passing through with fear but no trouble we found ourselves in the middle of the night looking for a bus returning to the US. We were told there was one waiting around the corner, a dark and lonely corner. Cautiously, peeking around one could see a lighted bus awaiting passengers. Thank God, He is so good. That bus took us straight to the airport—small miracles. There we sat until noon for our flight. We were both exhausted and stinky but filled with excitement. Soon we would be home with our families.

~Maybe you will choose to travel great distances by bus. Always be cautious; it is an adventurous yet tough way to travel.~

Home felt great. I loved visiting my family and being a part of their lives again. It seemed only a short time had separated us. Being back at church moved me; services in English were awesome, the messages powerful. It was great to not be able to see the podium when all those tall people stood up. By grace, I was invited to speak to two groups of people and one Bible study about my time overseas. My message was that we cannot be complainers in our prayers. God knows we in the US have been richly blessed. Our prayers need to be filled with many more thanks. This connection with my church filled my missionary soul. I was not alone. The Bible says that we were given our gifting to help the church, and we were given the church so we may have family and work together. My church was eager to keep in contact with me even though I was not a church missionary, just a Christian living overseas serving the Lord as I could.

The three weeks passed too quickly, but I didn't struggle with a desire to stay. Culture shock had turned on me; now I was uncomfortable in the US. Shopping in the huge stores was not enjoyable, Taco Bell had the best food, I didn't want to use the day and night teller, and waiting in traffic was stressful. The cold winter was coming and I didn't want to be there for it. It had been an awesome visit with my family and I missed them tremendously, but my life for now was in my new country.

The trip back felt even longer than the trip down, insufferably long. Even though the buses were not cheap, they were pretty comfortable, so we rode on through the nights to avoid hotel fees. Later we decided the inconvenience had not been worth the little amount we saved. Calculating in all the fast food we had to buy on the way and the expensive taxi fares, it would have been cheaper to have flown straight home. One good thing though, now we could say we had been through most of Latin America and we had our passports stamped to prove it. Two foreign women travelling by bus is no longer an uncommon sight, this is the age of tourism for all.

Once back in our little house by the airport, we were still friends and could stand each other—a miracle testimony. Soon we settled back into the teaching life and got busy. All were happy to see that both of us had returned from the US. It is difficult for international schools because a few teachers visit home and stay, leaving the school without a teacher at the last moment.

The overseas teaching experience is different than in the US. It's important to be flexible, really stretchy, and enjoy it.

"I'd like you each to introduce yourselves and tell what grade you're teaching."

"Hi, my name's Tammy, and I'm teaching first grade."

"Hi, my name's Kimi and I teach second grade."

A throat clearing. "Hmm, Kimi, we changed you to fourth grade this year."

"Oh. Well. I'll be teaching fourth grade!"

"And Kimi, you'll be in the classroom down the hill."

"OK, no problem."

"One more thing. This is Waldina and she needs a place to live until we get her into an apartment."

"Nice to meet you, Waldina. We have one room empty in our house so you're welcome to stay with us."

We liked Waldina. In her we found a good friend and fellow teacher from the States. She stayed with us for only a couple of months, but I will tell you her story because it is something you should hear. She came overseas to do her student teaching after graduation. She was a beautiful, well built, young professional black girl. Waldina fell in love with Mario—a handsome, smiley, muscular young man from the coast. She had stopped to buy something from him at his trinket stand in the open market. Other men, even a doctor, had courted her but she fell hard for Mario. They were an adorable couple. All were happy to see their romance develop into an engagement.

After taking a trip to the coast to meet Mario's family the two flew to the States for their wedding and began life near her family. Three years later I heard that they had returned with their two-year-old son, and

Waldina was again teaching at the school. Knowing how hard it might be for a Hispanic man to change countries, especially with no formal training, I presumed Mario could not adjust to life in the US and that Waldina had come back to try to save their marriage. On February fourteenth, Valentine's Day, they had their pictures in the paper. The story reported that Waldina had kicked Mario out of their apartment. Furious, he walked to a friend's house and got a gun. Returning to her, they fought. He shot and killed her, then he shot and killed himself, leaving their baby boy crying beside his two dead parents.

This horrible reality still affects me. Waldina was looking for love and life. Why couldn't I have been her protection, seeing that there was something sinister in their love? Why hadn't Tammy and I noticed anything awry from the beginning? Maybe it was because their love had evolved into this; it had not always been in danger, yet the danger was there waiting to come out. Waldina deserved the best, her son deserved the best, and she wanted the best for Mario. We miss them both. This tragedy could happen in any country to anyone. But as I encourage you to fulfill your mission overseas, I also want to make sure you are more careful than at home. Caution is the word.

The school year started out well in my fourth-grade class, but my visit to Johnnie's boys on the weekends saddened me. In the six weeks I had been away, three boys had disappeared from the center. No good-byes for me. I spoke to Johnnie.

"Can I go with you to visit the permanent center where they take the boys to? It's just too hard for me not to say good-bye to these boys."

"Sure, I'll ask the nun there if it's all right. She doesn't much like evangelicals, only tolerates me, but I'll see what she says."

Sister Mary Rose OK'd my visit. It would be my hope that you all get blessed with meeting a Sister Rose. We took off early Saturday morning as it was a two-hour ride into the countryside. The detention center was hidden away off the main dirt road, surrounded by acres and acres of wheat, corn, and beans. There were groups of mango, mandarin, orange, banana, plantain, and lemon trees with cows grazing peacefully under in the shade. It was a beautiful setting, this little valley divided by a waist-high wading stream quietly tucked into the side of a mountain range, lost in the belly of this nation. It was remote and therefore very difficult for most families to visit their sons.

"The boys plant and harvest food for all the other centers; it's an agricultural center," Johnnie said. A few boys could be seen bent over working in the field. On the other side of the dirt road appeared a very nice expensive but somewhat abandoned-looking hacienda encircled by a beautiful garden full of flowering plants gracefully planted.

We crossed a small wooden bridge and pulled up to the front of Tangala Rehabilitation Center for Youths. The vigilante came out to greet us and looked everything over. The front gates were just regular gate ironworks. The fencing holding the boys in was made of wooden posts and three rows of barbed wire that any child could get through. So much for my prison fears. He ushered us through and we parked the car near some large sheds. From the middle shed I could see a boy about thirteen peering over at us, his head newly shaved.

"If you do something wrong or try to run away, the punishment is to sleep in the shed. He's being punished."

We turned the corner and began to walk down a dirt pathway wide enough for a car, lined on both sides by small houses, maybe ten houses in all. Each house was painted a different color, and boys were sitting on the front steps. Green grass grew between the houses, shaded by an occasional tree. At the far end of the row was a grove of giant coconut trees loaded with coconuts leading to a concrete court, followed by classrooms and a huge library.

As we passed, the older, bigger boys greeted and jeered at us.

"Hey, Johnnie, where you been, man?"

"Hola, boss man. Who you bring with you?'

"Hi there, *gringa*."

"Hey, boys, I remembered to bring the World Cup Wrestling video."

"Wow, awesome, man. When can we watch it?"

"I have to take Kimi to meet Sister Rose. I'll be back soon."

"Okay, man, you know where we are."

"We'll be here."

The boys laughed and snickered a little.

"See you later, Kimi."

Looking between the houses there were three different soccer fields, all with games going on at the same time. Boys were everywhere, running, playing, chasing, joking, sitting, or just looking around bored. In this center there were 112 boys from the ages of eight to eighteen. All had closely shaven hair, most wore no shoes and only a few had shirts.

Sister Rose was a presence. At five foot eight she towered above most of the boys. Her nun uniform was always the same: a blue-gray color, long-sleeved button-up shirt and skirt combo trimmed in white. She had gray-white hair covered by her white nun head scarf. Her shape was round, topped off by an extra-large bust.

She smiled, welcomed me to the center, then invited me in to see where she lived. It was a small cottage maybe thirty by thirty feet in all. She had been in the center serving since she was thirty-nine, for over thirty years. To us she was a significant figure. When you live your life for eternal goals, daily values change. For Sister Rose, this was the only way to live. Her stance was as a positive yet respected and commanding nun. But she was ready to retire. She had completed her mission—the one God had given to her.

~Long-term missionaries are great people to hook up with. They know what works, how it works, and who can get it to work. Also, they have proven themselves as led by God.~

A quick gaze around found a five-room school, huge cafeteria, office, staff rooms, and large library. Of all the buildings, her pride and joy was the beautiful library. We left Johnnie to visit his boys and walked toward the back library entrance, which revealed a football field–sized pond stocked with fish alongside a basketball court. The library room was large and completely full of books, many in English. In the middle was a table for doing difficult one-thousand-piece puzzles. There was a boy at the puzzle, pausing, trying to find a missing piece. Alongside the table she displayed arts and crafts made by the boys. Showing these to me, she paused to recognize the talent shown in each one. Then the cowbell rang for lunch.

The cafeteria was within steps from the library. Boys came running, lining up in four lines by height in front of the cafeteria doors. The shortest and youngest boys got to enter first. Sister Rose barked commands, assuring the rules were being followed. Her orders included moral thoughts and family values, challenging the boys to remember that one day they would be going home and needed to be a valuable part of their family again, so rules are rules to be followed. When there was silence in all the lines, she prayed and then permitted the ones in the first line to enter. Quietly off to the side, an older boy hit the boy in front of him with his knees, temporarily buckling the boy forward. Sister Rose called for a teacher to count and sent the older boy running laps around the concrete court while the teacher counted the laps. It took him a while to finish, but he looked fine when he came in to eat.

She then introduced me to Gerardo, the teacher of the little boys, and took off toward the library. Standing in line, I followed the teacher through the kitchen, absorbing all the sights and sounds. The food looked and smelled good. They were serving baked potatoes (no margarine), beans, tortillas, and egg. All was cooked in great-sized pots and pans. It looked like a lot of food. We each got a natural fruit drink. The cooks were the only females to be seen besides Sister Rose. As I followed the teacher to the table, a cook handed me silverware.

We sat down near the head of a very long table seated with very long benches, all made of natural wood with no paint. None of the boys had silverware; they were using the tortillas in torn off bits or their fingers to pick up the food. They smiled at my gaze, not stopping. The cafeteria was gigantic, hollow, and very dark; its quietness engulfed us. All was broodingly silent, even as we ate.

An overwhelming sadness enveloped me; it seemed we shared the same heaviness of heart. Having been torn away from our families against our wills, thereby losing all—our families, homes, friends, future, we were united as prisoners of a weighted down soul. Freedom eluded them but gave hope to the future.

Gerardo introduced me to some of the boys by name. They asked me a few questions but quickly finished and received permission to dart out. The bigger guys from the next table were glancing over to see if the little guys still had any food on their plates they might not want to eat, and the negotiations began. It was difficult to tell if the little guys won in that exchange or not, but they seemed OK with it. The last table, full of the biggest guys, lined up again for the final leftovers still in the pots. They were grinning and talked lightheartedly while standing in line.

~Seeing the situation others are in helps you to understand how Jesus sees you and your situation more clearly.~

Once outside I asked Sister Rose permission to become a regular volunteer. She gave me her consent and my position as a family visitor for those who were never visited began.

My weeks were spent teaching and my weekends at the center. Saturday mornings I would take a taxi for eighteen cents to the bus station and then take the bus to Tangala about an hour outside of town. There the little bus would take me to the road leading to the center where the walk was about twenty minutes more to the front gates. On Sunday I would leave right after lunch in order to get back home before the sun set. Each trip took about two hours, depending on how long one had to wait for the buses. This schedule left me unable to attend my church in town, so Sister Rose and her Sunday sermons became my service. As Catholic as she was, very little of what she preached conflicted with my evangelical beliefs. Her messages for the boys brightened my days. She was there for them when no one else was. I called my mom and dad to let them know about my first weekend volunteering.

"Do they need anything?" my mom asked.

"Well, yeah. They need underwear and T-shirts."

"Maybe we could get donations for that. How many boys are there?"

"About a hundred. But now that I think about it, they probably don't want T-shirts and underwear. They seem more than happy running around as they are. What they really want and need are soccer shoes. They play soccer barefoot. And they need balls. One hundred boys playing soccer day in and day out wear out a lot of soccer balls in a year."

"I'll talk to Sherri and see what we can get started."

"Thanks, Mom."

~Your mission includes touching others in your life so they too can complete their purpose.~

My days there were wonderful. It was awesome to see a hundred boys being boys in their true natural habitat. No hair to comb, no shoes, no underwear, no socks. Various soccer games were going on all at once at all times. I noticed rocks whizzing by, insects being tortured, balls flying, cuss words slipping out. It was a unique place, but all knew where they were. Their little homes were not homes. Inside each house was a living room with benches in front of an old TV, and a small room with a gated front, where they had their clothes and all their earthly possessions stored in cubbyholes. Across the hall was the teacher's room where he slept. The rest of house opened up into one big room divided by a half wall in the middle. On each side were ten beds in a line. At the far end were two large bathrooms and a shower room. It was sufficient for the body but lacking for the soul.

Some of the boys without visitors took the opportunity to adopt me. They would seek me out to chat every Saturday; ask me about life in the US, tell me about their families, and entertain by asking me to watch them play soccer, go feed the pigs, or tell of interesting things they had learned. Some would clean the steps off quickly so I could sit, tell the other boys not to cuss around me, and share their hopes for the future. Each month I would try to bring one hundred of something to share: a hundred packets of crackers, a hundred little bags of dried papaya in sugar, a hundred pencils, a hundred apples for Christmas.

Once I brought a hundred marbles. It was my custom to share with the little guys first, as they were my group. Pulling out the bag of marbles from my purse and lifting it high to announce the gift I noticed Orlando, nine, our third from smallest in the whole center, standing squarely in front of me and closely inching in to ensure being first in line. He may have been small, but he wasn't going to be last. Orlando had caught my attention before. His clean hair, a little longer than the rest, shone black and his beautiful dark caramel-colored skin showed off his smooth little-boy muscles and native tropical features. His teeth were beautifully arranged and bright white. He had a nice, easy smile that he had learned to use. Orlando was the silent one, calmly quiet and obedient. He always seemed to be doing the right thing. That's how he began to win my heart, the heart of a mother. He was also one of the boys who never got visited.

One visit, the teacher called all the boys out of the house to line up. Someone had cussed and thrown food during lunch. No one ’fessed up.

“It is important to admit when you’re wrong; that’s what men do, so I’m asking one last time. Who cussed and who threw the food?”

No one moved; all their eyes looked innocently around, eyebrows high.

“It’s not fair to punish everyone when we know that only one or two of you broke the rules. Don’t make your friends pay for your mistake. Tell me you did it.”

No movement. The teacher waited.

“A team pulls together. When one member fails, he doesn’t make the whole team pay. He tells the truth.”

Nothing.

“OK, everyone line up for group punishment. Orlando come sit down.”

Gerardo had pulled Orlando out because he was tired of punishing him with the group all the time when Orlando had never once done anything wrong. The boys were fine with that too. The group started in on their squats, jumps and running in place while Orlando and I gazed on.

~You will get the honor of meeting and working with top-quality nationals who have a heart as you do and are already involved in the solutions.~

The groaning and panting started way too early. They knew the tricks—best to sound and look tired early so the punishment wouldn’t last too long. But the teacher did tire them out. Maybe even enough for them to not cuss or throw food next time. If Orlando had been bigger, the boys probably would have gotten mad at him later, but he wasn’t so they didn’t.

One night Orlando had been watching TV with the group but sitting next to me. I asked some of the boys who their best friends were. The three asked all said Orlando. So I asked Orlando who his best friend was and he said he no one. My heart melted for this wonderful, beautiful little boy who had no one.

Still I remember the first gift Orlando gave me. Entering the house to look for the teacher I found it quiet and empty. Turning to leave, a small sound came from the giant bedroom. Orlando was alone on his bed playing with origami animals.

"Hey there."

"Hi."

"Did you make these?"

"Yes. Kiko the Japanese volunteer taught us how to make origami."

~God bless short-term volunteers from around the world and the people who financially support their efforts.~

"Beautiful."

"They move like this."

He picked up the origami bird and made it fly by flapping its wings. Then the origami rabbit that he made hop. Each paper figure he moved expertly.

"You can have this one."

He gifted me the small bird. "Thank you, Orlando. That's very sweet of you."

Wanting to bend down and give him a big hug I held back, respecting my place in his life. His gift had touched me. I tousled his hair and looked around down the long row of beds on either side, imagining bedtime with all twenty boys getting ready at the same time and sleeping so close. Home it was not. "Where do you keep your clothes?"

He showed me the locked room containing the cubbyholes guarding all their earthy possessions. The teacher returned with a few boys and came directly to the room and opened it with his key. "Cubby check. All must be neat and orderly." The boys scrambled in to clean their cubby. Orlando didn't move. The teacher crossed the small room and commented, "Ah, yes. Orlando, yours is always in order."

Orlando smiled with his nice, easy smile that he had learned to use. His cubby was only half full yet it held all he possessed on earth.

Aldo also adopted me. He was a handsome boy and knew it. He was a little short for his age but stocky and strong. At thirteen years old he was a force to be dealt with and liked throwing his weight around. Aldo entertained with great stories of his wayward youth, abusive family, and recent escapades. He lived life to the fullest, he smiled, he laughed, he looked to be happy. Aldo played soccer nonstop, barefoot, but would take time out to show me around.

Once a small band of boys and I were looking up at the giant coconut trees planted by Sister Rose thirty years before, in the days when she never imagined she'd still be around to see them so tall, and Aldo offered to get me a coconut, Orlando was there too. Before I could discuss the issue of safely climbing a coconut tree, he was off, his bare feet curled around the trunk, his hands clasped in front and inching up. We all just looked on. At about halfway up he was tired and rested a little. He looked to be pretty high up, too high to jump down. Aldo put out the energy and continued upward, his hands and feet beginning to get scraped by the tree trunk. Up he went, really high up, then broke off three coconuts and threw them to the ground hoping someone would catch them, which they did. Inching down, he flinched a bit at the pain in his hands and feet but arrived safely. Then he asked the guards to loan him a machete, and yes, they did, in order to cut the shell off. With strong blows he hit the coconut well and uncovered the small brown center nut. He slashed one corner of the nut and handed me the drink. Then he started on the other two. After drinking my coconut water, he cut open the nut so I could scrape out the meat with the small corner he had slashed. Aldo was an expert coconut server.

~Accept gestures of love and friendship as they are offered to you. Try not to demand your vision of love and friendship from them, or you will be let down.~

Aldo lived in another house, one with older boys. It was his little brother Chano who lived in the little guys' house with Orlando.

Chano was a little short for his eleven years and had a finer build. Chano would stand off to the side when I was around and spoke little, letting Aldo lead the way. Sister Rose mentioned that Chano was difficult to handle, but he seemed to behave himself for me even though it was a reserved acceptance. He did appear to like to tease or trick the other boys; no one seemed to be Chano's friend. Aldo was his protection and connection to the world. Aldo's bouncing energy and encouragement to act better brought life to Chano. He really could not do without his big brother. Aldo had somehow survived the near burns, blows, and verbal abuse better than Chano had been able to.

One nice crisp day we were permitted to take the boys fishing at the back pond. It was a huge pond and lined all around by a high dirt mound that was wide enough to walk on. Tropical trees and bushes dotted the path, creating an ideal fishing site. I sat to one side in the shade of some trees monitoring a small group of the boys. Aldo ran from one side to the other, gleefully picking just the right spot to catch a fish chattering loudly the whole time. Chano hung around a group of trees a few feet from the pond. Orlando settled down in the sun on the bank.

Each boy had a roughly carved wooden H form that was about the size of their hand. Wrapped around the center of the H was a plastic fishing line with the hook tied on the end. I guess you might call it fly fishing. The boys heaved back their arms with the hook in their hand and threw them with as much force as they could. Sometimes the line landed well. No worms, no poles, no flashy flies—just hooks. Boy, were they happy, this may have been the most peaceful, free, happy time I ever saw them experience. It was just smooth, calm fun. And they did catch fish, planted there by Sister Rose's contact, and I suspect the fish were a little on the hungry side. Aldo caught the first one. With all the excitement Chano had inched his way to the edge of the water, close to his brother. Everyone was smiling. Aldo was laughing, yelling, and jumping about, following his somewhat small fish that flopped on all sides. He finally caught it and hit its head a few too many times to ensure it was dead. Then he took out the hook and scrambled to find a bucket to put his fish in.

This catch got everyone going; maybe they too would catch one. Orlando decided to get a little braver because he really wanted a fish and started to enter the shallow part of the water in order to throw his hook out farther, but it just got caught in the weeds underwater. His hook wouldn't come loose, and there were no more hooks. Orlando began to inch slowly farther and farther out to recapture his tied-up hook. Without a hook you couldn't fish, maybe ever. Nervousness set in; after all, I was the lifeguard of the moment but hadn't really planned on getting wet or muddy. Suddenly, he quickly dipped down under the water—swimming, I presumed. Before I could panic, he popped up. He had a great smile. It had been worth the risk—he held up the hook. For now he could keep fishing. Maybe five fish were caught that day—none by Orlando, but it had been a blessed two hours of life. They got to cook, clean and eat the fish they did catch so it was time to find branches to build the fire to cook, ask for matches from the guards, and then eat—all done outdoors, of course.

~This simple service of a pond and fish blessed the boys greatly. God bless those who made it possible.~

As the nation elected a new president, we at the center had no clue as to how influential he would be in our lives. President Canales made a new mandate a few months after being in power repealing the law that made living on the street a crime. His new law freed all those children living in confinement solely for being found on the streets. Only those who were admitted for crimes would stay; all the rest would be returned to their families. This new law meant that of the 112 boys in the center, only 39 would stay, and 73 would be sent home within the next three months. The center was in turmoil.

Sister Rose went into action. She contacted families by phone, sent teachers to find families that were "lost", and bound up folders for each one of the boys containing their education and religious diplomas, achievement certificates, and copies of their case stories. Every day or so one boy would leave. It was a tense time, as each boy wondered what would happen to him. Would his family refuse him? Was there still abuse to confront? Would it be best for him just to arrive and then run away? Would his old friends receive him or harm him? Would he have to work instead of go to school? Could he forgive them for abandoning him and not visiting? Would there be food and a bed to share or not? Talk ran wild as the boys assured each other with their grandiose freedom plans and the promise that they would stay in touch—which were all lies and they knew it. Families arrived, happy, celebrating, tears flowing, moments as touching as can be—freedom, no matter how uncertain, is magical. The boys left behind felt heavily burdened by the unknown of tomorrow, and deeply affected by the displays of emotion they had been denied seeing for so long. Month by month the center said its good-byes. Sister Rose responded, encouraging the boys individually to make the most of this opportunity given by God, reminding them of the boys before who had triumphed, studied, worked, went to church regularly and were taking care of their families. Sister Rose had been their lifeline to real life, creating within the center a constant reminder of family values, morals, and hope.

~With service you can make the sacrifice and enjoy the walk, knowing this was the mission made for you to complete. Sister Rose was an incredible God connection for hundreds of boys who had only her to look to.~

"We're still trying to find Franco's family. I sent Teacher Lando to his pueblo, but they weren't sure where his mother had moved to."

"What will happen with the boys whose families can't be found?"

"The law says they'll stay here until they turn eighteen."

"What about Orlando—have you been able to find his family?"

"No, he came in from Pedro del Sur, and they said his file is incomplete. No one has ever come to visit him."

Then I asked what had been in my thoughts for only a short time. "Can I take some of them home?"

My time volunteering at the center had just been a year but Sister Rose knew I had come into her life for a reason and now she understood. I had joined her. Service given out of love and with a natural passion is the only way to live.

God had a plan for my life, but I had to take the steps to fulfill it. It had to be my decision to leave all to know and understand Him in a new and intimate way that I could only experience here. Now I knew a few of my overseas brothers and sisters intimately and shared their reality with them. My prayers would imitate theirs and His answers would bless us all.

~Serving overseas gives us a united heart with all our global family. Jesus has invited us to know one another face-to-face so our prayers better reflect the desires of His heart.~

"If you want to, I can register you as a tutor with the government. Tutors can take the boys home. I think the maximum is four."

"Yes, I'd like that. Maybe I can take four."

Then thinking of my health questioned, "But what if I have to quit at some time or something?"

"Do what you can. Any time they have with you is more than they would have without you."

God was no longer a part of my life. He was in all of my life.

Time to ask Tammy if she would agree to let me share our home with four boys. She said yes and even continued to pay half of everything. We were both crazy. Memories came to me. I had regularly prayed for years in the US to get myself set up so I could live without an income in order to donate my time to the ministry. First, I had imagined volunteering for two or three months, then one year, finally it became five years. This would require me to sell my house, buy a small farm, then grow and can all the fruits and vegetables needed to last one year. There would be chickens ready for egg production and consumption. With savings I would pay for gas and insurance. My car would be paid for—I had always paid in cash for my cars anyway. As I have never used credit cards there would be no debt to pay off. The desire of my heart had been to work full-time in the ministry and now God was permitting that dream to come true in His own way.

Immediately, I began my paperwork with the government. Sister Rose picked out the boys, choosing those she felt could best handle free life with a foreign white lady who was not their mom and could offer no dad. There was no financial help or assistance for me, but my $325 a month as a teacher could provide for us all. The house was paid for by the school. Calculating $250 for food (five people), left us $75 a month for transportation ($5), clothes ($5 per boy), utilities ($25 for half including cable), and extras ($30).

Receiving permission from the school to add the boys to our home, I was given the papers on November thirtieth for Daron, fourteen; Aldo, thirteen; Chano, eleven; and Timoteo, nine. Timoteo was the smallest boy in the center, even smaller than Orlando. He seemed to be about nine, but no one knew exactly how old he was. Sister Rose guessed he had been four years old when he first arrived to her. Timoteo could not talk well because of a birth defect that left his tongue partially glued to his palate. He seemed to have brain damage resulting from resistol use (a sniffing glue) given to him by his mother. Apparently, both his young parents lived on the street. Just thinking aloud one day, I asked Sonia why a mother would give her baby resistol and she guessed it was to keep the baby quiet, especially if it's hungry and there's no food. Timoteo couldn't pronounce his name well but was very streetwise.

Collecting the papers I went to the center by bus, then picked them up with their backpacks and sacks full of personal "things." Sister gave them a short "better be good" lecture and bid them farewell. We walked the twenty minutes to the bus stop and awaited our first trip together as a free family—our trip home. Timoteo, Chano, Aldo, Daron, and I began the two hour ride home.

~Faith in God is manifested in our daily decisions which allow His will to become complete.~

Chapter 8
Living to Serve

Our small house was just feet from the division separating the neighborhood from a busy main street that ran alongside the airport. To the adults, the plane traffic was a constant bother, but to the boys it was heaven. They loved hearing the constant interruption of roaring plane sounds cascading down over us while landing. They would run outside to catch the great gusts of wind that blew at their faces, pressed their clothes against them, their eyes wide open to study to mechanics of the plane bottoms just as they hit the ground. In short order all the names of the airlines landing near us had been memorized. It was a male dream come true.

Tammy and I had to share the master bedroom and bath. There were two boys to each room. Together we nailed the wooden beds Tammy and I had bought at the open market for five dollars each and had hauled home on the bus. Each boy had a new bed frame, two-inch foam mattress, pillow, sheets, and a blanket. For dinner Tammy had prepared American enchiladas and we drank Coca Cola; we were giddy with joy. Afterward, we all sat down to plan the next day, as Tammy and I had to work until Christmas vacation. Who could we ask to look in on them?

Tammy phoned her boyfriend and asked if he would be able to drop in on the boys during the day. He did and found them dressed, fed, the kitchen clean, and everyone inside watching TV. Praise Jesus. Daron, the oldest, was the organizer of the group. He was a soft leader type. Tall, thin, and easygoing, he supervised the group in a quiet way. His mother, who had been a prostitute, had died of AIDS and left him and his older brother alone. His mother's family had rejected them years earlier because of her profession. While she was desperately ill, Daron had decided to live on the streets, distancing himself from his brother. He was soon sent to the detention center because he was caught sleeping near a store. The owner believed he was waiting to steal, which was very likely true. When his mother was on her deathbed, he was released to visit her on his own. He attended her burial on a small mountainside cemetery overlooking the capital and couldn't make himself leave. He had nowhere to go.

After a few days the police came and told him to go. He chose to return to the Sister Rose. He had a victim's outlook and attitude, but knew what was right and wrong and chose to do what was right most the time. He did most of the dishwashing and cooking; he loved cooking and eating but never put on a pound.

Tammy's boyfriend continued to help us out for four more days, his brother then helped us out for two more days until Christmas vacation began. We spent our time after work shopping—each boy picking out a new shirt, pants that fit just him, a belt, socks (each boy a different color), and shoes. We bought toothbrushes, shampoo, deodorant, towels, soap—lots of small items needed for daily use. Christmas seemed to have come early for the boys, but it didn't help Timoteo much. Timoteo sat with me in the bus and grabbed my hand when walking, all the time talking to the people around him in his slurred speech. "I'm outta here after Christmas. I'm just getting my presents, then I'll be with you on the street, *comrades*."

My calls to Sister Rose were almost daily that first week, just to let her know how things were going. She encouraged me greatly.

Other problems did crop up. Rules had to be made. The first request by the boys was for no more beans, rice, tortillas, and bananas—only American food: hamburgers, French fries, Coke, pizza, etc. My food budget would only stretch far enough for us all if we ate native, so amid groans they accepted reality. Rooms had to be cleaned, chores had to be assigned, and outside freedoms had to be defined.

Outside the homes here is a huge concrete basin kept full of water at all times for washing. The clothes are then hung to dry on the line. Each boy was responsible for washing and drying his own clothes, keeping his items picked up and washing his own dishes. In order to easily enforce this last rule I bought each boy a different-colored plastic cup (large sized so they could drink in a big way) and plate, and we marked the silverware. If they left their stuff out, I would know who it was from afar, no denying. And if they didn't wash their things well, they had to use them as they were. It worked quite well.

My dad and mom had sent seven hundred dollars for Christmas. We bought a two-foot-high dried bush, free of leaves, that had been spray painted white. We decorated the bush, put up stockings, and played Spanish Christmas songs from a cassette a Mexican friend had given me in the US. We even made popcorn to string for the tree, which, by the way, didn't last even a few days before being eaten. Each boy received a giant toy, ball, hat, swimming shorts, plastic sandals, comb, a coloring book, and a stocking chock-full of candy. We ate a great Christmas dinner of American and Spanish food in a mixed sort of way. We all dressed up for church and enjoyed the singing and message of family. We had a daily routine and things were well.

Cuss words still seemed to be slipping out in conversation so I worked out a rule: each time someone cussed, they would get a mark on the Good Speech chart. If at the end of the week they had no marks at all, that boy would get to go out to dinner at the corner taco stand. Chano immediately started jumping up and down on the couch chanting cusswords and using up any chance of going out to dinner, making him free to disobey the rule all week long. I was stumped.

The next day he told me how much he hated Timoteo.

"I hate Timoteo. He's stupid."

"Timoteo gets to live here too without someone hating him."

"I'm going to shove him outside."

"Timoteo hasn't hurt you."

"I'm going to hurt him."

With that Chano grabbed a pair of scissors and ran into Timoteo's bedroom, where he was quietly playing, slammed the door shut, and locked it. I was petrified. I called to Chano to come out. His brother, Aldo, helped too. Finally, he opened the door. Timoteo was safe, but I vowed this would not happen again in my house. Sister Rose told me to bring him in the next day. Luckily, that was a Saturday so I didn't have to miss a day of work.

A quick plan had to be made in order to get him to cooperate. The next morning we told the boys that Tammy and her boyfriend were going to drive all of us to the movies. While everyone waited in the car, I gathered up all of Chano's belongings into plastic bags and quickly stuck them in the trunk. On the way, we stopped by the open-air market where the buses were leaving for the center. I got out and found a guard to help ensure Chano got onto the bus. Aldo and the other boys were aghast. There was no time to explain; I followed Chano onto the bus. Tammy did her best to clarify to the boys why Chano had to leave.

Even though Aldo understood all the whys, he was losing his brother—it was the worst thing for him. They were all saddened and nervous by the change, but safety could not be negotiated. Tammy and her boyfriend took off with the boys to the movies.

On the bus, Chano promised to be good over and over, but as a single woman with older boys, I could not handle the mental problems that he had manifested. Sister Rose was furious and bawled him out for losing such an important opportunity. Aldo had taken his place as a protective older brother seriously. They had been a pair against the world. Now Chano was again at the center, this time without him. Knowing they should be together I questioned my decision in front of Chano. Sister Rose declared, "Aldo deserves his chance at a home." I returned alone.

~Take all responsibilities of your ministry very seriously but don't accept more than you can handle.~

By Christmas the center had been left with only the permanent group of "until eighteen" criminals and a few "free" boys whose families had not shown up or could not be found. On December twenty-fourth of each year, Sister Rose celebrated the birthdays of every boy whose birth date was unknown. Orlando celebrated his tenth birthday on December twenty-fourth with Sister. Visiting a few days later, Sister Rose took me back to her tiny house and quizzed me on all that had gone on since Chano had left. All was well and the boys were happy. Then she told me there was one more boy who needed a home and could fill Chano's place if I wanted him. It was Orlando. My heart was thrilled, but also filled with a quiet reservation thinking that I could not offer him all that he deserved. His life with me would be full of boys coming and going; we would not be a normal family. I had missed Christmas with Orlando, but he would be home for the New Year.

The first question Orlando asked on the way home was if he would have to eat beans every day. He has never really liked beans and was ready for real American cuisine-junk food. Quickly he learned that we would eat beans three times a day just like every other household. But truth be told, even today he still isn't too thrilled about eating beans.

Orlando liked his new bed in the room he shared with Timoteo. Timoteo was feeling more comfortable in his new surroundings and began the habit of walking out of the house and not coming back. He didn't seem to understand the boundaries of a home. This was scary for me, as he was so little. One day he disappeared in the morning, and we looked everywhere but couldn't find him. He came home after lunch with money. He had been begging at the bus stop. Angrily, I took the money and told him we would give it to the little old lady that sells gum on the corner and share the gum with everyone. The boys were excited and ran him down to buy gum.

My talks to Timoteo about our yard limits began to include more details. The other boys were put on lookout for him, but he disappeared another time—for six hours. He bought fireworks with the money from begging and set them off (with matches?) a block away from the house before he came home. How could people give money to a little boy dressed in new shoes, jeans, and shirt? The boys told me he had said he was going to buy resistol (glue) to sniff the next time.

We were all on "Timoteo watch," but he disappeared again. We looked all over for two days this time with no sight of him. Then, on the third day, a neighbor told one of the boys they had seen him two blocks away living in a half-finished building with the vigilante family. Aldo went to get him and returned saying the people wanted money for looking after Timoteo for the three days. Extortion.

~Many see us as having an endless supply of future dollars. Unsavory characters will show up eventually trying to get a few dollars for themselves.~

Tammy and I grabbed ten dollars in pesos and went to confront the couple. When we arrived, Timoteo was not there. While conversing, it became clear they were hiding him from us. I was talking my way through the negotiations when Tammy saw something in the background. She moved quickly and grabbed Timoteo from the corner. Making my last offer of ten dollars to the man for their time and provisions I added that if they refused this time the police would be summoned to help. They took the money and let us take Timoteo.

The next morning all seemed fine when we took the bus across town to go to church. Two of our boys and little Timoteo were outside playing with the other children when he walked off. Aldo came in right away to tell me, and we all took off looking down the streets. We looked everywhere, but he was nowhere to be found. We never saw him again. He had followed through on his word—after Christmas he was "outta here" and back on the streets with his *comrades* telling great tales. If he had really wanted find us he could have at any time because one can see the planes landing from anywhere in the capital, but we never saw him again. Street life can ruin a kid in a few months. After that, they don't want to obey any rules: no baths, no bedtime, no school, no family, no limits. We need to make sure no child lives on the streets. It's incredibly dangerous too. Bless the people who donate for street children.

Right away, I reported him missing to the police and Sister Rose. During my next visit to the detention center Sister Rose asked me if there was room for one more. I said yes, still crazy. Cruz was a free boy. He looked to be about fourteen years old and strong.

"Hey, Cruz, come meet Kimi."

"I've already met her."

"Sister tells me you are good enough to come live with me."

"I'm not so good."

"Oh." I paused while thinking quickly. "Why are you here?"

"My father is in prison; they say he killed my grandfather."

"The records say Cruz is here for his own protection. His uncle threatened to kill him in revenge," Sister Rose said.

"Do you want to live with me?"

"I want to be with my sisters and brothers, but the orphanage won't take me."

"Well, you can stay with me until we find out about your brothers and sisters."

"Can I visit them?"

"Yes, I'm sure we can do that."

Cruz packed his bags. Sister gave me the papers, and we took the bus home.

~Make sure you take no child into your home without legal papers. Each country is held responsible to know where all the children are and with whom. It's the law.~

Everyone appeared glad to see Cruz, mostly because they had to. He was now the oldest and strongest of the boys and let them know it. Because

Daron had already established himself as the informal leader, some adjustments had to be made. The boys easily conceded to Cruz, but I did not. Daron was the leader on my side, he was compliant, he pitched in to help. Cruz was vying for my position. Would the boys be faithful to him or me? Cruz was as tall as I was. Good thing he let me win . . . most of the time.

Cruz had joined us at the end of vacation, and it was time to organize the boys for school life. The scholastic year starts in February; we had one week to get ready for public school. They were excited and unsure. They were on the outside now but not part of a regular family. We all spent one afternoon walking the thirty minutes to the nearest primary school to enroll the boys. Single file we passed the airport, the military base, and finally entered a somewhat poor looking family neighborhood. The school yard was swept clean and dotted with a couple of bushes and trees that had managed to survive the impulsive touch of many hundreds of school children while playing. We were led to the office and handed over to the principal. I was immune to the surprise of the staff.

"Hi, how can I help you?" Thinking: *What's a gringa (foreign white woman) doing here?*

"Hi, I came to register my boys for school. We just moved in by the airport."

Noticing all the boys are *not* gringos, don't look like me, and don't look like brothers, a quizzical look appeared on her face.

"Oh, do you have their transfer papers?"

I handed over the detention center school papers. A weak smile appeared.

"All in the same grade?"

Second-graders normally are aged eight or nine. I was registering a fourteen-year-old, two thirteen-year-olds, and a ten-year-old—all for second grade.

Cruz, Aldo, Daron, and Orlando all smiled. I smiled.

"Yes, they finished first grade at the center."

"Wonderful. I'll speak to the teachers to see where there's room." Thinking: *We already have classes of forty-five; what did we do to deserve this? Can't say no to the government.*

Two boys were assigned to each second-grade classroom—Daron with Aldo, and Cruz with Orlando.

~You must have the previous school's documents to enter a child in a new school. They also request a birth certificate and there are vaccination requirements.~

Our new schedule began. At six thirty, Tammy and I would leave for work, walking the twenty-five minutes through the neighborhood and onto the dirt road leading to our international school. The boys would get up, cook, eat, clean the house, study, get on their uniforms, cook lunch, eat, clean the kitchen, and walk thirty minutes to school, arriving promptly before noon. Tammy and I would come home around three to correct papers, rest, cook dinner for the boys, and await their arrival at five thirty just as darkness was closing in.

It seemed a good idea to hire a lady to come every morning to check on them, help with the homework and make sure they left for school on time. Just to ensure they were school-ready at the right time. She was hired to work a couple of hours doing easy work, but after three days quit. Hiring another lady the next week, she lasted only two days. We had to talk. If they were in agreement, I would hire them. Instead of paying the ladies, they would get a wage for watching themselves if they obeyed the rules to a T. At the end of the month they could spend their portion of the earnings on anything that was healthy and legal. They were ecstatic. Each boy was promised five dollars a month. The rule was unequivocal—the house must always be perfect when I got home, and they must always be on time for school or I would hire someone else. It worked like a charm and an extra bonus was that I was relieved of all begging.

"Kimi, buy me a ball."

"You can buy one with your own money."

"Kimi, I need more erasers for class."

"Buy some when you get your allowance."

"Kimi, I'm hungry. Buy me an ice cream."

"Save a little of your money next time so you can buy one when it's hot."

But the real test came when the social workers gave us a surprise visit. As the ladies were approaching the side door entrance, the boys were on their way out, leaving for classes. Bathed, fed, in uniform, lugging their homework with them, they smiled and invited the ladies in to quickly do their review. The house was spotless. The ladies were in shock. "How did you get them to do this?" We became famous for the day at the Children's Protection Services. Yet, on weekends things seemed to go awry; the house was always disheveled, things thrown here and there. Tammy and I would wake up first, letting the boys sleep in, as they did every day. We would cook a special Saturday breakfast, clean the kitchen, get them up to share our special meal, then let each boy wash his own dishes. But the house seemed to always look a little too messy. After lunch it would look even more unkempt.

"Boys, why does the house look so bad on the weekends?

Daron smiled a big grin.

"Every morning we get up really late, watch TV, cook, eat a big breakfast, then get dressed for school. By eleven fifteen we haven't cleaned anything. So on the way out, we clean our rooms, then the living room, then the kitchen, and then we close the door as we back out of the house."

Bingo. The house was kept clean and orderly during the weekdays; we had had no knife incidents, no rage factors, no bad reports from school, nothing stolen nor sold on the open market as far as I knew. So far so good.

~You will be held legally responsible for the safety and welfare of everyone staying in your home. Foreigners brought to court for any reason, guilty or not, are generally fined for all related expenses for everyone, as the judge knows the poor person is less able to pay.~

Saturdays we had to make the long trek to the store to buy provisions for the week. Although this was fun, it was also intimidating. During these times we were seen regularly out together as a family in public, reminding us that we were different. Each of us wore a backpack to carry our purchases home; Orlando had the littlest backpack: the Transformers. We walked thirty minutes to the store—"cheap food at a high price"—and loaded up on everything we could fit into our packs, then walked home with our heavy loads. I did try twice to get a taxi back home, but they were either unwilling to fit us all in one taxi or asked me for exorbitant fees, so we ended up walking. Cruz, Daron, and Aldo filled their packs with the heavy items: sugar, beans, rice, dry milk, vegetables, and lard. Orlando filled up his little pack and I took the remaining things. Anything you carry by hand for thirty minutes when you're walking becomes heavy—even bread or toilet paper. We did this every weekend with only one incident that I can remember. On our way out the door of the store, the other boys told me Aldo had stolen a lemon. Yes, a lemon worth about two cents. My guard had to be on at all times and so did everyone else's. Poverty is a reality and a mindset. It takes time for one to believe in change and confide in a better and safer future. Sometimes it's easier to retain the patterns you believe have protected you through thick and thin, especially if you are a fourteen-year-old boy.

~Some of my boys were later caught shoplifting. It is a serious crime. Make sure you do not accompany people who shoplift or you will be arrested too.~

It was important to me that the boys learned to feel comfortable in a fast-food restaurant. Eating out should be a normal activity, not done often but not unknown either. Once a month, Tammy and I took the boys out to eat. We visited Dunkin Donuts, McDonald's, Burger King, Church's Chicken, Pizza Hut, Wendy's and Taco Bell. The Taco Bell finally closed. Paying top price for tortilla and bean meals didn't really take off. The boys became accustomed to standing single file for ordering, saying "combo number five," knowing which questions would come next and how much saying yes to these might cost them, waiting in line, then going to the condiment counter or filling up their own drinks and throwing away their waste in the hidden garbage sites.

We really enjoyed taking the boys out—our gringo break. The toy rooms for the little kids looked very enticing, but only Orlando was still short enough to enter. The boys tried to coerce him into entering, but he wouldn't go alone. I couldn't convince him either. None of my boys got the chance to play in the areas set up for kids, ever. But they did enjoy all the other extras and made me proud in a restaurant ambience. My hope was that this exposure would help them to reach for a higher standard of living than they would have been accustomed to.

On one of my weekly school visits to pick them up—well, walk with them—the principal informed me that while awaiting the records from his original home school, Cruz had shown the teachers he was well educated so they had bumped him up to fifth grade. Cruz was much happier in fifth grade and still excelled in class. Aldo was struggling in second grade. He had a hard time concentrating and was more interested in socializing; the girls in school were lovely. Orlando and Daron were doing average work and enjoying their new school out of the center. At home every night we would turn off the TV around six and study together for one hour. For us, these times were to discuss the things that mattered. We talked about relationships, science, languages, professions, the past—anything we wanted. It was quality time spent getting to know one another. Then we would watch one more hour of TV, Tammy and I would pray for them, and they'd go to bed. We thanked the Lord for our blessed family in Christ.

~Pray with your beloveds every opportunity you can. It is a way of conveying your love for them and uniting all as family in Christ.~

Aldo was a bigger-than-life kid. He did everything in a big way. He was messy; his part of the room was a pigsty, really—hidden food, stinky clothes shoved in between clean ones—a real mess. He was a cuddler; he gave bear hugs—long, very strong, painful hugs, all the time smiling in a huge way. He was a romantic and fell in love every week. He loved girls, and even one of their mothers. He had a secret cigarette habit that he couldn't hide but did manage to keep outside. He loved fat and would put great gobs of lard in his soup or chunks of butter in his bread sandwiches when I wasn't looking. He sang in a great big, wonderful voice—loud, cheery, free. He loved listening to the radio. Every night he would call up the station to request a song, the same song: "Moño Colorado" (colored hairband), a song for preteens. Every night the radio announcer would ask who was calling and from where. Every night Aldo would make up a new name and place, then he would dedicate it to one of his many infatuations. One night he called in. The radio announcer already knew him by his great voice.

"I want to dedicate a song."

"What's your name?"

"Harry Lion."

The announcer paused, probably laughing to himself.

"Who do you want to dedicate the song to, Harry?"

"My wife in Santa Barbara."

We all were laughing.

"What song are you requesting?"

Both voices—his and the announcer's—were in unison: "Colored Hairband." And the music would start. Aldo would crank up the music so loud that the neighbors finally sent their guard to complain.

Another night he was sitting in the middle of the hall quietly talking to the radio announcer. I thought, "Great, what's he up to now?"

Then I heard Aldo say, "I want to guess how much the pig weighs."

"All right. If you guess exactly right, you'll be the winner of the pig. It'll be yours."

"*Oooooy*! I think it weighs 215 kilos."

"Sorry, Mr. Rich, 215 kilos is not right. Thank you for playing to win."

Thank goodness. I thought, *What would we do with a pig!*

Aldo did miss his little brother, always feeling the role of big brother protector, but understood why Chano was with Sister Rose in the center. One day when I came home from work everyone was acting really weird. I noticed they were running inside and out a lot.

"Hey, guys, what's up? What's going on outside?"

"Chano's back. He escaped from the center."

"Aldo's been taking him food."

"He's over by the road hiding."

Calling Sister Rose she contacted the authorities for me. Taking Aldo aside I explained that Chano could not come back into our home, but it would be OK to take him some food and Kool-Aid for now. Chano stayed outside that night by a shed near the main road, but parked himself right in front of the house all the next day. He yelled at the boys inside, cussing, ranting, and even telling them to bring him something to sell. That night he came around the gate with a flask acting like he was drunk, yelling that he would kill my cat, kill me when he was grown up, and cussing so loud the neighbors could hear. I called the police directly. They said they would come, but when they found out he was only eleven years old they lightened up, said they would come but didn't.

The next day was the same. Calling the police again they mentioned they had no gas for the car so I offered to pay the five dollars or a taxi. Finally arriving, they almost laughed looking at little Chano. Handing them the five dollars, they then put him in the taxi, and took him to an overnight house for street kids, promising he would be returned to the center.

That next morning Chano was back in front of the house, yelling that he would kill whoever came out first. I called the police asking why he had been let loose. Evidently, he had cried so much they felt sorry for the little guy and decided to let him go if he promised not to bother us. I was furious at the mismanagement of the situation. This time they came in the patrol car and took him away, still chuckling at the idea that he was a threat. This scene broke Aldo's heart, but there was nothing neither he nor I could do. Chano had chosen to rebel when he should have chosen to embrace.

~Police are underpaid, exposed to dangerous people and situations, and not well funded. It is difficult to get police protection much of the time.~

My hope was to involve the boys in church now that they felt comfortable with the Sunday services. They had an outsider's mentality and maybe meeting some Christian kids their own ages would change that. The only friends they had been around the last few years were all from the detention center and, honestly, they felt more comfortable with them. It was hard to take the stigma away from their hearts. They never knew when their past would publically or privately curse them again. They still had to be tough to the core. Sunday after Sunday we attended church, getting to know the regulars by sight, but never once did they meet or talk to any other young people.

Spring break camp came, so I took advantage of an opportunity. A living-together situation always brings about bonding that cannot take place any other way. Unfortunately, that's exactly what prisons do. Fortunately, that's what retreats and camps do too, in a healthy way. I wanted to forge a new path and signed them up for camp, paid for the meals and extra activities, and got the list of things they needed to take for the weekend. We talked about what camp would be like, and they were not eager to go, but I encouraged them to give it a try. Even though they were highly apprehensive, they agreed. Any new situation where they were not in control or where their "leader" was not in control felt highly stressful for them. Their tragic life experiences had taught them not to confide in adults, any adult—not even their moms and dads. They had to be ready at all times to do what was best for themselves. But I was able to convince them to give it a try by buying lots of cool treats: chips, cookies, crackers, donuts, fruit, and sending juice, enough to share too. Besides, I was traveling to Texas the same week to meet up with a great friend in the ministry who was showing interest in me as a wife. The boys had met him during his last visit here and liked him too. Our trips were coinciding.

Asking a lady church friend to take the boys to and from camp and stay in our home would cover me as my trip would take two days longer than their vacation.

~A rule of thumb overseas is to never leave your house empty. As long as someone's home, the thieves stay away. If you leave your house alone for even an hour or two you could be robbed.~

The boys were nervous because the list said they should bring sleeping bags or mattresses and we didn't have sleeping bags, even though most people here don't either. We did have mattresses, but those seemed to be what the poor kids who didn't have sleeping bags would bring. These boys were very sensitive about being different even though we were different in most every way. They were concerned about fitting in even though we didn't fit in. Convincing them to take mattresses I let the main leaders know about them and left for Texas.

The boys arrived fine at the church camp. It was a picturesque spot in the mountainside outside the capital, called Betel. Acres of forest were well maintained and dotted with cozy cabin-like homes. It was a beautiful, refreshing place to be. There was a soccer field, basketball court, playground, and a huge convention room all actively used by the youth. A live band played Christian music, and the boys were encouraged to really enjoy themselves. Feeling anxious, they ate all the extra food I had sent right away that Friday evening, so they didn't go to dinner because they were full and shy. Then on Saturday morning lining up for breakfast they realized everyone had plates, forks and cups and they didn't. They left the line and went to the side and waited. After everyone else had eaten, one leader asked if he could bring them plates but they said no, it was OK, and walked away. They never asked for nor were they offered food again. They didn't eat Friday dinner, Saturday breakfast, lunch, dinner, or Sunday breakfast the next day—all of which I had paid for.

That Sunday, when the buses got back to the church, my lady friend didn't show up to give them a ride home. Everyone else had been picked up and they were left waiting. But they didn't wait long. After not eating for so long and feeling embarrassed, they decided to take things into their own hands. So, incredibly hungry, angry, weak, and hot, they set out across the capital walking with all their stuff on their backs and bags in their hands. Three hours later they arrived home. My lady friend was inside but hadn't noticed the time. They were furious and didn't feel one bit blessed. Their time at camp had made them feel like outcasts, a feeling they had expected to feel and may have even embraced.

~When working with groups of people, try to be sensitive to their feelings of rejection. Needy people are not happy to be needy. They desire to be equal.~

In Texas, I had had a great time and met many wonderful people but did not feel I was meant to be the future wife of my very special friend.

Getting off the plane returning home, my boys were waiting for me right outside the first gate. They were supposed to be in school but had all decided to skip so they could surprise me and help me get home. They were also a little uncertain, wondering if I would ever really come back. My homecoming couldn't have been sweeter; I was greatly touched. We filed out of the airport and they dragged my suitcases on wheels the three long blocks to our home. We were together again and contentedly happy.

All of us had survived the separation except for my cat, Piggy, a wild barn kitten who drank with her paws in the milk. She had made it to our home from the detention center on one of the trips with the boys. Being a little ferocious, she was able to defend herself against four big boys. But my absence had cost her, I couldn't find her anywhere. Finally, I heard a small sound in the cupboard under the sink and found her hiding (or trapped—I will never know). Trembling, she meowed a weak cry and cuddled up in my lap, eyes wide open and dilated. Then the Piggy jokes began and they laughed recounting all that had happened to her, the funniest being when they tied a block to her tail and she climbed clear up the curtains to the ceiling. Boys and cats can mix, but the cats lose. I was back and aggressively defending her every moment. She would not suffer like that again on my watch, poor baby. The boys said cats were not cool; they wanted a dog.

We were walking home after a night out for pizza, a great treat, when we noticed a large dog following us home, attracted by the smell of the extra pizza in my hand. He was half my height, shorthaired, a golden color, and very thin with sores on his body. He had been on the street awhile but obviously had been raised in a family. This great dog nicely walked alongside us and seemed to be smiling, thinking he had found dinner. When we got to our gate, he tried to enter, but we blocked him out. His face just dropped; he couldn't believe we were locking him out. He sat and stared at us, silently begging for entrance. We went in but he did not move. Giving up I let him sit on our front porch and gave him some rice with milk. He needed a veterinarian.

The next day he sat calmly on our porch, gently barking in a soft low tone to people who passed by too close to the gate. I named him Baby, as he was huge but gentle. The vet came in the afternoon when the boys were all in school to attend to him. He let me know Baby had signs that he had been on the streets without food for some time. He probably had been set loose by his family as he was dying of what looked like cancer. The vet suggested he could be let loose on the street again. The other dogs would fight with him until they killed him. I offered pay for a shot to put him to sleep instead and he was very positive. It would be seven dollars, a little costly for most people to spend on their pet when they might need that money for medicine for their child. He offered to carry Baby away to the dump yard for me in his pickup afterward. As the vet was getting out the lethal injection, neighbors came to observe. Things were a little tense.

"That your dog?"

"No, he followed us home last night."

"You gonna pay for his medicine?"

"No, he's dying. The vet can't save him."

"He has cancer," said the vet.

"She won't pay for the medicine?"

"Yes, she's paying for this medicine," he responded.

"You have to look for his family. You can't take someone else's dog."

"He's been on the street for a long time," I added.

"Better ask around to see if you can find his family."

"This medicine will make him sleep so I can take him to my clinic and try to contact the family," the vet interjected.

The vet and I glanced quickly at one another. The neighbors did not seem to understand that the cancer was untreatable. They were not in agreement with what we were doing. Gently I talked to Baby until he was asleep and the vet took him away. The neighbors left feeling confident the vet was doing what was right. When the boys got home from school I told them the truth. They seemed to understand.

~Seeing starving animals is a very difficult reality here. But there is a saying: "For every starving dog you see, there are a hundred starving children nearby." Our focus must be on humans.~

The days passed. Aldo was found with cigarettes in his room. Cruz said he would not do his chores. Aldo hid during chore time. Daron decided cooking was fun and cooked whatever he wanted with all our provisions while I was gone. Love notes written by Aldo to various girls were scattered around the house. Orlando was good as gold. My time at home he would sit on my lap, hold my hand, ask for a bite of whatever I was eating, and share a spot on the couch with me. As he was the youngest, I was forever aware of his presence and tried to ensure he got his turn. It was a joy to have a little guy around too.

Cruz asked me if he could sign up for drum lessons at the government-run after-school program. He had learned to play the drums growing up and missed practicing. He would be able to get to the school by taking only one bus, so I agreed. Later that month the First Lady was visiting the school on her birthday. His group had practiced some songs, but as he was the newest member, he was not going to get to play. Cruz decided to show up anyway and, sure enough, the drummer didn't. Cruz jumped into action and played the drums for the First Lady. He was pumped up and I was proud of him.

Things were working well for us all, except Tammy. Her boyfriend was suffering from some extreme mental problems and they broke up. She was totally distressed and decided to return to the States. She had been a super support for me and the boys from day one. She had paid half of many expenses, opened up her home, and had helped us all lovingly during our most important stage. Her friendship could not be replaced. We walked to the airport to see her off and said good-bye forever.

The school year for foreign teachers was ending. I prayed to God that if these boys were my family, I would adopt them, but if this was a ministry then God had to fund it. The Children's Services had asked me to take six more boys. They had found a house and agreed to provide furnishings, utilities, and some food but said the wait would be another month. I prayed and with faith turned in my resignation to the school then gave notice on our house. The ministry had begun.

~Your mission completes you, using all your life experiences to prepare you for the challenges of today and tomorrow.~

The same week I got my final check from the school, the Children's Services told me the house had fallen through; it might take many months to find me another. Not knowing whether to be in shock or to calmly trust the Lord, I decided to stay calm and trust as much as possible. Suddenly, we had no future income and no home. I asked the landlord to accept us again, but he said he already had found other renters, very likely without a bunch of boys and willing to pay more. Then a miracle happened.

A check arrived in the mail from a couple I had met in Texas. The amount was three hundred dollars—exactly what I had been making at the school. There was no promise of support, just a check sent to help us out. We had what we needed for one more month's expenses. I felt blessed and stressed and started looking for a house. For thirty days my heart was in my throat, I was confident yet tensely wondering how we would manage the next month. Miraculously, another check came, and the next month. Is my Father God good or what? We had an income from heaven.

Chapter 9
A Life Alive

To find a new home was a little difficult. There were no real places to find rentals—it was all word of mouth. I would get on the bus with Daron and Orlando and we would travel around for a while and then get off and ask at the mini store *pulperias* about houses to rent nearby. Many of the houses were too small or prices were inflated because I was a *gringa.* Additionally, no one was too enthused about renting to a group of teenage boys. Changing my story, saying a lady in our church with four boys needed to rent a house, the prices went right down. Finally, we found a nice house in Colony Centro. It was a two-story home in the middle of the capital in a mountainside community. We were half a block away from the primary school and five city blocks from the buses, taxis, and a grocery store.

All the homes were like townhouses, each one built on the side walls of the next. Dark wood framed each room's white walls, and tile floors reflected the coolness provided by the windowless sidewalls. The small kitchen and living room opened up to a courtyard on the ground floor flanked by a bathroom and an extra bedroom. We all slept upstairs. To get to my room you had to pass the two boys' rooms and bath and cross a small open-air bridge-way above the courtyard to my door. This gave me a nice feeling of the outdoors and private space. I had a walk-in closet and a bathroom with a bathtub! This was a luxury; few homes have bathtubs here. The rows of homes were joined by both sidewalls and back walls. It felt safe. The owner assured me that there was no gang activity nearby. He was charging seventy-five dollars a month—my price.

We began the job of moving. I had to find a pickup to hire to move all our stuff, boxes to pack everything in and provide meals for the boys while we were moving. The boys were getting nervous; big changes were happening and they felt lost again. They wanted to decide, do other things, or hide. But I was in charge and if asked to do something they would have do it. Things were getting stressful. Aldo had disappeared at the sound of work, leaving to say good-bye to his various girlfriends for the third time already. He didn't want to help, and the other boys were feeling used.

Going out to look for Aldo, I found him at a house a few yards away and called him home to help. He really didn't want to come but did. Inside he made it clear he was not going to do anything, and when I insisted he resisted more. The rules were that he must help to be a part of this family and he must help now as we were moving. He raised his hand in a gesture to hit me, only showing that he could do it. That was it. Aldo had to leave, but it would have to wait until we had finished moving. Without a word I let it pass and we finished packing moving into the new house before dark. The next morning in the new house he continued with his power struggle, maybe thinking he had won the previous day.

"I don't have to do anything you say."

"To stay here you do. I am the authority."

"You can't make me do anything."

"To stay here you will have to obey me unless I ask you to do something illegal or something that will hurt someone."

"You're full of sh--" He glared at me.

I grabbed him and pulled him toward the door.

He fought but not too much. I could not give in. In my home, I could not have a thirteen-year-old boy turning fourteen, fifteen or sixteen who might eventually hit me. I pushed him out the door.

Outside he cried, “I need my stuff!”

The boys gathered his belongings, and we passed the plastic bags to him through the door.

“Sorry, you don’t belong here with us anymore. You decided you didn’t want to be a part of our family.”

I contacted the Sister and the police, but he was gone before they came. Four days later he returned to ask for his papers and school grades from the detention center. He told me he had found a place in a home funded by the Catholic Church. Thank God they took him in. Aldo will always have my love. It was not my desire for him to be on the street, even for one night. My greatest hope was that he would make it. Aldo has so much to offer the world.

Cruz, Daron, Orlando, and I continued our life. Things seemed pretty OK until Friday and Saturday nights came. Late at night, we could hear youths yelling in the street, machetes being swung, scraping the pavement as they walked by. More than one night we heard footsteps running across the rooftops of our connected houses as we slept. Anyone could drop down onto my open-air bridge-way and be at my bedroom door or the door to the boy’s hallway in a flash. We were a little tense during the noisy moments, and it took a little getting used to. We heard stories of people being held up when leaving their homes or in the narrow pathways made for us to go up or down the hill to the bus. One weekend the street gangs supposedly ran off the vigilante guards. We were always on the watch. We knew we could be targets when entering and leaving our own home. But, all in all, things were OK.

We had to change churches, as our old church was now four buses and two hours away. I chose Betel, the same place where the boys had gone for church camp. It was a twenty-minute ride in church buses out to the ten-acre retreat center. The air was fresh and cool and the plants abundant. The church services were perfect for youth, except they expected you to bounce a little and clap with the music—you know, loosen up and enjoy the beat. There was a dance team of girls who twirled and swayed, stringing long, thin colored fabric strips in the air.

Everyone in the whole church bounced and enjoyed the music, clapping continuously, except for one group of very staunch boys—mine. Finally, I began to point out to them that they were not even clapping in church, so the next Sunday they clapped, most of the time. But my complaining never convinced them to move a little to the music or, heaven forbid, sing. Singing in church is only fun IF you sing. Listening to other people sing is just not fun every Sunday. They needed to sing to themselves, not really loudly drowning out the other voices, just quiet lips moving enough to make themselves feel good, a part of the praise. But it never happened. It was more important for them to not embarrass themselves in each other's eyes than to embarrass themselves every Sunday in front of the other three hundred members of the church. Their group was strong and their unwritten laws solid. The church was active, alive, and positive. We enjoyed the services anyway, every Sunday.

The boys were registered in the new school. They had to meet all new friends and I again had to buy new uniforms.

Daron came home from school filled with excitement.

"Kimi, I think my mom's cemetery is right up that hill. It looks the same."

"Well, we can go look. Do you think you can remember where her grave is?"

"Yes, it's next to a white wooden cross by a tiny tree and near a concrete tombstone with some name on it I can't remember."

Not much to go on. "OK, we'll go look."

The hike up was short, maybe five minutes. The cemetery had changed a little since he had been there. It was a run-down, uncared-for plot of land dotted with handmade gravestones, plastic flowers, and stick crosses marking the resting spots. We looked all over for the grave he remembered, the wooden cross by the tiny tree and the tombstone with some name on it, but we couldn't find anything that resembled his memories. Daron was sure it was in the place we were looking, near the little withered tree, so we enjoyed having found her cemetery and the visit. He told me much more about his childhood than he had before. His soft leadership, the jokes he would bear, and his joy at being in second grade with a bunch of little kids began to make more sense. My guess was he had been sexually abused as a child. It sounded as if his mother had maybe sold him for sex while prostituting. He was confused. I wrote immediately to one of my pastors, Pastor James in the US, and requested the book his wife had written that dealt with overcoming childhood sexual abuse. This assistant pastor of a very busy church with eight thousand members sent me the book for free. Oddly enough it was pink!

The book helped me a lot to talk with Daron in an effort to help him overcome his past. It was then that I realized all that my church in the States had prepared me for. My training had started years before while listening to awesome preaching every week. Not only did I gain a great ear for the truth as expressed in the Bible, listening to preaching and teachings, but each service over the years had spoken to different groups of people about different issues. Now I had to know a little about most of those issues in order to raise my boys with wisdom, and I had learned how to do that at church, thank God. Everything learned and experienced in my entire life was being used to raise these boys, allowing them the choice to become godly men, great husbands and fathers, and responsible citizens.

~God is continually preparing you for His purpose. What you have already learned may be sufficient to put you in action.~

It was necessary for me to be aware of everything, handle anything, and promote traits of godly men, great husbands, and loving fathers. Some things I would not be able to handle, and I prayed that I would be able to tell the difference. The book helped me a lot, but it was in English and Daron was not able to read any of it. My responsibility was to help as much as possible to free Daron from his abusive past to become the godly man Christ had planned for him. Protection was utmost. My home provided the protection he deserved, and I had to keep it that way.

Cruz, Daron, and Orlando had to divide all the kid chores between just the three of them. I heard Cruz sweeping the kitchen and repeating to himself, "I am not a slave. I am not a slave," although, he did feel like a slave. One day after asking him to do his chore he fired back at me.

"I don't need to do anything for them [the other boys]."

"But, Cruz, it's your turn."

"Do it yourself."

"I'm cooking, Cruz. You have to do your part."

"I'll do what I want around here."

"No you won't. I am the leader. You can be the leader of your own home."

"You're not a leader; you're a waste."

"Cruz, you know the rules. You have to obey or leave."

"You can't make me leave."

"If you can't do what I ask, I'll go next door and ask the father to come over."

"Right, you scare me."

Cruz crossed his arms; his flexed muscles showed from his sleeveless T-shirt. I went next door and asked the father to come over right away to help.

"So, what's the matter here?" he asked, looking at Cruz at eye level.

"Cruz won't make Kool-Aid for the other boys," I responded quickly.

The neighbor looked my way and raised his eyebrows in surprise. "Cruz?"

Cruz looked down and choked up.

We stared in silence.

Tears began to form in his eyes. He looked much tougher on the outside than he was on the inside.

"Cruz, make Kool-Aid for the boys. Help your mom out," said the neighbor.

Then he left. Cruz made the Kool-Aid and the conflict was over.

Other people called me their mom but the boys did not. I met my boys as Kimi at the center—that's what they called me before coming into my home. Plus, I was, after all, a foreign lady with an accent and limited Spanish vocabulary, and I did not look like any of their mothers anyway. People would most likely react strangely, firing questions at them, if they introduced me as their mother. At all times they tried to avoid looking or being different, because we already were so different. This did hurt me occasionally and denied them the right to say "Mom" like regular kids, but we couldn't really worry about it as there was so much more to focus on. Yet, it was always nice when the people closest called me their mom, and eventually they would decide to slip it in, if it seemed to fit safely at the moment. Confidence was a hard thing to earn from my boys.

The church had an excellent medical assistance program. There was a very small doctor's office inside the church building. Since my boys were older and not about to share anything too intimate with me, I decided to have them visit our doctor just to assure myself there was nothing too serious hidden from me. Orlando, Daron, Cruz, and I took the bus and walked the thirteen blocks to the church office. Waiting there were three ladies with their small children. No one in line spoke much; there was just the occasional pleading and crying of the children echoing from inside the doctor's closed office. The longer we waited, the more anxious Cruz got.

"What are we here for anyway?"

"The doctor is going to give you a checkup."

"I'm not sick. I feel fine."

"A checkup is to record all the illnesses you've had, record which shots you've gotten, list which medicines you are allergic to, weigh you, and measure you."

"I've never been sick."

"Well, you need to tell him that."

"Daron and Orlando have to go in first."

A pause.

"I'm not going in there alone!"

Another pause.

"And if he tries to touch me, I'll punch him a good one."

Everyone waiting in line started laughing, even Cruz laughed at himself. Cruz did go in but he also came out quite quickly. I later learned the doctor had only asked them questions. He even didn't check anything.

~Doctors are used only for sick patients. Well visits are not done.~

Cruz would push me around verbally at least once month. We had our confrontations, but he would always let me win in the end; that's what made the difference. Ultimately, each and every boy had to let me win or they would have to go. The nice thing about Cruz was that he always spoke what was on his mind right to your face. This could be tiring, but also it gave me a chance to defend myself or clarify a belief or mature the ideas surrounding a conflict. There was space for learning and sharing. Cruz put up a strong front to protect himself because he felt the most threatened by life. Each time a boy came into our home, Cruz would quickly dominate him by challenging a fight. The new boy would back off, and Cruz would then offer friendship, gaining him on his side. Cruz never did hit or try to hit anyone; the threat was enough. He fought only with words and appeared ferocious. He really was a peaceful leader—all things considered.

Johnnie visited us in our new home to ask if we had room for one more boy who was fourteen. He was registered with the Children's Services, had been in a home, but needed a different home because of sexual issues with the daughter there. We would make room. Going to meet him at the government building, I entered the main office, passing by a blond fourteen-year-old who was praying over his plate of food. He had me. One more came home. Within a few days he displayed sexually abusive behavior toward Daron. We all believe the Holy Spirit led me there at the right time to avoid a more serious situation. Calling Johnnie immediately, I asked him to take the boy back to the Children's Services. He came right away and the threat was gone. Under my roof no abuse would be tolerated. The boys were in my care to avoid and not repeat past abuses. They were to be protected and safe from harm.

Later that day Johnnie returned and together we talked one by one with the boys, clarifying what sexual abuse was, reviewing options of avoidance, and asking about their sexual histories. We told them that sexual abuse would not be tolerated in our home and opened the door for later dialogue at any time. They could count on either one of us. Johnnie was awesome. It was shocking to realize what had almost happened under my roof yet my determination to protect the boys only strengthened.

Chapter 10
Always an Extra Pillow

Four weeks before Christmas, Johnnie returned and asked me if I could take in three of four brothers whose father and mother were in jail for selling marijuana. The oldest son had raised his brothers alone for the first year following the arrest of their parents, with one of his cousin's cooking and helping out. Their father met Johnnie at the prison fellowship and asked if he could find a family to live in his house and care for his boys. Johnnie found a church couple and provided the food for them all. But the house parents decided they really didn't like the boys—not boys like that, anyway—so the situation was deteriorating.

Their home was smack in middle of a neighborhood known to be dangerous. The house was run-down, small, but just sufficient enough to live in. The two little guys, Deni and Lorenzo, were there peeking out the bedroom as I entered—cute kids of about nine and eleven years old. Nolan, thirteen, had just run out of the house in order to avoid a head-shaving punishment by the house father, so I didn't get to meet him. The house parents agreed to send me the boys. As we were leaving, the oldest brother, fifteen, walked out of a nearby house—the cousin's—swaggering a bit and dressed like a gangster in large clothes and a plaid long-sleeved shirt and bandana.

"That's Riki."

"I won't take him." Johnnie nodded in agreement.

Later that day I returned to the cousin's house by bus to pick up the boys and take them home. The next day we went to the Children's Services but no records of them where found, so we started on the papers right away. Nolan had been sick with meningitis when he was one. Of all the babies in the hospital with meningitis at that time, he was the only one to survive. The doctors warned that he could be blind, deaf, retarded, or unable to walk. Nolan was blessed. He grew strong, beautiful, happy, and showed difficulties only with learning and conceptual ideas. Lorenzo was a handsome, quiet, angry boy who worried a lot about what other people thought and made friends only with those who hung around with his brothers.

Deni, the youngest, was a happy, smiley, friendly, personable kid who excelled at most everything he tried, which kept Lorenzo hopping. Deni was the kind of kid who would find a backpack, steal anything of value, take the money, read the ID, and then return it to the lady who lost it, claiming nothing was found inside, and collect a reward. Since he was such a cute little guy he got away with a lot. We were happy to receive these brothers. After all, my boys thought these boys were pretty awesome with both parents in prison and all. How cool is that?

It was so different receiving boys from a home atmosphere. They blended in, did their chores, shared toys, spoke without cussing, and took care of their possessions and those of others. They had bad habits too—selling things from the house, hiding wrongdoings, stealing, and choosing improper friends. But through this change my boys were the ones who really showed what they were made of. We now had the same amount of money and space, but double the boys. My boys had to share their rooms, blankets, toys, turns, bathrooms, and TV. Nightly, we all crammed in front of the TV tightly together, lying on thin mattresses. Orlando always paired up with me. We ate simpler food, had to divide more, ate out less, broke more things by accident, and bought less. We had to vote on where to go and what to do. Some had to stay home while others got to do errands for me. My three boys never once complained.

Maybe it was because it was more fun too. There was always someone who would play what you wanted to play, something new going on, and lots of fun and jokes. Because our family was made of boys who were not all brothers, they took greater care in not angering each other. Best just to leave a touchy situation alone or there might be unforeseen trouble.

Now that we had another father in prison, we began a monthly tradition of visiting them. I didn't think there was much involved to visit a prison, although I never had been to one. It was necessary for all my boys to have contact with their parents if possible and feel loved by them. We had to go where they were. Cruz's dad and Deni, Lorenzo, and Nolan's dad were in the same prison, which was located in the center of town. I remembered passing by on the bus and looking out with pity at the women standing in line to enter, imagining how sad it must be to visit a loved one inside. Now I was to be one of those women.

Each visit was a weighty experience, but the first was simply a shock. I was so naive. The four boys and I took two city buses to arrive at the prison door. It was just two feet from the street, built in the early 1900s, and was a formidable fortress. But the city had grown and encroached on its premises, closing in on all sides. The brick-and-mortar round corner guard towers gave it an appearance right out of the movies. The double doors were very high, about fifteen feet, and were of heavy wood decorated with metal, just like castle gate doors.

As the boys lined up with me, the other women informed us that boys over twelve had to line up on the opposite side with the men. This meant that Cruz, Lorenzo, and Nolan had to enter by themselves and just Deni remained with me. The men's line was faster, as fewer men visited the prison, so the boys were ushered inside quickly. As Deni and I entered, we saw the men on one side of the hall and the women on the other. Luckily, the older boys were waiting, insisting that Deni go with them on their side—little did I know why. I was ushered into another side room just for women and their small children. The walls, high ceiling, and floor all looked the same: cold gray concrete bricks from the century before. The end of the room had been divided by tiny wooden thinly walled booths about chest high. In each space was a lady guard. Waiting my turn I entered into an empty booth.

"Show me your undies."

"What?"

"Show me your undies."

She looked bored.

I looked around over all the other half booths. Evidently, this was procedure.

I pulled down my pants.

"Pull down your undies."

"What?" My eyes popped open. I was flabbergasted. I couldn't be hearing right.

She looked at me over her glasses. "Pull down your undies."

I did and I tried not to look around, my face burning red.

"Squat three times."

My eyebrows shot up and I froze.

"Squat," she repeated.

I squatted three times.

Then she OK'd me to leave.

No wonder the boys had called Deni to the other side! Leaving by the back of the room, I hoped no one would notice my beet-red face in the light of day. I was totally shaken and trying not to show it. The boys were waiting for me at the double-door metal gate. What I didn't know at the moment was that they check men too. The boys had gone through the same thing on the other side—all of them. But we didn't ever talk about it. ~Prison ministry is a positive movement; join in with a group to serve. Do not go alone.~

Visitors then waited at the inside gate until their prisoner was notified and came to invite you in. This is because guards don't pass the main gate. The prisoners are running things themselves without police presence behind the big walls. That means the guests don't have guarded protection once they pass the gates—just the protection offered by the prisoners themselves. This protection does seem to work, because if even one guest has any problem behind the gate, the guards can choose to stop all visits indefinitely. As you can imagine, these family visits are sacred to the prisoners, so the risk seems to be minimal. At this moment I didn't realize there was no guard protection passed the entry gate, possibly because I was still in shock from the squats.

The announcement that we were visiting spread from prisoner to prisoner until one of the fathers received the news. Cruz's dad heard first and came forward to claim us. His smile couldn't have been wider, his face aglow. We entered, my heart pounding with stress, and began walking among the crowded groups of men. It was difficult not to accidentally bump into or touch anyone while passing by, or look anyone in the eyes, as there was not much room. We just squeezed by through the never-ending crowd of men. Lucas, Cruz's father, led us to a patio tent room placed on the concrete that had a small kitchen-like area and one chair inside. He insisted the guest use the only chair so I sat down while they excitedly began talking.

Cruz's father was a very thin, small man who had a weeping sore on his forehead. He had a soft voice and looked to be around fifty. Cruz asked me in a whisper if he could borrow twenty pesos. Secretly I passed him the pesos and he went to buy us all juice. Cruz's dad had no money to "invite" us, as is the Latino custom, and he was embarrassed by this. The talk started—father and son desperate to fill in the news of their lost family, making them more complete and united by these moments to share.

~If you "invite" someone to eat or go on a trip, you pay for both. Many newcomers get shocked as they are asked to pay for the whole bill because they were the ones who said, "Let's go."~

Soon we got word that the three brothers' father was around on the other side of the building. We all left in single file, trying to pass through the heavy crowd again. There were more restaurant tents, some tents used for conjugal visits, and others selling food or necessary items for the prisoners. No open, empty spaces. When we found the other father the two families separated, each boy with his dad. I sat with Cruz and his father, Lucas, first. He wanted to hear all the news about Cruz and of his six other children living in the orphanage together. Lucas had become a born-again Christian in prison and hung around with the Christian group of prisoners. He spoke like a Christian too. His stories included the claim that he was innocent, he should not be in prison, and he did not kill Cruz's grandfather but was assumed guilty because of a long hatred between the two. It seemed a good time to let them be alone, so I moved a few feet over to join the brothers and get to know and visit with their father too. Pablo was tall, about five foot seven, and very thin—no butt in those jeans. He had all white hair even though he was only thirty-five.

"Boys, you must attend school."

"We do, Dad."

"And do your homework."

"Yes."

"School will give you the money you need for the future."

"Yes, Dad."

"Remember to do your chores in the house."

"We do, Dad."

"Remember that no matter how poor you are, you must be clean."

"We wash our own clothes."

He must have thought the idea of boys washing their own clothes interesting as he turned to look at me.

"Nice to meet you. Thank you for taking in my sons."

"You're welcome. I enjoy having them."

"Their mother abandoned them. She left them on the streets alone."

"Yes, they told me. I'm glad they are with me now."

"We both ended up in prison at the same time, so there was no one to care for them."

"We can go to visit her next month, at the women's prison."

"Oh, didn't they tell you? She escaped and fled to the United States last year. She's in New Orleans."

"I'm sorry. I didn't know."

"That's all right. She was a bad influence on them anyway. They're better off without her."

A voice pleaded to him inside my head: *Please tell them not to lie or steal, to stay away from drugs and alcohol. They need to hear that from you. Tell them to make themselves into young men of moral quality in order to not end up in prison like you. To study, earn money, and be clean are good things, but they need so much more.* These moral issues were the important ones for me, but he continued on repeating his advice that was sound for one part but missed the bigger picture. Our visiting time was ending. We promised the dads we'd return every month, which brought them great hope. Leaving the front gates of that prison with incredible relief I turned around just in time to see the tears welling up in the fathers' eyes and the intent to cover the pain in their faces as they said good-bye. It seemed at the moment that it might be their last good-bye.

Johnnie called me about another boy, Roberto, who was fifteen and went to his church. He had been in and out of the detention center near Greg's house for stealing. I had met Roberto at Johnnie's church and OK'd his arrival. My only concern seemed to be his size. He was a big boy but not fat—just very strong and thick. He could overpower me if he chose to do so. Roberto had a pleasant attitude and had completed sixth grade. He was a little taller than me, maybe five foot four. He loved Johnnie and had spent a lot of time in his home with his children, but Johnnie needed to find a place for him to go permanently. Roberto wanted to learn English and dreamed of visiting the US one day. What I did not know was that Johnnie had promised Roberto that if things didn't work out with me, he would try to find a *gringo* couple to adopt him. That promise set me up. It would almost impossible to win Roberto's loyalty with seven other boys and little funding when a magical couple was waiting to adopt him with fistfuls of money and a US future. Roberto joined us but it was just a matter of time until he would decide there was something better than what our family could offer. Arriving as the "new" oldest boy, he left me a little unsure as to how the head boy status would work out, but Roberto accepted Cruz as his sidekick leader.

With Roberto's arrival, Johnnie and his wife Vicki invited me to join them in serving boys as one ministry. Maybe working together we could offer more to each one of the boys and be in a more secure position for the future. In addition to visiting the detention centers their service had been focused on community contact with teen boys; being the church connection, creating a soccer team, taking them out to eat, helping with home problems, and inviting them for a sleep over every Saturday night. This last activity kept them off the streets on Saturday night and ready for church Sunday morning.

The boys loved it. Every Saturday afternoon Johnnie would go to town and pick up eight to ten boys. He'd take them out for cheap tacos, then bring them home for the night. Vicki would cook special foods, they would watch movies, play ball, and go on outings together with Johnnie's and Vicki's own children. Sunday morning, after a superb breakfast, they would all pile in their two vans and go to church.

The idea of joining forces was excellent. It would feel better to be a part of three than alone as one. We met at their house to decide how to proceed and combine our ministries. The vast blue sky was bordered by a great grass lawn area covering the ground—maybe five hundred yards to the cliff and vast valley view. Their children, my boys, and the dogs played in the sun and cool breeze, running and throwing things in all directions as we sat in lawn chairs and tried to follow what Jesus had in mind about the future for our ministries. The idea presented by them was that we would pool all our resources and donation connections together to create one center. Johnnie saw a farm with manual labor skill-building opportunities for the boys: working horses, milking cows, raising goats and chickens, harvesting vegetables and fruits, and a center school which would include training in construction and mechanical repairs. It was a perfect vision.

Then the dream started to enclose me. They envisioned me living in a home with the boys. Not only would I be doing all that a "mother and father" would do but I would have to do it all before and after school hours as I would be their full time teacher also. My schedule would be 24 hours a day, seven days a week in ministry with no breaks. Johnnie and Vicki would live in another house with their six children. Johnnie would run the ministry, farm, and school. I would not run anything, not even the school even though I would be the only one there teaching. Considered only a volunteer, my donation connections would be used to help fund the center.

It sounded a lot like what Sister Rose had done in the detention center, only she lived alone, hired the teachers and ran the whole place. This idea seemed to doom me. I would not be in charge, but would pay with all my time and finances. My position was based on the assumption that I would never have my own space, remarry, have a family, decide things for my boys, and/or be an equal in the ministry. My responsibility was to be the volunteer mom and teacher until I couldn't. I backed off. We never did have a second ministry meeting, but Johnnie and Vicki continued to be good friends and a great support and model for us. Eventually, we completed our missions separately and to the benefit of many children. The Lord blessed them with all that the beautiful vision held and they have done a superb job at being faithful in their ministry.

But without them security was not in my immediate future either. Once home from the meeting, the landlord told me the rent would be doubled. All my insecurities returned. How would I be able to care for all these boys? I prayed for help and put aside my underlying fears. We had been in Colony Centro only six months, but we were off again. After giving our advance notice, the owner astonished me by commenting, "See, there are gang youths above this street and gang youths below but no problem here, like I told you." That explained his "no gangs around here" comment he had made when we first moved in. It seemed that every person I spoke to over the years claimed their own neighborhood was safe; it was the other neighborhoods that were dangerous.

~ If people warn that you are in a dangerous neighborhood or place believe them and leave or take all precautions.~

We began scouting for another house. I told the Lord I could live anywhere as long as I had hot water and my own bathroom. We used the same plan as before. One or two of the boys and I took the bus and got off "after a while." Then, we walked around asking if there were any large houses to rent nearby. Most of the time there were not—the only large houses available were for sale. Rarely would we hear of one, and if they didn't quote me an outrageous price, we'd look at it. I had heard of a small town—Branzano—about thirty minutes from the capital, where all the rich people had their weekend homes because it was cooler and greener. There was a national park too. A friend from church gave me the number of a *gringo* that lived there who could maybe help me out with the boys. They called him Big Jerry, a larger-than-life Christian, a one-of-a-kind hero type. He invited us to visit him and his family in Branzano. We jumped on the bus and went to look around one afternoon.

It was a cozy, quiet country town; a great place to raise boys. Big Jerry's wife, Jessica, ushered us around, helping to locate a house big enough for us all without the added price hike for foreigners. We found an old, somewhat large crumbling house with a yard for only fifty dollars a month. The house was a little rough-looking; inside it reminded me of a dark airplane garage: low lights, bad painting, and cracked concrete floors. And when it rained there were leaks all over the house. It had a few other problems. There was no phone line, only one bathroom for seven boys and one female, no hot water, and no lock on my bedroom door (which was entered by walking through one of the boys' bedrooms). But for fifty dollars a month I would manage.

Remembering what I had said to the Lord before: "I can handle anything as long as I have hot water and my own bathroom," I knew He was chuckling now. I still hadn't learned it was best never to set limits on the Lord. As lacking as it was it would be our new home and everything felt right. Temporary circumstances would not affect our happiness; there was always hope for tomorrow and contentedness with today. We were together and joyous, living life as a blessed family. Possessions do not make life worth living—they are what we use to live life. Doing what I was able to do at the time was all I could offer and nothing more, Jesus would make sure it was enough.

Chapter 11
Just Regular Folk

Our life would become simpler in Branzano. There were only six dirt main streets in the whole town. Small homes ambushed by tropical leafed trees, beautiful bushes, and flowering plants dotted the dusty roads. The main entrance was a pebble stone road that ended after the third block. This place seemed to have a quaint country movement: people walking, donkeys carrying loads, horses trotting, adults passing by on bikes, all at a safe speed, a casual meander. The little town had a high school (grades seven through nine), and farther out the other end of town, lost in the hills, was a military training center that offered night classes for older students finishing primary school. There were eight churches in this small town and no alcohol sold. I gave a verbal agreement to rent the house, took the bus back to the capital, and celebrated my second Christmas with the boys.

The weather became a little too cold for me in November and December. Cold fronts lowered our temperature to the high fifties during the day, probably low forties at night. But these few last days had been perfect, the sun shining and temperatures rising to almost eighty. My parents surprised us with money sent before Christmas for a Nintendo. Cruz and I jumped on the bus to the capital to try to buy the game in secret. Because the sidewalk areas in the downtown are narrow, everyone walks single file, one line passing the other. It is rare to be able to walk side by side in the city. Cruz agreed to walk one step behind to better protect me from robbery. It was still Christmastime, after all, and a lone *gringa* could look like easy prey.

As we got off the bus and crossed the bridge, we took up a brisk pace trying to get through the crowds. Glancing back from time to time I would make sure Cruz was just a step behind. There were lots of people out. In the middle of the bridge I glanced back and saw that Cruz had stopped to talk to a friend. Turning around I marched back to admonish him.

"Cruz, I need you to be watching me."

"I just got robbed." He smiled hugely.

"What?"

"He cut me here with a knife."

He opened his shirt and we both looked at the light one-inch-long slightly bleeding cut.

"My God, Cruz. He could have really sliced into you."

Cruz was shocked. "I never thought they would rob me. I'm their *compadre*."

Cruz's system had let him down. He had felt protected thinking he was "one of them" and they would be able to tell he was.

"What did he steal?"

"Only my watch," a gift from Johnnie.

We were shaken up but had to continue on. This sacrifice we made for the Nintendo was more than we had planned, but it was worth it. We found the last Nintendo in the store, and since there is a "nothing can be returned" policy, I prayed that the machine would work, which it did. Never had the boys seemed so happy. It was a real American Christmas Day in Latin America. We had a grand celebration full of good food, another leafless-bush-sprayed-white Christmas tree, clothes, and lots of cheap toys.

The next day we took a trip to the prison for their Christmas. It would be a mixed blessing, as I had to tell the two fathers "Merry Christmas" but that we would be moving farther away. We all went, in order to reassure them that it would not mean they were going to lose contact with their sons. This visit I made with the prison social worker because we would not have to enter amid the prison population or pass through the panties-down area if we asked to meet in the office. This was great news for me for obvious personal panty reasons, but also alleviated my silent fear that the boys could at some time be falsely accused of passing drugs to their fathers during our visits and I would have no way to protect them.

From then on we always met in the social worker's office. This day when we passed the huge gates into the patio area, the prisoners were all gathered around listening to Cruz's dad play the marimba with his prison group. Musical joy filled the air as the high bell notes tumbled at lightning speed within the gray brick walls. Lucas had played professionally for years and was an outstanding musician. He was known for his great talent and blessed us all with a joyous musical day in the capital's prison. After a nice holiday visit we returned home to begin packing.

Johnnie helped me tremendously during the move. He rounded up a truck and a pickup to load all our belongings and boys on, and we arrived in Branzano New Year's Eve day. This move was easier on them than the last, although Cruz did put on a gang bandana for his arrival, trying to look tough. To celebrate, we had brought Burger King's two-for-one burgers, and later that night we were ready to light fireworks, some big ones. Lecturing the boys on safety they responded, "Yeah, yeah." Cruz was pretty much in charge, as I wasn't going near the fireworks, just yelling orders from a safe distance. Everything was great fun, even when Cruz's firework flew up, arched overhead, and landed in Orlando's fireworks bag, exploding all his fireworks at once. They were ecstatic; they loved the show. Life couldn't be better. We met and prayed at midnight, thanking God for our new home, and then went to sleep, as it had been a long day.

~US safety standards do not exist here. You will have to decide when it is too personally risky for you or decide to join in with the nationals.~

The small town was just right; everyone knew everyone and talked about everyone. They would all be watching my boys. Our home was right across the street from the back wall of the primary school. If the boys forgot something, they could yell to someone at home and have them throw it over. Teachers knew where to find me, and the boys knew I could be over in a jiff.

Every week it was time to make the bus trip into the capital to do errands with one of the boys. The thirty-minute bus ride through the countryside was a joy. The bus wound down our hill into a beautiful bowl-shaped valley encircled by high encroaching mountain ranges on all sides. Once on the other side, the bus would climb steadily up the mountain range to top off at a wonderful 320-degree panoramic view of the capital. The air was fresh, blowing in from the dusty bus windows. Even though the ride was a little too bumpy (as the buses were very old, repaired but not well kept up), for a dollar you couldn't complain.

We were then dropped off right at the entrance to the open-air market. It was a huge market divided by streets of small stalls all selling what looked to be almost the same things. Mounds of fresh vegetables, fruits, and basic food items begged to be bought. Smells of fresh foods mixed with rotten garbage filled the air, mixing pleasure with required tolerance. Hundreds of people walked about filling their plastic reusable shopping bags full of heavy cooking items, lugging these weighted-down bags around block after block, then all the way home. Most had someone extra to help them, as I did. Some days were hot and sweaty, some days cold or rainy, and some days windy and dusty. Shopping was an outside experience. Caring for seven boys required a large quantity of items, so it was important to stock up on cheap fruits and soaps, cleaning items, cheeses, and pasta. We would buy in the big market what was hardest to find in our *pueblo* (little town).

~ Hauling provisions for a week for a family weighs more than you might think. Always take help and plenty of plastic woven bags made especially for carrying fruits and vegetables.~

The boys adjusted well, making friends with the neighborhood children and getting to know the town. Before long kids were coming over to meet and play with the boys in our yard. Yet, after only a few days, Roberto decided he wanted to leave. He rounded the boys up by the washing tank outside and was talking to them in a low voice. I secretly listened and watched from an inside window.

"Johnnie wants to give Kimi a house right next to him for us, but she doesn't want to move there. I'm going to go and live with Johnnie. Who wants to move to Johnnie's house with me? Raise your hand."

Everyone raised their hands.

"OK, everyone act normal. We'll pack our stuff secretly during the day and tonight we'll escape for Johnnie's. No one say a word to Kimi or there will be trouble. Boy, will she cry, waking up all alone in the morning."

"Yep, sad I will be." I eased out from my spot, "Especially because Johnnie doesn't have a home for us. The house he had picked out is already rented. He doesn't want us living in his home; he wants us to have our own house. You need to let the adults decide these things for you. We are taking good care of you and want what's best. You all are free to go if you want. Pack your stuff and walk all over the countryside looking for a place to stay if you don't want to be here. But you need to choose now because I'm not cooking dinner for boys who don't belong to me. And if you leave, don't ever come back. This is a home not a hotel."

The boys decided my offer to eat was the best option as they didn't really know if Roberto knew what he was talking about anyway. Roberto left the next day for Johnnie's, who did take him in but only for a night. Roberto's adoptive mother invited him back to her home hoping things had changed, but he was soon caught stealing again and was out on the streets.

Arriving for the monthly visit to the government offices, I was asked if we had room for one more. My answer was no, we were full with seven.

A fifteen-year-old boy sitting nearby said, "It's me."

"Where are you from?"

"A Christian center called Christ Reigns,"

It was the same center where Cruz's brothers and sisters were. He had been raised Christian.

"Why aren't you there?"

"I ran away."

"Why?"

"I got into trouble."

"What's going to stop you from running away from our house?"

"I moved to the center when I was seven, and have never lived on the outside. I don't know where to go."

How could I turn down that request? We had no more money or room for one more. But this boy's life was more important than our provisions and comfort at the moment. We would manage.

~Support from the US very likely will not increase just because you've taken on more responsibility. Count on managing without.~

Freddy joined us. Cruz was very happy to hear real news about his brothers and sisters who had lived with Freddy for years. And Freddy was a great storyteller. Now we were eight.

For our first few months in Branzano, Johnnie and Vicki aided us greatly by helping with food. They went to the open-air market once a month and would bring us lots of food, about a hundred dollars worth. They brought grains, vegetables, fruit, cereals, meats, and milk. Some of the meats were strange. The worst was cows udder—"udderly" rubbery. I didn't recognize the meat but the boys did. How to cook it perplexed me as I refused to touch it. Finally, I got it fried by flinging it around a lot with two forks. Lorenzo loved the udder, but he was the only one. He would make a good husband—his wife could cook him anything. Cow's tongue was also gross but we ate it. Well, I didn't but they did.

One day Johnnie even brought us a hundred-pound bag of donated powdered milk from a dry milk company in McMinnville, Oregon. It had been expired for over three years. Bless the hands that got it to us. We served it up regularly, feeling really special. And I swear in those six months the boys all grew a lot, really. But it didn't get the nickname the "farting milk" for no reason.

We made the monthly trip to town to visit the dads in prison but entered only into the social worker's office, calling the dads into the protected space. Lucas was cheerful and gave his approval of my place in Cruz's life, as his *gringa* mom. Deni, Lorenzo, and Nolan's dad, Pablo, quickly greeted us then called in another prisoner who almost bowed down to him. The man hurried off to bring us each a plate of food and a drink. It seemed Pablo had some kind of income. The boys began their lively chatter, thrilled to be with their dads. Listening to the boys recount their stories with my added interjections, Pablo seemed pleased with our new living situation. He gave me a sideways glance and paused, holding his eyes locked on mine. A personal glance.

Classes resumed in February, so it was time to buy two school uniforms, black shoes, socks, T-shirts, underwear, a belt, and PE clothes for each boy, which included another pair of tennis shoes in the required white color. This took some time shopping by bus and foot. The first day of school the teachers would give them a list of supplies to buy and we'd be off again, hoping to find everything needed. It could easily cost $100 per boy, so February is a big expense month for parents.

School is required by law up to sixth grade, but the costs of attending leave some children or families out. Shoes are required in schools in the city and most schools in the countryside. Some children do not have shoes. Uniforms are also required. Some children do not have a white shirt or blue skirt or pants without holes. But all children are required to attend school, even though if all the children in this country showed up to our schools we could not house them; it would be impossible. To rectify this problem in the cities, many schools run a double shift in order to teach all the children in their area. One group starts at seven a.m. and leaves for home at noon. The second group starts at noon and returns home at five p.m. Some teachers teach both sections, seven to five straight through with no lunch break, earning a double wage, doubling their $325 a month. Classes average over thirty students in the cities, while in the country one teacher may have two or three grades in one room for a total of seventy students.

Some country schools have no chairs or desks, or not enough for everyone. Some of their students arrive with no pencils, paper, or erasers. This leaves the teachers responsible to help out, occasionally buying extra supplies with their own funds. The teachers and students alike may have to walk one or two hours to class every day and then back, no matter how hot, cold, wet, or windy it may be or how bad they may feel. Many students arrive without breakfast. But the people are working hard to overcome these obstacles to a successful education by providing breakfast at school, involving the community, and trying to get government assistance. We need help in our schools.

At the end of each year we confront a teacher's strike, sometimes cancelling more than a month of classes. The teachers demand their back wages from the government before they will pass the students on to the next grade. Combine this with many days of classes cancelled because the teacher is sick, has a sick child, went to visit someone who was sick or having surgery, went to the bank, went to a funeral, needed to travel, was at a teachers' conference, had car or transportation problems, had home visitors, travelled far for the holidays and was not back yet, went to the dentist or took a family member to the dentist. School is cancelled much too often. There is no substitute teacher system;

the class simply gets cancelled. Other class days are lost because the students arrive and have to do projects. Sometimes the students are requested to paint chairs all day, do the gardening for the school, prepare for a celebration, practice marching, or go on a field trip. Lately, our country has made improvements to its educational system by enforcing new laws, and some parent groups have been powerful enough to get some positive changes made. Our new school welcomed us into their community despite all the obstacles they currently faced.

~ If their children can live with the system, so can yours. Speak up only if you are able to help and accept their decision to approve your idea or not.~

Meeting specifically with Nolan's teacher I explained his difficulty in learning and advanced age. The three brothers were all put in the same third-grade classroom, while Orlando was placed in fourth grade. Daron opted for the military night school as he was too old to attend day school, and Cruz began high school (which is really seventh through ninth grades—US middle school) at noon. Freddy hadn't yet decided what to do, as he did not want to go to high school. This schedule meant that there would be more individual time for each one of the boys; half had school in the morning and half in the afternoon or evening. It felt more like a regular family of four most the day.

After morning school a small group of neighbor boys of all heights would huddle outside my kitchen window with my boys playing marbles in the soft dust. The competition was a bit intense. A large outside circle was etched into the dust, its center wiped clean from as much dust as possible, leaving the hard ground bare. Every boy would put a marble in the center. Then, with their remaining five marbles take turns flicking them hard, hoping to knock someone's marble out of the circle without theirs following. The intensity was created by the rules. The one who knocked out another's marble would get to slam-blast the knuckles of the loser with his hardest flick shot. Big boys were the best and strongest hitters; little boys walked away from the game with swollen knuckles from being hit so many times.

Another popular game was top throwing. There was one old wooden top maker living in our town. The boys frequented him, asking for twine or a new top to replace the one they had lost. The top maker entertained the boys by showing them how to do new tricks. They spent hours rolling the tops up and down on the twine, practicing sideways throws, and showing off handheld tricks. They got quite good and could even show you a few tricks today. It was perfect to have my boys in our yard playing with others because it was easy to keep an eye on them. It was always interesting for me to see how they acted in competition with others. This can tell you a lot about one's character. One day became quite a sad day—the old wooden top maker had died. Our tops and tricks would have to last forever.

~Part of the pleasure of a simple way of life is living as exactly they did in the past.~

Freddy had decided he did not want to continue studying. He had finished sixth grade in the orphanage and could have gone to school with Cruz but refused. He wanted to work.

"No way I'm gonna study anymore."

"But sixth grade is not enough."

"My dad only went to second grade."

"Could he read?"

"Not really, my mom read for him. She graduated from sixth grade."

"There's not much work to be found with only a sixth-grade education."

"I want to work in the field."

"How much can you earn in the field?"

"Reynaldo earns 1,800 pesos ($90) a month."

"That's not enough to raise a family on."

"I don't have a family."

"But you will. How will you support them all?"

"I can be a construction's assistant."

"How much does that pay?"

"2,300 pesos ($120)."

"Freddy, if you study you can get a better job *or* be a construction's assistant; you can choose. If you don't study, you'll be in competition with every guy in this country that doesn't have a good education."

"It'll be good enough for me."

~ Choose who and how you will help carefully. They may not always be ready to be successful.~

To Freddy the work looked like freedom, but as he got older and had a family he would realize it was not. We were receiving donations, so I had to make the rule that a working boy would have to live somewhere else, find a room to rent. The people donating were not supporting a teenage boy so he could work and spend all his money on fun, while eating, sleeping, and dressing himself with their gifting. I offered to charge him room and board but would take his wages and put them in the bank for him to take when he left home, and I agreed to give him a small allowance to spend now. He didn't think that sounded like a fun idea. The effect on the other boys of having one of them with so much money would be negative. They would remain penniless, studying every day while watching him leave for work, returning to spend his money on fun stuff, unintentionally encouraging them to believe it was better not to study. My decision was that he could stay one month after finding a job, then he would have to rent a room from me or someone else. We began asking around to find work for him.

Because of Nolan's learning difficulties he was a bit sporadic when following rules, but he would let me win whenever I confronted him. His pattern to get what he wanted was to lie first, so I would pause, smile, and say, "Nolan, that's not the truth." Then, he had no time to invent a second lie, so he would tell me the truth and smile widely. He had a catching smile that would get him far and knew it. Nolan seemed to be very wise concerning the wrong things in life for a thirteen-year-old. He was very attracted to all girls and loved to hug, he liked picking up things that weren't his (commonly called stealing), one of his best friends was the local drug seller, and he liked talking about people—the sordid things, of course. Strangely enough, he was very good with money. After visiting the school office one day I went to visit the third-grade teacher. Class was still in session so I patiently waited outside the door.

Nolan was standing next to the teacher by himself in front of the class.

"You know that's not right."

"Uh, thirty-six?" Nolan responded.

"You are bigger than the rest of the students; you must be the example."

"Uh, twenty-four?"

"Nolan, how much is three times seven?"

"Twelve?"

"Nolan, *why* don't you know any of the answers? *How* you do your homework every night?"

She was angry now.

I spoke up from the doorway. "I work with him every night on his homework."

It's important to show up to school in person for the best communication with the teacher. Nolan was good with money but multiplying was beyond his grasp. Evidently, she forgot our talk about Nolan' meningitis and learning problems. My heart ached for Nolan. When the students left, I again explained about his learning disabilities. Maybe she would be kinder to him.

That night I let Nolan know that he was doing his best and that I was proud of him for trying. It should have been difficult for Nolan to get up every morning and get dressed for school when it could be so embarrassing for him, but he loved school all the years he was able to attend and I helped him every night with his homework. After watching *Sheena the Princess Warrior*, and *Samson*—our favorites—on one of the three channels available, we would turn off the TV and all study for one hour. If one of the big boys had no homework, he would help the little guys do theirs. If they were done with everything, they could read the Bible until bedtime. No one ever read the Bible, but they did finish their homework. This time helped me focus on their individual abilities and scholastic needs.

Before bedtime we would all sit down in one of the bedrooms, some of us on the floor, and have prayer time. We began with a theme for the day, such as "If someone wants to fight with your friend, what can you do?" or "What do you think is OK for your friend to lie about?" The discussions were focused on how they could advise their friends who had these problems. That way I wasn't preaching to them but seemingly preparing them for being a positive friendship support in difficult situations, all the while defining important moral issues. We would discuss things for a while, giving the boys opportunities to talk and me an opportunity to know them much better. Then each one would pray.

Because it is a little tense to pray in front of others, I began the practice of just asking “Who wants to pray?” and then waiting in silence, maybe for a few minutes until someone offered to pray. They soon got the idea that quickly volunteering to pray made the prayer time end a lot sooner than waiting. Before long they were all quickly volunteering to pray. These were special times for us; we were bridging the gap and becoming a real family.

Deni was always the first to fall asleep and the first to wake up. I would privately pass by his bed at night and give him a quick kiss on the forehead in secret since he was hard to catch in the daytime. At nine years old he would be mortified if the others saw. At six a.m., he was always awake and making his bed very carefully while still in it, slipping out at the last minute. Then he would go to his shelf, pull off all his clothes, and rearrange them carefully, each morning. Shelves had been chosen to be built instead of dressers so that we could see everything at all times. This helped avoid problems with hiding dirty laundry among the clean clothes instead of washing them, losing socks, or hiding illegal substances. It was also easy to see who needed to straighten up their area and who didn’t. Besides, we did not have many clothes. The shoes were all lined up against a wall, easy to find: a dirty, dusty, musty twelve-pair collection of worn footwear.

Furniture was pretty sparse in our home. In the living room we had one couch and two chairs to sit on. These we would also sit on to eat meals, as our kitchen table had no chairs. But the TV was the highlight of the living room. Our dining room was empty. In the kitchen I used the large dining room table to cook on. With no countertops or shelves I used a dual burner camp stove for cooking. My first purchase was a small half refrigerator that was never full; the boys always ate whatever was available.

~Getting by with fewer possessions for a while teaches us how much we really don't need.~

Each day I spent about five hours cooking—mostly large pots of beans and rice. In the morning I would walk to buy tortillas from a lady across town. Before lunch I would walk clear out to the restaurant on the highway and buy two large French bread loaves freshly baked. It was important to be on time because they always sold out, sometimes before I arrived. This combination allowed us to survive on fifty tortillas a day. For breakfast we would drink coffee because of its great taste and because it's so inexpensive. Coffee is not served black—sugar and/or milk have been added before perking. Coffee is served to everyone. I've even seen it in baby's milk bottles. With this we would eat sweet baked breads (with a very bready taste and very little sweet) with a serving of mush. We loved mush: oatmeal, flour, rice, or corn. I would mix it with milk, sugar, and occasionally with chocolate or banana or strawberries or any sweet item around. Mush was always served with a little surprise flavor.

All the boys came home for lunch. Normally, I prepared beans, rice, French bread, and something else like spaghetti or cheese and avocados or tuna mixed into the rice. For dinner we would eat almost the same: beans, rice, tortillas, and something else. My limit was one pound of meat per dinner meal. I invented many combinations: ground beef with cabbage, eggs with rice and mayonnaise, chicken in soy sauce with potato. It was also necessary to include many vegetables or fruits unknown to me: *guayaba* (wonderful fresh or in juice), *nance* (sour but eaten fresh or in juice), yucca (boiled like potatoes or fried and incredibly wonderful), and *pataste* (used like zucchini in soups or on the side).

The monthly visits from the government would include a donation for us: a cake, a sack of oranges, a bag of oatmeal, a bag of milk, or cheese. With the continued support from the miracle couple in the US of $300 monthly, contributions from Johnnie, my church and family connections and the government, all worked together to allow me to care for the boys. Everyone helped. I could not have done it alone, not for a second.

~ Even small support amounts help out greatly. Some believe we must choose between US support and global, but the truth is we can do both effectively.~

The more comfortable the boys became in their new neighborhood, the more they began disappearing without asking permission. This quickly became a test of wills, so rules had to be invented. No one could leave our yard without asking me or they would have to sit on their beds as punishment for hours on end and would be grounded from going to the corner store for a week. They laughed. That night two boys were gone. We went looking, as the other boys thought they knew where they were, and found them ready to spend the night at a friend's house. That's when the next rule was made. No more going out into the night to look for anybody. Any boy outside of the yard perimeters after six p.m. would not be allowed home; he would have to sleep somewhere else and wherever that was would be his new home. Cruz tested the rules the next day. He went to the corner store without permission. I grounded him, confining him to his bed.

"Ouch, this punishment hurts." He laughed.

"If you get up before I say it's OK, you'll have to pack your bags and leave. To stay here you must obey the rules."

"Don't hurt me more!"

"No playing or talking to anyone or I'll start your time over. One hour beginning now."

"Time to take a nap!" He smiled and lay down.

Five minutes later: "Am I through yet?"

"I have to start the time over Cruz, you talked."

"You mean I can't even ask the time?" Smiling. "No, you can't say anything to anyone."

"Can I talk to myself?"

"No, Cruz. You must be silent."

"OK," he whispered, raising his eyebrows and putting his finger to his lips.

Ten minutes later he stated: "I really don't want to sit here anymore."

"Sorry, you talked. I'll have to start the time all over again."

"No, really, this is driving me crazy. I can't just sit here for an hour."

"Sorry. You now have one full hour."

"Hey, brothers!" he yelled, "This is torture. Listen to me. Don't do it."

Deni looked at me with wide eyes.

"Yes, I know Deni. You could never sit for one hour, so watch out. Just ask me permission before you leave. I almost always say yes."

Grounding became a thing of the past. It worked wonderfully the first time. The boys remembered to ask for permission before leaving the house.

~ The Children's Services law states we may not physically punish the children under our care. You must obey the laws in place or don't volunteer.~

Life was good and safe for us in Branzano. Everyone was busy studying, and Freddy had found day work as a ditch digger and left early every morning with a group of men. Big Jerry's wife, Jessica, started a Bible study for us at their house every Tuesday night, about a ten-minute walk away. She was excellent at recounting the grand adventures of the disciples and Jesus in real-life terms and action. She always had a sweet treat for everyone, and afterward the kids got to play awhile outside in the dark yet warm tropical nights. Big Jerry was there for us as a strong Christian model. He would lay the law down for the boys and explain where all that was said in the Bible. Big Jerry's dedication to the Lord included waking up every morning at three to go outside and pray under the starry expanse while the world slept. He loved Jesus in a big way and would lay his life down for his belief in a flash.

On Sundays we would take the bus over back roads to Betel, our old church. This trip passed through a beautiful countryside of small towns hidden inside deep valleys or on top of high mountain ranges. We also passed the national prison, newly reserved for gang-affiliated prisoners only, and the coffee plant that always filled the air with perfect coffee-brewing aromas. It was a joy to be able to stay with our church with so many home and school changes. At least we could still count on a familiar worship service each Sunday. To get to church all eight of us would file into the bus and Orlando would usually sit with me. The bus attendant would pass by, rapidly repeating his spiel.

"Where to?"

"Betel."

"Seven pesos each."

"There are eight of us." I handed him a hundred-peso bill.

He paused, looked at me, and headed to the back of the bus with the money. He was having difficulty calculating how much change to give back.

The next trip I was ready. Handing him the 100 peso bill and offered, “I’m paying for eight. That’s 56 pesos. I need 44 pesos back.” He smiled and counted out the change.

~Many people cannot always accurately calculate large sums or lots of items, so you must remember to count too.~

One Sunday Cruz decided he wanted to walk back home from church. My rule for the bus use was that if they wanted to walk and didn’t hitch a free ride, I’d give them the fare they didn’t use to spend as they pleased. Most often they spent it on food. Seven pesos was about eighty cents; you could buy a Coke and a tiny bag of chips. But our church was about a thirty-minute bus ride from our town. Farther than they had ever asked to walk before. Two of the other boys decided they wanted to walk back with him. I was skeptical—it was a *long* walk home, but figured if they had so much extra energy to burn, it would be better for me to OK the trip. It looked pretty daunting, at least eight miles, maybe three straight uphill. Their plan was to secretly hitchhike, thereby getting a free ride home, sit down under a big shade tree, eat with joy, then show up looking really tired and beat.

They took their bus fare and watched as we boarded the bus; the other boys laughed at them from their windows as the bus sped off. We got home quickly in time to eat a late lunch. Three hours later the walkers had not arrived. By the fourth hour I was beginning to worry. But they did finally arrive, really hungry, tired, hot, thirsty, and smiling. Car after car had passed them by but no one had picked them up, but they had great stories to tell about their adventure getting home. The seven-peso snacks were not enough for the long walk, so they had looked for fruit along the way. No one ever asked to walk home from church again.

Boys are always hungry no matter how much they eat. To satisfy them without having to listen to constant groaning and begging for food, I made a deal with them. They could memorize any two consecutive Bible verses, once a day, for one peso, or about fifteen cents. Memorizing the Bible would give them the gift of life; throughout their years they could compare other doctrines or real-life truths with what they had learned from the Bible. The fifteen cents would not buy much, but it would buy one egg, maybe three tortillas, juice in a clear bag, a few tiny sweets, a cheap sweet bread roll, or a tiny bag of chips.

It worked. The boys were reciting Bible verses every day. The best part was that they would spend time looking through the Bible in order to find the shortest two verses. They would read through various pages, deciding which verses would be the easiest. Great Bible time! They would then spend a few minutes memorizing and then recite the verses to me while I read them, finishing up with a few questions for comprehension checks. The most difficult part for me was remembering which verses had been memorized by whom. Cruz, Deni, and Orlando memorized nearly every day for most of two years. This paid off at school too, as their short-term memory skills improved for retaining any memorized material, and their grades were going up.

~Learning takes place at home too. Adding fifteen minutes a day of homeschooling can help any child more be successful at school.~

Another visit to prison gave the fathers relief and assurance that I would continue protecting their place in their sons' lives. Cruz's dad had moved into the older men's area and felt safer, a little separated from the main prison population. He always talked about his strong belief in Jesus and his dreams he longed to fulfill once outside again. He wanted to begin a marimba band made up of young people and tour the world. Marimba is a dying art; most our marimba players are in their sixties. A young group would gain popularity.

Pablo, the three brothers' father, shared with me more of his life and what had happened to the boys. This was his third time in prison, all for marijuana possession, each time for a longer term. This last time he had been imprisoned for being the owner of the home where marijuana had been found inside one of the rented rooms, although the police had no proof of trafficking. Once his new sentence began his "wife", Dolores, had been arrested and put in prison also. This left the four brothers at home alone without an adult or any income. Soon after arriving, Dolores escaped, trekking all the way to the US. Pablo said he felt blessed that I had come into their lives. He also shared that he had been attending church on Sundays in the courtyard of the prison. Maybe it might do him some good.

~Historically most couples have not formally married but publically refer to one another as husband and wife.~

Emergency medicine has a different meaning in a small country town as I was soon to experience. Living right behind the school gave the boys constant opportunity to enter whenever the gates were open, kind of like a second backyard. For some reason Cruz, Deni, and Nolan were inside the school grounds one afternoon. Orlando was in our yard perched up on one of our concrete gateposts, sitting high above everybody else. Cruz could barely see Orlando's head from inside the playground. He decided to impress the bunch with a super pitch of a rock aimed to hit Orlando far on the other side of the brick school wall. He hit his target. Orlando yelled out in pain and halfway fell down the concrete post, blood dripping from his eyebrow. It had happened when I was gone buying bread. By time I had returned, Orlando had put a bandage over his eyebrow and wouldn't let me see the injury. In order to give him the chance to calm down I didn't push, but the boys insisted I look right away. Sure enough, he needed stitches; the gash was very close to his eye. By now it was nearing five p.m. and getting dark quickly.

We had to look for a doctor immediately, but in that instant Orlando had disappeared. We looked all over and finally found him in the darkness of dusk crouched behind the washing basin outside. He was terrified. When things get out of control for these boys, the fear of the unknown dominates and they revert back to the tragic feeling of being vulnerable with no protection. Deni stepped up to offer to walk with us to look for a doctor. This perhaps was the only reason Orlando got up the courage to agree, and we took off on foot.

The three of us went around town asking our neighbors where we might find a doctor. They guided us to the other side of town into a poor area of wood and adobe homes collected together but divided by dust and dirt. Inside a real shanty shack, lit by candlelight, a friendly man told us the doctor was not in. Quiet relief came over me; it was too dirty there and not likely he had any anesthesia anyway. We headed back into town and were told about a nurse who lived out the other direction. It was now dark and we were walking to another new area. We found the nurse and she invited us into her home and convinced Orlando to let her stitch him up. After all, because he was such a handsome boy, she wouldn't want to leave him with an ugly scar right there in plain view on his forehead. She took out plastic gloves, a needle, and medicine, all in sterile bags. She gave him a shot for numbing the area and stitched him up. She took no money for her time but requested $2.50 for the supplies. She reassured me the scar would fade with time, and she was right. As we walked home peacefully in the dark, I had the feeling of being greatly blessed. Being poor makes you quite vulnerable to emergencies, but there are really good people in every corner of the world ready to help. One can go anywhere and find acceptance and emotional support from our Christian family. Orlando's scar would fade with time, inside and out.

~With no buses running at night, minor medical emergencies are served by those nearby if possible. Keep medicines and supplies on hand.~

For Mother's Day, the school put on a special program. The students prepared many drama and song presentations. Because we were Christians, the boys told their teachers they weren't allowed to dance, a good excuse to use because Christians here in this country don't dance (except for the Catholics), but that meant none of my boys were in the program. I went anyway, trying to enjoy the celebration atmosphere. Nolan served me mango juice and Orlando served me some great *campesino* finger food—fried chicken wrapped in tortilla with a special sauce.

The food I enjoyed, but for the program, none of the children were seated with their parents. The mothers were left alone together. The presentation was not really OK to me. It was full of sexy dancing to crude but popular songs presented by fifth- and sixth-graders dressed as if they were in a bar. Feeling uncomfortable I tried to hide my displeasure.

~It's important to celebrate with the community and best not to voice any disagreements as it could easily be received as an insult to the culture or their financial status rather than a concern.~

One of the sexy sixth-grade dancers was kidnapped weeks later by a thirty-three-year-old man. She was thirteen. This man had been seen earlier drinking beer in her father's little store and stating that he liked only thirteen-year-olds. It was rumor his sixteen-year-old "wife," whom he had stolen when she was thirteen, had had a mental breakdown just the month before and had disappeared. This man kidnapped the little sixth-grader and took her into hiding at his family's house on the other side of our small town.

Everyone was on the lookout for her, but he was able to hide her there for weeks. A few knew where she was but were so afraid of him and his family no one dared do or say anything. The rumors grew until even the police had suspicion of her whereabouts.

Finally, Big Jerry heard the story and couldn't believe no one had done anything to save this little girl. He got the support of the police, got his gun, and they stormed the house. She was taken to safety and her kidnapper was hauled off to prison to await trial. She had become a "woman," so his actions had caused her great harm. Virginity for females is necessary to be considered a respectable "wife," but for men, promiscuity is believed to be a necessary attribute, so you can see the dilemma. If you are a young respectable girl saving yourself for marriage, most likely the offer will never come. For some reason we rarely have weddings here. Therefore, the public promotion of male promiscuity and public requirement of marriage for women creates grave problems for the women in this country.

During the next week the kidnapper wrote his victim from jail declaring his undying love for her and asking her to become his "wife." She dropped the charges, he got out of jail, and she returned to his house to live as a "married" woman, which saved her reputation but put her in a vulnerable position. About two months later she showed up at my front door.

"Hi, I have a question to ask you."

"Yes?"

"Can I stay here with you?"

"I don't take in girls here, sweetie—only boys."

"It's just that I have nowhere else to go." She paused, looking nervous. "He's abusive and I can't return."

"You can't go home to your mom and dad?"

"No, my stepfather said I couldn't live with them anymore."

"I can only accept boys."

"I'm pregnant. He'll hurt me."

"Then you can't go back to him. I want to help you but I really can't."

"Maybe I can live with aunt in Pedro del Sur."

"Yes, maybe she can take you in. It would be better if you lived far away from here anyway."

"Can't I stay here just for tonight?"

"I'm sorry. Ask your parents for help. I know you don't want to, but they will help."

And she left. The guy was reportedly seen weeks later boasting that he was looking for another thirteen-year-old to make his wife.

~How will you handle abuse situations that come to your attention? Use great caution and seek wise counsel. Don't act alone.~

Mother's Day was also celebrated at the high school. Cruz was on fire; he was touched that I was there but was not about to show it publically. He faked a loud fart, drank out of the mouth of the three-liter Coke bottle before offering drinks to the mothers, and ate his finger food after dropping it on the floor. Boy, was I proud. Well, maybe not proud, but happy to be there for him as his mother. Cruz has a great sense of humor and is always joking around. He is a joyful person. It pleased me to be counted as his mother, no matter how many jokes he made.

Later Cruz asked me if he could visit his brothers and sisters in the orphanage as I had promised. It was time to take a visit. The bus ride was quite long (about three hours) and ventured into a part of the country we didn't know. We got off the bus in the small town, started walking, and asked for directions to the orphanage. It was about a thirty-minute walk from the bus. The main gate entrance to Christ Reigns was simple beauty: green rolling hills spotted with fir trees, a little still blue pond, cows grazing in the far-off fields.

We entered taking the path that led to the orphanage property, walking until we crossed a small hill to see a huge white church surrounded by a group of small white wooden two-story houses. A volunteer came up to the gate and ushered us in. It took us a while to find Cruz's brothers and sisters since there were so many children running around. The center had 250 at the time, plus we hadn't advised them we were coming. His older sister (sixteen), littler sister (thirteen), and two little brothers (ten and nine) were gathered together and allowed to sit with us at the picnic table. They had been living in the orphanage for five years. His littlest brother was four the last time Cruz had seen him.

The family reunion was touching. The older girls were in charge of taking care of the little brothers even though they lived in separate groups within the center—girls together and boys together. They talked about all that had happened to them, remembered their life as a family, and told many childhood stories, laughing, teasing, and reinforcing their family ties by history. They insisted we take family pictures, and ate the snacks we had brought. Cruz gave them a little money to buy treats from the orphanage *pulperia* once he was gone. They were very sad to see Cruz go; they were dying to be together. We promised to visit again. Cruz really missed living with his brothers and sisters. We still don't know why he was singled out for the detention center instead of the orphanage, but Sister Rose said it was probably for his protection. That pain of separation never left him; he missed his family united. Weighted by the loss yet thrilled by the reunion, we headed for home.

People around town would hear about our family and come to our door asking me to help them out with their kids. We worked through the government so, of course, I couldn't help.

~You will constantly have to choose not to help; we are a nation of a million needs.~

"Hello, I wanted to know if you could help me with my daughter. She's thirteen."

"I don't take girls. What problem do you have with your daughter?"

"Well, she wiggles when she talks to men."

"Oh."

"We thought about sending her to the women's prison in the valley."

"I don't think they'll take her there; that's for real criminals."

"Well, she must go. I can't have her in the house with her stepfather anymore."

Or:

"This is my son, Andrew."

"Nice to meet you."

"I was wondering if he could live with you because he doesn't obey anyone."

"I don't take boys who don't obey."

"Well, could you train him to obey? He ignores me because I'm a woman."

"I'm a woman too. He should obey his parents."

"He doesn't have a father."

"I only take boys who have neither mom nor dad. He should be a real man and take care of you."

"Yes, I need his help."

"Maybe you should help your mother. Isn't that what the man of the house should do?"

It seemed I had a reputation for taking in problem boys and making them good. What a nice compliment, to me and my boys. But if the opportunity opened up, I would always set them straight. I didn't take in boys who had problems, but boys sent to me from the government whose parents had problems. That would always get me a smile. Truth be sweet.

~You do not have legal authority to accept children into your home without legal permission. Find out who has that authority and contact them.~

Country life is not complete without a swimming hole hidden somewhere in the countryside frequented only by those who live nearby. About seven city-sized blocks from our house in Branzano was one of many swimming holes around. It was a beautiful, refreshing spot on a chocolate-colored creek surrounded by tropical greenery gone wild. Because our topsoil is so fragile, rains constantly carry off the top layer of dirt into the streams and rivers. All are chocolate colored all the time, but still great for swimming.

The boys asked permission to swim at least once a week during the summer part of our year, from February to June. We would usually find others there swimming, though not many were girls. One big reason for that is that the boys would swim in their underwear up until the age of about fourteen. Once I sent the boys ahead of me in order to finish cooking their lunch first. Within ten minutes I arrived, just in time to see Nolan in the water, grabbing a sixteen-year-old girl around the waist and lifting her so high his hands almost covered her whole chest. There were no adults around. Her nickname was "Pistol," and it was rumored she had been kicked out of school for hitting a teacher. She could leave, accuse them of anything and there would be no adult able to testify to the truth. I couldn't leave them alone even for ten minutes. My boys didn't realize how vulnerable they were to rumors, and how easily they could be hurt, especially if the stories involved girls. That night at prayer time we discussed false rumors and how to avoid them. I guess Nolan wasn't listening. The next day he walked out the front door to the road in a towel to talk with a girl; I'm sure her father would be thrilled. Calling out "Nolan!" became common.

~Rumors and accusations of sexual misconduct abound. Be extremely careful because they are almost impossible to defend. Try to be constantly accompanied.~

Daron loved his daily schedule. He had nothing pressing to do all day. I tried to keep him busy cleaning and doing chores, but you can't push a teenager much. He dawdled a lot, spent some time each day studying, and left every night for fourth grade at the military base. A camouflage jeep-like truck would come to town at five p.m. to haul all the students out. The students were thrilled to jump into the back of a military truck with two guys in army fatigues supervising, then off they would go down the dirt road into the countryside. His classmates were also finishing primary or middle school at an older age so he enjoyed night school and got passing grades.

As one of my oldest, most trusted boys, Daron helped with my chores when needed. For Orlando's and Deni's combined birthday party, I sent Daron by bus to the capital forty-five minutes away to buy two-for-one Whoppers to celebrate in style. It was a Sunday, so we all went to church and returned home awaiting Daron's arrival with our birthday lunch. We waited and waited. Orlando got fed up with waiting and began to get testy. He would act like a lion when he didn't eat on time. Everyone was hungry. I insisted we wait as nothing more had been prepared to eat; tortillas, rice, and beans don't cook in a second. Finally, we could wait no more and ate bowls of mush for dinner.

As birthday meals are the only gift received on one's birthday, Deni and Orlando had had the worst birthday of their lives, even worse than having no one remember. Daron never came home, not even the next day when we celebrated the birthdays with BBQ beef from the only restaurant in town. Days went by and we didn't hear from Daron. Then the fourth day he appeared looking ragged and dirty. His story was that he had been mugged, the money stolen, and had slept on the street those nights too embarrassed to return home. He went on and on. Not wanting to believe him I said I did, deciding to find out later what had really happened. He agreed to pay back the money I had sent for dinner by forfeiting his monthly allowance for a year. It would take almost half that long to pay me back at $1.50 a month. Daron would also have to do the chores of the others who had been forced to do his while he was gone.

A few days later the boys whispered to me that Daron had not been robbed as he had said. He had entered Burger King, and instead of ordering for us, ordered for himself the most expensive super-sized combo on the menu. Then he went to play video games in the *pulperia* around the corner until he had spent all the money. When all the money was gone, he hung around for three days doing nothing but living on the street, returning only when he had gotten too hungry and dirty. I was furious.

He had taken advantage of my confidence. It is important to recognize those who choose to do what is right and admonish those who choose poorly. The best solution is to have a fail-safe system in place so bad occurrences happen rarely if possible.

It is considered unpardonable to accuse someone of stealing here; we just don't do it. Openly accusing Daron of stealing would accomplish nothing. These issues are best resolved by ever so slightly inferring that next time you will have to investigate and prosecute. Be politely upset, show your great concern at the loss, and retreat for the moment so you can inform yourself better and work behind the scenes. Foreigners have lost their lives arguing over stolen items.

~ Latinos generally choose a non-conflictive approach to problem solving. This may be because there is not always police protection available. You may be right at the moment but pay heavily for it later.~

Now that I knew, it was only a short time before he was tricked into reciting the parts of his story over and over until the lie departed from his own lips. The rule in our house was that Daron had lost his right to return. Wherever he had slept that night had become his new home. I agreed to give him one more chance, but in addition to the other paybacks, he had to shave his head just as they did in the Tangala Detention Center. That might not be a punishment for some, as it is a little popular in the States now to shave your head, but for my boys at this time it was not cool. Head shaving became an additional clause to the leave-home rule, with the stipulation that you could not spend the night out—but you could leave and come home in the same day. Daron was safe for now but had no more chances. And a shaven head did not compliment his looks.

Our homes promote indoor-outdoor-type living. Tropical fauna breeds tropical bugs. This country is full of *animalitos*—small animals, they call them. These animals are not the mammal kind; they are insects as big as small mammals. Our seasons are identified by insect groups: ant season, fly season, unknown flying kamikaze bug season, mosquito season, *cucaracha* (cockroach) season, and tarantula time.

~ Billions of really big insects abound in tropical countries. If you like camping you'll get along fine.~

Tarantula time occurs when the hot, dry summer is ending and the warm downpours begin. Tarantulas live mainly by and in banana and plantain orchards in the countryside. We now lived in the countryside, and sure enough, the first great downpour began as night was settling in. Washing the dinner dishes in the dusk I noticed what looked like hundreds, maybe more, of soft small moving rocks marching down the streets. The sight petrified me. No one was walking down the street; maybe everyone already knew. It was a moment right out of a horror movie. Fortunately, no tarantula ever entered the house (that I'll admit to).

There were many small churches in our town where the congregation counted maybe ten to twenty faithful followers. A friend invited all my boys to the youth service at one of these small churches. Seeing this as an opportunity to escape by myself and do other things, I gave my permission, but walked them there. It would be too easy for them to get sidetracked on the way to church.

We arrived a little early, but they ushered us in to sit down while we waited. Soon, people were entering and greeting us kindly, happy to see us there. An old neighborhood drunk swaggered in and sat down too. Before I knew it, the service had started, and I felt awkward getting up to leave so I stayed put. They began with a few songs, and one teenage girl from the audience offered to sing an additional song. She sang horribly, belting out her heart to God. The drunk sitting in the isle began to look around, making faces, letting us know he thought the singing was horrid. She noticed too, and a look of pain swept across her face. He then began insulting her singing, talking loud enough so that we could all hear his opinions. The church put up with him rather than throwing him out or rebuking him openly. But the girl had been publically humiliated.

Latin American churches tend to believe in something that is beautiful--anyone can sing to the Lord in church; it is a gift for God and not to be judged by man. So everyone is encouraged to grab the microphone and howl away, if your heart is in it. Since singing makes your body healthier and your spirit lighter, they are right—everyone should sing, not just those who are talented singers. It is an honest pleasure to listen to bad singing in church. But the drunken man had forgotten this wonderful truth.

After her song a few youths got up and recited verses. One young man recited the verse that men should not wear women's clothes and women should not wear men's clothing. I froze. I had come only to escort my boys to the youth group, not attend church, and was wearing a T-shirt, jeans, and tennis shoes. After church an elder came over to me and asked me not to wear pants to church next time. The criticism shocked me. They put up with a drunk in church but had to comment to me about my clothes. Besides, I was wearing a ladies T-shirt, ladies jeans, and ladies tennis shoes. My boys would not be caught dead in clothes marked "ladies"—even jeans or tennis shoes. After all, Jesus wore a tunic and sandals and so did the ladies at that time. I imagined they had men's tunics and women's tunics.

It is not what is on the outside that makes you a Christian but what is on the inside, and that is all that Jesus sees. Do not judge another culture by what you see on the outside. Jesus has permitted you to be in your new country to have an intimate view as to what is on the inside. He is sharing His love for His children with you. Respect differences and be sensitive at all times. The Bible will be your guide and unifier; we are all His children. And as it was my new country, I never wore a T-shirt, jeans, and tennis shoes into a church again.

Everyone would always say that my boys must be bilingual, living with a *gringa* and all. But they were not. They were being pressured from the outside to learn English, but they were too proud to do it—if you can imagine that. English is required at the high schools, so it seemed natural to begin classes at home.

"Azul is blue. Repeat: blue."

They repeated as I pointed to the blue sky.

"Blanco is white. Repeat: white."

They repeated as I pointed to a white T-shirt.

Cruz interrupted, speaking quickly. "Verde [green] is red." They all repeated red as he pointed to the green cap he was wearing. "Red."

Cruz shouted in triumph, laughing grandly and awaiting my next word ready for the power struggle.

Class ended. So much for English.

~It's very, very difficult to speak two languages at home. Usually one dominant language wins, even with our best intentions.~

It was again time for the Independence Day march. Our primary school would march around town in a little parade for all the parents to see. My two third-grade boys, Deni and Lorenzo, and Orlando, in fourth grade, were too "cool" to want to march with their class but were forced to participate. They complained and complained. They never really did get over being too cool, as far as I know. Nolan wasn't complaining; he was proud. He had been selected street officer and given an orange vest to wear and a bike to ride on. The boys did march—well, not march but walked awkwardly among those in their class through our small-town dirt streets, parents lined on both sides applauding at the sight of their children.

After the march we all met in the town center in front of the school for a fair. There were many special booths of great-smelling foods, arts and crafts to buy and a face-painting booth. Singing and dancing competitions were performed on the permanent wood stage. My favorite of all was the horse riding competitions. The horses were quality breeds, well trained and expertly handled. My boys decided to compete in the greased pole climb. A grown man stood on the bottom, grabbing the post in a half-squatting position. Cruz, shirtless with all his muscles showing, climbed onto the man's shoulders. Daron passed Cruz while climbing up on top of his shoulders. The fourth climber, a younger boy, started the climb up, but as he inched up past Daron, his extra weight caused Daron to begin to slip. Blindly, Daron stuck his toes into the waistband of Cruz's jeans in order to not fall. But his weight began ever so slowly to pull Cruz's pants down. Cruz figured out he couldn't let go to pull up his pants. Realizing his crack was about to show to all the people, he began talking to the audience about his dilemma.

"Uh oh, I feel I might be exposing more than I planned on."

"But I won't give up; I'm a winner."

"Or maybe I'm a loser who thinks he's a winner."

The audience began to chuckle. His crack was showing a little.

"I just want you people to honor my request and turn a little away from this embarrassing sight."

Pause.

"Except for the women—the single ones anyway."

They were laughing now.

"If you are still looking and you are a single girl, please give me your phone number when I get down."

They did win the greased pole climb, our smallest boy climbing clear to the top to grab the scarf. And true to his word, Cruz did take the opportunity to ask a few girls if they had written down their numbers for him. It was a winning moment for us all. We walked happily home, one block away, reviewing the high points of the fair.

Big Jerry dropped by our house occasionally to check up on everyone, feeling that a woman alone with boys would need the help. He would order the boys around and threaten to punish them or throw them out of the house if they didn't do what he or I said. This didn't please me. Others had no right to threaten my boys with living on the street unless I said so. It was up to me to know all that had passed in our house, and I would decide if it was the last straw or not. Then Big Jerry's threats to Daron could be heard coming from the kitchen.

"Who ruined all these pictures in the camera?"

"I did."

"You're too old to be touching things that are not yours. You knew not to touch it."

"Yes, I know."

"This shows that you have no respect for Kimi or her things."

"I'm sorry."

"Well, 'I'm sorry' won't solve it, will it?"

"No sir."

"The next time you do something like this, I'll dig a hole so deep, when I put you in it, you won't be able to climb out."

"I understand."

"Let's hope you understand very well because I'd hate to have to show you."

I let it pass but it upset me. Ruining pictures was not a great worry of mine; we had much more to handle here. Big Jerry approached me in the living room.

"These boys need to study as soon as they get home from school."

"We study at night."

"That's not a good system. They need to sit down and study right when they get home from school."

"I have morning and afternoon students; we all study together at night."

"The best thing for them is to study right after school when they're fresh from learning. That's what we do at our home."

I was a teacher, these were my boys, and he was telling me when we should study in our own home.

"Our system is to study at night."

"You're not listening to me."

"Did the Lord give you a home for boys?"

"No."

"Well, he gave me one."

"Fine. I'll never set foot in your house again."

And he didn't. He remained a good friend and support but he never crossed our door threshold again.

~Others might try to dominate your project or ministry in order to help you out. Keep a hold of your authority.~

Weeks passed before we got a call came from Big Jerry.

"My neighbors tell me your boys have been smoking cigarettes in the trees near their yard."

"Thank you for telling me."

"What are you going to do about it?"

"I'm not sure."

"Bring them over to my house. What they really deserve is a good paddle."

Later that night we ate dinner, and I made some lame excuse about all of us needing to go to Big Jerry's. Then we set off on the ten-minute walk in the dark. As we neared his house we saw Big Jerry standing on the front porch in a statuesque pose with his muscular arms crossed on his chest and wearing a large colorful Japanese kimono awaiting our arrival. He gathered the boys together to talk in the living room. I went into the kitchen to visit with his wife. Then I heard Big Jerry quietly talking, and a whack of wood being slapped against his palm. Running in it looked to me like he was ready to give out real consequences. He told them he was just doing what a good father would do, and he was right, but I couldn't let him spank my boys. It was against government policy. Maybe Big Jerry was just scaring them, he scared me. The boys believed they came very close to a mighty paddling from a mighty man, and that was good enough punishment for me. The smoking stopped, and not one of them tried again for years. But the experience shook me up. Big Jerry and I would have to keep our distance.

One morning, Riki, the three brothers' older brother, came to visit to see where we lived. He was wearing the same oversized plaid long-sleeved shirt that gang kids wear. The girl next door noticed too and came out into the street wearing a red bandana to impress him and try to get his attention. He was polite enough with the boys. Deni, Lorenzo, and Nolan were thrilled to see him, but my hope was that he wouldn't visit too much. He was more streetwise than any of them, and we didn't need that kind of leader around; things were hard enough.

Riki asked permission to take his three brothers to visit their dad in prison since it was only a thirty-minute bus ride from our home. Their visit would save me a trip so I OK'd it and quickly looked around the house for some provisions to send for the dads. We never had much but I shared what we could. They went and came back on time, but I heard rumors months later that they had smoked some marijuana in the hills on the way. Marijuana is a plant that one can grow for free almost anywhere. Always best to be on guard, every minute, with my boys.

Life was full for me, and I enjoyed being a busy mom for my precious sons given to me by the Lord. Our little town, country life, our spirit-filled church, the food, and language, everything was perfect, but things would have been better if I had a husband to share everything with. Others felt the same. One man talked to me about this.

"You shouldn't be raising boys."

"Why not?"

"They need a man to raise them."

"You're right. If you find someone, let me know and I'll give them to him."

The man chuckled.

"I do the best I can. You know boys need a mother too."

"Don't worry about me. I think you're doing alright."

"Thanks. I do love them like my own."

~Few people will talk well of your project or ministry; many more will criticize.~

Summer came and I could not fly home. It had been four years since my last visit. Desperately wishing to see my family, I was locked in by responsibilities too big to leave. With no money for airfare, no one to watch the boys, and no legal permission to leave them with someone else it seemed an impossible wish. My needs included a visit home, but that would just have to wait. My mom also felt the separation had been too long, but maybe the Lord needed me more than my family at home did. She was right, because when you are motivated by love, no sacrifice is too big. My boys deserved a mom and Jesus had sent me, but I had given up precious time with my own family.

Our days did brighten up when the boys finally got their dog. As I was cooking in the kitchen, a purebred bloodhound passed by our fence. She looked awfully thin as she cautiously ran by, glancing my way for only a second. Minutes later she ran back by in the other direction, glancing my way, probably smelling the aroma of the beef, red and green bell pepper strips fried with spices.

Finally, she passed by again but stopped by the fence and longingly looked in, silently begging for a bite to eat. I invited her in the yard and offered her some scraps with meat juice poured over them. She gulped it down, looked me in the eyes, and then turned around three times in a circle and sat down by the door to rest. The boys were excited. Our dog! Three of them gave her a bath, which she tolerated quite well. Naturally, they then invited her inside the house now that she was clean. I invited her out, but that didn't last even for a second. Living in a tropical climate makes doorways just a pathway from the outside to the inside. It would be impossible to keep the dog out, especially with so many boys running in and out. We named her Stinky, as bloodhounds stink no matter how well you wash them. She settled down to life with us, and we enjoyed her easygoing manner. No one came looking for her.

~If you lose your pet, it could be almost impossible to find it again so watch over it carefully or be prepared to get a new one.~

Chapter 12
A National Disaster

That same week every living thing in our small community would be threatened, and honestly—our whole nation. All was flattened by the hurricane gone wild—Brutis. I had seen the warning on TV in the bank, watching the hurricane hovering over the land, never imagining it would have the force to cross our whole nation and cause such great destruction. The boys warned me that danger was coming, but I rejected their fears, reminding them in my teacher voice that hurricanes begin over water and usually hit the coast every fall. This was a normal seasonal concern.

Later that afternoon we knew Brutis had crossed over onto land and was not losing velocity. It was coming for us and it wasn't just the tail. Our home was old, and the roof was not only very old but made of red adobe tiles laid one upon another—no nails. The typical roofs you see in all the pictures of romantic adobe homes are removable. That's how we get inside when we leave our keys in the house. Just lift a few tiles and lower yourself in. Daron was our roof climber—long, thin, and limber. A hurricane could throw those tiles and topple our old roof easily.

As the rains began to really pound down and the wind picked up, the floors in the house began to fill with water drops. The roof was leaking in every room. We tried to move beds and furniture away from the drips, but the number of leaks continued to grow faster than we could move things. In my bedroom I found Stinky sitting on my bed completely wet and hiding from the storm. Trying to move her off she threatened me with her eyes, so I rolled her off using the whole bedspread. A dry bedspread to keep me warm was needed now more than ever, but it would not dry out for nine more days. Stinky sat in the corner wet and shivering. We mopped and mopped and mopped, keeping the floor an even wet but at least not flooded. That night we all went to bed insecure of what the darkness would bring. There was no safe corner to protect ourselves in. All I could do was pray, hoping that the roof would not collapse onto the boys, and we went to sleep. Our prayers were heard over the howling wind blasting down the rain. "Father God, protect us tonight." God was in charge of nature and, boy, was He mighty. Man's power is nothing compared to His. God is to be respected.

In the morning we were all fine, and relieved to see our house intact. But the storm was still tormenting our nation, hitting the capital tragically hard. We heard the sad news that one couple from our town had lost their lives in the hurricane that night—a mom and dad died at home in bed. A landslide had landed on the parent's side of the room and left their four children orphaned but safe from harm. But the national news did not reach us for a few more days—5,000 lives lost with thousands more missing. We prayed for all the good people and families who had suffered so much from Brutis. May Jesus fill the emptiness in their hearts left by the loss of their loved ones. Our hearts went out for the victims. We felt powerless.

~ In a national disaster communication will likely be down, you probably will not be able to call or e-mail to the US.~

The storm had caused our electricity to go out, and we had no water, as the pipes were broken. Since it was still pouring down rain, we set about fifteen different water-catching bottles and containers under the roof overhang and began a water collection effort. The water off the overhang was sparkling clean, as the roof had been very well washed all night during the storm. We then hauled the containers in and dumped the clean, drinkable water to store in the sinks and plastic garbage cans. I could not cook anything for breakfast, so I fought my way through the storm to the *pulperia* store next door to buy some cereal.

All was quiet inside and all twelve shelves were looking pretty empty. Others had been shopping and decided to buy extra. I did too. As daybreak arrived, we could see a silent movement of people in the constant downpour. Soaked and in shock, they started arriving one by one to the school, carrying their only remaining belongings with them: a bag full of clothes, a chair, TV, or a wet mattress and blankets. In our kitchen was a pretty full 100 lb. bag of rice donated by one of Big Jerry's friends. We had not much else. I paused, trying to decide what to do. It would not be worth the risk to help others out with food, as my responsibility was for the boys, and it was uncertain when we would get food again. But looking at the 100lb bag, I could not refuse these people food for today; they needed to eat something. Besides, if help came early it would haunt me knowing I had left them hungry just out of fear. My belief had to be that food would arrive in time for us all.

Immediately, I sent the boys to the school to find out who didn't have food or money. They were great spies, chatting with the people and finding out their circumstances. We had no tortillas and no containers, just rice. So I cooked up batch after batch of rice, dumping them into used plastic shopping bags. The boys eagerly ran back and forth from the school delivering the freshly cooked hot rice. It was then that I noticed there was not much gas in the tank for the stove. As dinnertime approached, I began to get nervous thinking of how to cook without gas. Looking out our back door through the heavy rain I saw the neighbors cooking on their outside woodstove under the awning. They gave permission to shove our pot of beans onto the corner of the grill—praise Jesus, we had beans cooking. It became quite embarrassing though since I'm allergic to smoke. As the smoke came in my direction I would try dodging it, but my eyes began to water immediately anyway. I cooked the beans, tears streaming down my face, the neighbors laughing. They now had proof: *gringas* really weren't able to cook even beans.

The days and nights continued the same: no electricity, no water, a lot of wind and rain. Finally, after three days the wind died down and the rain disappeared into a mist, but the sun still could not break through. We were out of clean clothes but had only muddy washing water and nowhere to hang the clothes to dry. So we washed the clothes in muddy water (and surprisingly they came out clean, even the whites!) and then strung cord inside the house, draping the laundry, hoping the wet clothes might dry eventually.

News from the outside began pouring in. We found out we had the only surviving bridge between our little town and the capital. Anyone farther out than our town was totally cut off by road to the capital because there is only one main road connecting the north with the south. There are no other transport-ready accesses—no cars or trucks were on the freeway. None. We were all in shock. There was nothing we could do but go about doing our daily chores, exchanging information, and looking at one another, thinking, "I have enough food to survive for maybe three more days and so do you. Then it will become a violent, desperate place."

~If your new country is in an emergency, it may

be best for you to leave immediately for the US rather than compete for critically needed basics. There are many responsible native leaders who can organize any help you can send.~

The next day, day four, a few trucks started showing up on the highway. Life was returning, and hope filled our cautious hearts. The farmers were in action. In groups they had gone out into their fields and collected all the blown-down or flooded vegetables and fruits and were heading to the capital to the open-air market with their rickety pickups overloaded. On day five a bread truck came. We were ecstatic—the roads were opening up again. Soon the buses were in action, taking people from one blocked area to another, letting the passengers cross by foot over the damaged roads and bridges to another bus waiting on the other side. I stood out on the highway and caught a bus to the capital, silently hoping that a bank would possibly have electricity and be open, and hoping to get to the open-air market and home again.

Traveling by bus through the countryside one hardly notices any damage, but entering the capital presents a different picture. The river raged and was still so high it looked like it might spill over onto the freeway and wash us away at any moment. We passed areas where all the homes alongside the rivers had been carried away. These people were the fortunate ones—they had been evacuated. But the real shock was looking over hillside after hillside that had been sliced in half by a landslide, leaving half houses or houses teetering on the brink, with clothes and furniture dotting the cliffs. These people were thought to be in the safe areas.
Whole neighborhoods had disappeared along with their families. The good and the bad died, the old and the young, the believers and the nonbelievers, too.

The bus was silent as we all looked out, taking in the horrid reality of Brutis. As we approached a bridge, I strained ahead to catch a glance of a home I had visited just weeks earlier. It was completely gone. A family in our church had lived there in a nice-sized home. Now there was just an empty space filled with water. No trace of the house. The air from the open windows had a stench—a bad, dreaded smell—the smell of death that the river carried.

The first bank we passed by was open. I jumped off the bus and ran in and stood in line, nervously listening to the deafening noise of the nearby gas pump providing the electricity. We all stood motionless. A friend from church was there. He asked what neighborhood I was from and I asked him, both of us worried the other one would say one of the disappeared neighborhoods. Once outside, it was only five blocks to the open-air market. A nearby rice distribution center was mobbed by a block full of people waiting in line to buy. There were thousands of people in the market, fresh fruits and vegetables heaped high as your head, but there was an eerie silence. That's when I noticed that no one was talking. The lively sounds of the market were absent. There were thousands of people buying and we were in shock. All of us.

In the distance overhead, we could all see three large US army aircrafts coming in for a landing at the airport. Thank God we had international help and things would not develop into bloody chaos. Thank God it was in time. Relieved and sickened by the sights, I was able to buy some needed foodstuffs and headed home in silence. Once home the boys and I prayed for the families who were grieving for their lost loved ones. Brutis reminded us of how unruly nature can be, of how powerful the God who made it must be, and how quickly what man has made can be destroyed. About six weeks before Brutis hit, the Christian community had gotten together to make a singing advertisement. It was prophetic. A group of top singers, one each from five different churches, made the ad in the city center park singing, "I Ask You for Peace," written by our greatest Christian Spanish singer, Marcos Witt. The chorus is:

I ask you for peace, for my city.
I ask you for pardon, for my city.
Now I humble myself and I look for your face.
To whom will I go, Lord, if not to you?

We believe this act of singing for our city may have saved us from greater disaster. Asking for pardon from God is big in the Bible. Asking for peace gets answered. The thirty-foot-tall Christ statue overlooking the city did not fall. Thousands of people lost their lives in one swoop that night. Our nation had been changed forever. In all this, we see God's great protection for us.

Announced by a loudspeaker, we heard that our small town had 1,100 broken PVC water pipes between us and the water reserve. They asked for volunteers in the community to help. Maybe the boys would volunteer.

"Hey, guys, your country needs your help. They want volunteers to repair the water pipes."

"They don't want us; they want men."

"You guys are as big as men. They need anyone who can help to show up."

"I'll go if they pay me."

"They need volunteers. This is your chance to help your nation in an emergency."

"I'm busy."

"School's been cancelled. You're free all day. What are you busy doing?"

"I'm on vacation. No way I'm going."

"I don't believe it. You don't want to help your nation in a crisis?"

"Only idiots will go."

"No, only real men will go. They need everyone to help. There are 1,100 broken pipes to repair."

"I'll go if lots of other people go, but they need to be in front of me."

Insecurity befell them; they did not want to look silly by offering to help. Disappointed and a little sad knowing they had to be coerced into assisting their own country during a crisis I stood my ground. We watched the next day as some men passed our house on their way to volunteer. My boys were still apprehensive. Then some more men passed. I nearly shoved them out the door. They did work hard, had fun, felt like men, and served their country in a crisis. But the 1,100 pipes would take over a month to fix. We had to find water to wash and bathe in. Quickly, it became great fun for the families to go down to the river and swim to clean up. Big Jerry's wife stopped by our house and offered to take our ten-gallon drinking water jugs to the natural spring a few miles away to fill up, praise Jesus.

Big Jerry helped organize, recruit, make connections, dig, haul away, and deliver as needed. As the engineers were nearing the final portion of debris-blocked piping, Big Jerry was there to help out. This part was the most dangerous, as removing the last blocked boulders and rocks would open up a super-pressurized torrent of water that had built up on the other side. The engineers above were quickly realizing that this was the spot where the water would break through, and in that moment it did. The water burst rushing down the canal, unbeknownst to the two workers below.

Big Jerry ran alongside the canal, then jumped into the racing, unwieldy torrent of water, risking his own life, and swam across the canal to grab onto one of the drowning men, bringing him to safety on the far shore. The man he rescued suffered broken bones to most every part of his body, but he lived. The other man died. Big Jerry is a man of God to the core and constantly proves it to us. He lives a purpose-filled life. Big Jerry and Jessica are also independent missionaries. They get donations from the States but are not sent by a church.

~You may be put in a position where you have to decide if you will risk your own safety to help another. Choose wisely since your country may have minimal medical resources.~

The flooded-out families living in the school returned home or had to find a new place to live so classes could resume. Truckloads of clothes came in from the US for the victims. They handed out jackets, sweaters, shoes, shirts, and pants. The donations were overwhelming and gratefully received. Many men had been out of work for days and some had lost their workplaces. Others had no incomes or savings at all.

We had heard that the city prisoners had been moved closer to us during the hurricane. The main prison had been completely flooded during Brutis, part of it carried away by the river. We were worried about the fathers. My heart skipped a beat, I was afraid at what might have happened to Pablo. All prisoners were now in the country prison previously reserved for gang members that we passed on the way to church. If they were still alive, the fathers were closer now but had been locked in with the worst of the worst—the killers—a new threat. This country prison accommodated 150. Unbelievably, it now had 3,500 more prisoners. We decided to visit as soon as we could believing they were alive and might be without food or medicine. We were greatly relieved to see both the fathers. They had made it through the hurricane and the move.

Pablo told us what the prisoners had gone through.

"Brutis was right on top of us. The sound was deafening. The rain and wind were blowing everything around, and we had roof leaks all over in the prison; everything was soaked. The outside prison wall closest to the river began to crack. We froze watching it split. We couldn't believe it would fall—then it cracked open wider. The guards announced to the prisoners through the winds and pouring rain to gather all their belongings and line up in front of the main gate. We knew they had to move us out fast. We all lined up with our belongings; suitcases, bags, and beddings within minutes. I grabbed our family photos and put them inside my pants.

Then the wall cracked completely open and fell. We could see the river racing by and trying to take the office buildings with it. Mud gushed in, filling up the lower cells almost to the top. Some prisoners began running for the break and jumped in the river, but the guards didn't shoot at them. Then more prisoners began to run. I aided some in escaping, but decided I wouldn't jump. It was better for me to stay and finish my time than to escape and always be on the run—maybe I'd get caught and have to do my time all over again.

Suddenly, we heard gunshots. The guards were firing on the escaping men. The other guards ordered the rest of us to put down all our belongings and quickly get loaded onto buses which took us to the soccer stadium. They never returned anything to us. All we had we lost. I saved what was most valuable to me—my family photos. Thank goodness I was able to find them quickly.

When we got to the stadium, it looked like they were not ready for us. There was no food or water, so we collected rainwater to drink. Some had brought a little food from their restaurant prison businesses and shared with a few others. There was no place dry to sit or sleep, so we tore apart the bleachers and made lean-tos. They kept us there for three days, giving us nothing. We had bathrooms but no toilet paper. We were finally taken to El Hollo—the gang facility. When we arrived, we were wet and hungry.

We soon found out there were not enough floor mattresses for us all to sleep on. Most had not been able to bring their bedding so they had to sleep on the concrete floor with nothing. Thank goodness there were so many of us. We outnumbered the gang guys 150 to 3,500, so things have been pretty quiet so far. We don't have towels, pillows, plates—nothing. No clean clothes, no soap. All of the men have lost their prison businesses. We were given some blankets and beds today. Can you help us a little? We hate to ask, but we have nothing." Of course we could help. He held his eyes on mine and I on his. We were all safe but had been greatly shook up.

The boys and I helped out as best as we could at the moment. We donated a little money for beginning a tiny prison tortilla business, and brought some extra food. It wasn't much.

Our country began the long road to recovery. The US government took three months to decide how much funding would come to us. Unknown to me, my cousin was put in charge of dispersing the funds, and he had three weeks to write up the papers. Because Greg has lived his life preparing for moments like this, the funds were in safe hands. He got ulcers worrying over how to word the disbursement provisions so no funds would "get lost," and if they did that no more funds would be given. There could be no accusations of stealing. It was a delicate and precise legal language that needed to be written in order to ensure that no one except the affected peoples actually got the aid. The legal wording would have to solve the problem without pointing any fingers. He invested all his experiences and expertise into writing an impressive plan that in time proved to be watertight. The reconstruction took place with the help of international funding.

~You will get to see both sides of our governmental and ministry influences: the good and the bad. It will make you a wiser server and a unified prayer warrior.~

The next day the boys went again to the prison to give their fathers a little more cash, some clothes, and more food. Nolan returned grinning, the biggest grin I had ever seen on that handsome face, as he handed me a note in an envelope from his father. I took the note and began to read; Nolan walked off. It said many things, but the clincher was the words: "Will you marry me? Come visit me alone." I was stunned. As I gained my composure, Nolan was whispering to the boys in the back room.

"Nolan, do you know what this letter says?"

Grinning grandly. "No." Nolan could not read.

As he always lies first I backed up my question with another.

"Did someone read this letter to you?"

"Yes, maybe."

"Did your father tell you to read it?"

"No." He grew serious, now thinking that his father would hear of this.

"It is against all rules to read someone else's mail. Mail is a private communication."

"Are you going to say yes, Kimi?"

The boys knew the news. I would not answer and would not visit Pablo alone. I did love the boys dearly and would love to be their stepmother, but marriage was not even a possibility. Pablo and I had no relationship except through the boys as their parental caretakers. We all knew when Pablo got released, he would take the boys with him; and he would take them from me forever. Deciding not to think about it was better than pondering the idea. Pablo didn't know anything about me as a person. What a crazy idea.

~Culturally common, men propose to a woman they don't know well to begin a courtship. Statistically, they will never marry.~

Just a short time after the hurricane my landlord decided to almost double our rent. We would have to look for a new home, again. Another move, another change schools, another time to lose and gain friends. Later that week a carful of *gringos* suddenly pulled up in front of our house. It was Pam, Brett, and Carol from Maranila. They had come to visit because Carol's husband, Peter, was deathly ill and needed to return to the US immediately with her. She wanted to know if the boys and I could stay in their house and run the farm for one year. Of course my answer was yes, it would be a blessing. Now Pablo would be hours away, at safe distance if I was falling for him. The news that we would be on the move again thrilled everyone except Deni, my youngest at nine. He started complaining.

"I don't want to move."

"It'll be fun."

"It's not fun. I've had to move too much."

"But this is only your second move with me, Deni." After all, for the other boys it would be our fourth move in two years.

His eyes widened for emphasis, "Yes, but I moved twenty times before I came to you."

The words of his truth hit me. I said in silence: *You heard him, Lord.*

"Well, Father God sent those people here to invite us to watch over their farm. Let's go and see what He has for us."

We did need our own home, a home for them forever. A home like everyone else had where they could grow up, return to from time to time and bring their children to for a family visit at Christmas. A real permanent home for them no matter what ups and downs their futures might hold. Our Lord had heard this small boy's honest request. We began packing up our things into plastic garbage bags with the faith that God was with us each step of the way. And I couldn't complain; we had been well cared for so far.

Chapter 13
Life Back in the Hills

Brett sent a flatbed pickup that had hauled donated food items into the capital to help out the Brutis victims for us. We piled our belongings a mile high and tied it down with twine. Then headed off for a new unknown together. We passed over the ridge that looked down on the valley of San Jeronimo and began the decline down the great mountainside, then crossed the valley and headed up the opposite side winding from left to right. It was getting dark and a bit foggy. We stopped alongside the road for a short break as there are few bathrooms available in the countryside; only males took advantage of this break even though these stops are not sexist, females may have to too. I couldn't unless it was really, really an emergency.

Cruz opened up the driver side door and leaned in to chat.

"I have a girlfriend that lives here in San Jeronimo."

Unable to speak for the moment, my head nodded yes. It seemed that Cruz had opened the truck door from the driver's side and had already said those exact words to me before.

Suddenly and quite vividly, I remembered the dream as it had come to me a couple of months before. In the dream we were all moving on a flatbed truck with no sides, an especially strange idea since I don't pay attention to types of trucks, and a flatbed would certainly be the last type one would dream of moving with. But that is what I had dreamed. Our possessions were piled quiet high, tied down with cords. The furnishings precariously shifted from side to side as we drove. Deni had had on a yellow T-shirt, jean shorts, and white tennis shoes—exactly what he was wearing at the moment.

Realizing the dream was repeating itself I froze. In the dream Deni was sitting on the very top until it swayed so much that he fell off. He landed spread-eagle on the pavement, instantly dead. Fear took over. I prayed and prayed all the way up that foggy, windy, dark country road sure the Holy Spirit had given me this warning. I prayed every minute until we arrived at the farm around eight p.m. Deni made it just fine. If this dream had just been a figment of my imagination, I had wasted my time praying. If it was spiritually real, my son's life had been protected. Best to act on the side of caution. I had seen and felt it all before it happened, so I do not doubt that my prayers carried God's power.

Arriving to a new home in the dark is difficult and a little eerie. We found our way to the door and entered a big house designed to work as a church too. The boys' rooms were along the open-air outside hall. I stayed alone in the big central part of Peter and Carol's house. In the morning we were able to look around. This large home had an acre of strawberries ready to eat on one side. In the corner lot there was a small house owned by a pastor from this little town—the TV evangelist Luis Yoro's father. Behind the house were about two acres of potatoes soon to be harvested. Guarding the house was Jamaica, a black lab. She proved to be the finest dog I've ever had. She was great with the boys and protected our farm, never running off around the countryside with her pack of friends. Our house was set on top of a small rolling hill, and we looked out over the neighboring country fields from every view. It could take your breathe away.

Maranila was truly a country *pueblo*, untouched by the nearing modernization, and one of the most picturesque places I have lived. Every inch was just naturally beautiful. Rolling hillsides were dotted with small *campesino* homes: cows, horses, goats, chickens, dogs, and small children ran and wandered about their ample surroundings. Males of all ages walked along the roads carrying their machetes to work. Men passed by on horseback; women chopped wood and hauled water. There was no electricity apart from a few homes in the center of town; candles lit up the homes at night, exposing a spacious, deep sky full of stars so innumerable only God could count them. The best in modern science say if the universe was the size of the US our solar system would be the size of a quarter and the Earth a pin head size of the quarter. Incredible.

~Science continues to prove an intelligent design is the most likely answer to creation no matter how immense or how minuscule the discoveries are.~

The Catholic Church, located right in the middle, was the largest building in town. It was a very old, inviting, and majestic edifice. Entering the double-wide, two-story-high wooden doors, one felt the freshness and coolness offered by the great vaulted ceilings. Large plastic figurines dressed in elegant attire poised along the side walls. The church was strangely empty, filled by only a few pews. A beautiful and obviously handmade Christ hung in the center of the podium. Because our small town had so few people in it and we lived so far out in the country, a real Father would visit to preach just once every three months. He was their connection to the rest of the church.

A small telephone office gave us instant access to the outside world—no Internet, no cell phones yet. Settled in a large empty room, it had one desk, two chairs, one telephone and one man ready to serve. Beside the phone was a working telegraph, if you had someone you wanted to send Morse code to. Telephone calls were difficult to complete, as the signals were bad or the lines were busy, but it was available, if you had the time.

Another room in this small house served as the mayor's office, sheriff's, and jail all in one. Most days no one came, but if they did, the need was urgent—a legal dispute that could erupt into death blows, a drunk passed out in the street or a meeting needing to be called for all the country folk to receive informational help from the government with their crops.

A tiny clinic was the central point of activity within the community. Some of the country folk lived so far out they had to walk hours, maybe three or more, while ill or carrying someone ill to visit the doctor or nurse. It is incredibly difficult to walk a few miles or so when you're sick, especially so sick you finally decide you must see a doctor. Or try carrying a medium-sized child that distance in your arms. We see that in the country regularly. The truly blessed man has a burro or horse to help in emergencies.

In the front office were a few plastic green garden chairs all filled with patients quietly waiting to be seen—mostly mothers with small children. The walls were a mix of old paint and dirt which had settled with time. It was dark. A tiny table with a humidifier that worked but had no medicine in it, fumed out cloudy wisps of air made of water that seemed to help the patient. The doctor and nurse were dedicated professionals working in a difficult situation, praying for medicines or better equipment to serve their patients. They knew what their patients needed and offered what they had as they could do nothing more. Every day the country folk would fill up their clinic with serious needs, and every day they did their best with almost nothing.

Any small gifting is appreciated by medical staff serving in areas like this. They are almost embarrassed by the lack in which they serve, but they boldly do their best. If you are a medical professional and wish to help, first visit to find out the exact needs of that clinic. If you are able to get a donation, try to be there later when the gift is handed out or ask someone you know to be in charge. Many short-term missions team do just this and greatly bless small communities. To those in the US these may seem like small offerings but for a sick adult or child without any common medicine to take it is a small miracle. These gifts are very likely the only medicines these people get or have in their homes.

Another way to help with medicine might be organizing a Bible-memorizing coupon clinic. You could ask for help from a local church. Hand out beautifully decorated numbered coupons with an expiration date and a Bible verse to be memorized. Those who cannot read can have someone else help them memorize it. Maybe pick a theme and hand out five different verses. You hold a coupon clinic in the room of the church. They tell you the verse from memory and hand you the coupon which you date, write the number down, and hand back. Then they get to buy an item with the coupon: Ibuprofen, cough medicine, antibiotic ointment, cute Band-aids, colored toothpaste, or head lice shampoo from the “in church” clinic. Make sure to check with the medical personnel to ensure you are not unfairly competing with someone or some group that sells to this community. If so you might just buy from the vendors in country. Because of the expense I would only advise a church or group to invest in a project like this. You can be a medical blessing. Your coupon project has had the people memorize verses, united them with a local church which is helping to serve their community and has blessed their families with common over the counter medicines.

~My recommend for individuals would be to investment of no more than $300 in any project.~

Across the street from the medical clinic was a pool hall located in the living room area of a home. At night loud worldly music blared from the house, an invitation to men and wayward women to dance, play pool, and drink. You can also find tiny restaurants located in living rooms. The family puts a few tables with collected chairs about and waits for you to come in and order. They are a little hard to find because there may be no sign. That, of course, I have been told is because everyone knows where they are. You walk in, sit down and notice a menu lightly scribbled with white chalk on a small overused chalkboard. The house is quiet and no one comes to serve you. Thinking you may have made a mistake and have walked into a private home, you think about leaving and presto, the father of the house enters to attend to you.

"Do you serve food?"

"Yes, Dora is the best cook around."

"What can I order?"

"We have a lunch plate, fried chicken, intestine soup, or beef strips in spices." He repeats word for word off the menu.

"I'll take the beef strips."

"We don't have those today." He turns, glancing quickly toward the kitchen, as if it just happened.

"Oh, I'll take the chicken."

"Sorry, we don't cook chicken until after three."

OK, Dora might wait until dinner hour to cook up chicken. "Oh, I'll take the intestine soup."

"We only serve that on Fridays."

Exasperation crosses your face. The waiter seems oblivious.

"What's the lunch plate?"

"Rice, beans, tortillas, cheese, eggs, and avocado."

"I'll take that."

~Restaurant menus don't tell you what's available, they tell you what might be available.~

Old cars, old buses, beat-up-but-still-running trucks, horses, donkeys, and oxen with carts all shared the roads though there's not much traffic. Each one gets to hog the road as they wish. In the rainy season, which is most of the year here, the oxen really tear up the road. The large wooden wheels laden heavily with weight cut into the muddy dirt roads, sliding great amounts of mud to one side or the other. In a few parts of the road it was so bad I could not walk around, through or over the deep mud on all sides. This makes it a constant battle for the tractor road-repair man, called out to re-flatten the roads so someone can pass besides oxen.

Oxen carts with car tires do less damage, but because of their heavy weights still tear up the roadways. It is a great wonder to see these massive animals that weigh tons lumber down the road. As they pass you can feel the pressure of their hooves trembling the earth, hear the deep grunt as they breathe and the shift of the old wooden cart pulled from behind giving in to each sway. The truth of the past sometimes becomes a reality in this land: I saw a white ox that was yoked by a thick wooden plank to a black ox—the two stood still waiting comfortably. The white ox then decided to sit down, not without great difficulty because of the heavy yoke and his great size. Once down, the black ox stood with his head twisted downward because of the yoke but remained standing. Yokes are best worn in harmony, everybody up or everybody down. Jesus warned us not to marry unequally yoked, believers with nonbelievers. This was meant not to exclude people, but to show that if one is sitting down, the other is stopped in his tracks too, with his neck twisted. Best to be pulling the weight together.

Maranila is in one of the coldest parts of this country. Sometimes the winter chill can reach thirty-four degrees, almost freezing. It enjoys a short summer of highs around sixty—a nightmare for me. It rained nearly every day most of the year so the plants flourished. But being from the North, I was mortified to be freezing cold in the rain in a tropical country. Everyone else seemed to love it. Cold weather was a dream come true for many US visitors from hot-areas.

Carol had offered us her home rent-free; she was a blessing. The home was lighted with a gas-powered generator. Our first month we ran it in the early morning and for about four hours every night. The bill was high—we were spending a hundred dollars a month for gas, more than our rent had been! We had to limit the lights to just two hours at night. The rest of the time we used candles like everyone else.

The refrigerator, stove, washer, and dryer were gas machines connected to a human-sized tank outside the kitchen window. When the tank ran out we were in trouble. The closest place to exchange the tank for a refill was the next town about twenty minutes away by car, but we had no car. It was necessary to ask for help, we couldn't do it alone. I had to ask someone to pass by on their way to town with their truck. Two of my biggest boys could lift the empty tank onto the truck. The man would have to lower it and help lift the full tank at the gas outlet. Then we needed the man and one of my big boys to lower it again at home and hook it up. It was a big deal. I really hated asking for help. This bothered me, but we had no other choice. Timing was always our enemy as we would have to run out before I could ask someone to help us on their way in to town. We would always spend a few days without gas in these exchanges. A second gas tank would have been wonderful but was too expensive for us.

Electricity was difficult to attain. Many people are praying to God for electricity. Because of the expense of even the two hours of lights a day by generator we eventually had to cut all use of electricity in the house and use only the gas stove, refrigerator, and washing machine. Clothes were hung out to dry. Candles became our light. A pencil drawing of a frumpy, wispy-haired older man writing by candlelight came to mind. Just like decades ago in the Old West, the boys were left to study by candlelight.

We got used to using candles at night. They were cheap but we used so many it cost a lot. Just once we had an emergency. We were all inside the big part of the house when someone smelled smoke. I won't say who it was, but Lorenzo had left a candle burning in his room. When we opened the door, the curtains were on fire, burning the wood shutter, and the bed mattresses were touched by wispy black marks. Smoke hung in the air and choked our throats.

The boys jumped into action—pounding out the fire with their shoes, bringing in water to throw on the fire, pounding out sparks with the sides of cardboard boxes. We got the fire out quickly and sat down to analyze the damage. Lorenzo had placed the candle on the cassette tapes before leaving; all our Christian music had burned. Praise our Lord, nothing was irreplaceable. Our pastor came the next day and offered to help. He put in a new wood shutter and painted the wall with the boys' help. It would take us years to build up our Christian tape collection again, but things could have been worse.

There are few fire stations anywhere in this country—mostly because the houses are built of concrete blocks and the roofs of tile. Not much there to burn. In the larger cities there is always one fire station, manned with valiant volunteers but limited by lack of funding. In the countryside we have to put out our fires ourselves. Bigger fires are the whole community's problem, so we act immediately together. Each person's help becomes valuable then. It happens rarely, but sometimes we do lose a good man while fighting fire. Our whole community mourns together united in our loss. While we were living in Maranila one man did lose his life to fighting fire, to honor him we remember his sacrifice and that of his family. We dearly need each man in the country. Life is more basic, but the work is heavier.

~Country life can make you strong, the work can be heavy. Enjoy the challenge.~

Living with no TV is perfect for me. Without a TV, electricity, phone, or computer, daily life was, well, quiet. But the house was full of books. I read most of the over 300 books in the library, except the thousand-page biography of Billy Graham. Not that I didn't try to read it—it was just so detailed it was difficult to get through the first chapter. My favorite novel was an account of what happened on the ground with the A-bomb attacks at Hiroshima. It was horrifying, really, but history is to be learned from. I loved the library, but as candlelight is not bright enough for reading, only the sunlight during the days permitted me this luxury. On the sunny days I would go outside to a protected corner of the house and read, hiding from the wind but enjoying the sun.

The nights and mornings were pretty cold for us, so we always had a fire built in the fireplace. Most times it was so cold that your front was warm from the heat of the fire, but your back was freezing. The boys had no heating in their outside rooms. We just piled on the blankets. It rained a lot. It was at these times that my prayers in secret were for a new location, as this part of the country was too cold for me.

~Your service may be in an area that's too hot, too cold, too wet, too windy, or full of allergens.~

Pam and Brett were our great support. They helped us get settled in, buy food, and get to church. They lived about a one hour's walk from our farm, farther out into the country. We were invited over for Thanksgiving dinner and enjoyed celebrating together. I had nothing to add to the dinner except seven hungry boys. We ate on their outside porch overlooking the exuberant beauty of nature that surrounded us. Their girls were wonderful hostesses, serving turkey with dressing, green salad, pies, and a variety of Southern dishes new to me. The boys were thrilled with their American Thanksgiving dinner. All the excitement got Freddy off on another tangent which he decided to share with the girls.

"I hate Christians."

The girls opened their eyes wide and giggled nervously glancing at one another.

"I do." He looked bold, gathering their attention.

"No you don't."

"I'm going to kill all the Christians I have ever known."

Wonderful. Freddy had to go. Having a ministry that attends to homeless children limits your effectiveness as a moral role model—some people are not in a place to take advantage of the gift. Jesus told us not to throw pearls before swine. We servers have few valuable jewels to gift thus it is not wise to throw them before people who are not ready to win. We must pick and choose our fights.

Homeless children are not asking to be taken in as they have been forced into that situation. You are their best option at the time. They bring a lot of emotional baggage with them. Change may be slow. These children are sometimes like the little decorations that hold water and snow-like flakes. When shaken up the outside doesn't flinch but the inside is all awhirl.

~In your time serving you may not see the fruit of your work, but all parts of the body are needed for success.~

We offer to be a family to these children because all children deserve the love of a family, a safe place to sleep, adequate food, education, and a moral example. Even as just a new authority in their lives, we offer unconditional love, yet demand the best from them. Sometimes one must choose to protect the safety and quality of life for the majority in the home rather than leave them to the powerful whims of the minority. Some children are so strong and upsetting in their behaviors that we must send them to another home. It is an especially tough decision to send a child away.

Please distinguish this difference when you decide to serve. Is your ministry for those who have chosen to follow Jesus or for those who have not? As Christians we do not force Jesus on others, we allow them to choose. If you minister to those who have not made the decision to change their lives, you are preparing the ground and planting the seeds, but you may see little gain. Be happy in your part of the ministry. Don't let anyone tell you it doesn't count. It takes millions of seeds to make a harvest. That's why He needs you to be active.

That night the boys were all outside talking in the dark in the little shed. Approaching, I decided to stay aside and listen in a little. Freddy was entertaining them with stories of his life at the orphanage. "The guard wanted to sleep with the Christian girl and she said yes and ran into the forest with him. They didn't come back for hours." It seemed his stories always centered on how bad Christians were. I wondered how to get him out of my home so far away from the government office in the capital.

The next day he made comments toward Daron that were sexual. That was it, he had to go. Before lunch Freddy and Nolan went to play basketball in the *pueblo* center. When they got back they told the other boys big stories about how Freddy was purposely touching the girls playing basketball with them. That became my excuse to tell Freddy that he was out. He had to pack his bags and leave right away. My reason was that he had ruined the reputation of us all and the families would not want to have him around their daughters. As he was of age he would have to find work and begin his life without us. I gave him some money, he packed his things, and left on the bus for Branzano. The boys were unsettled every time I kicked someone out, but they understood, it was better to have me in control than Freddy. The government was informed that now we were six.

A medical brigade came to Pam and Brett's to service our little town. The boys and I took off walking, crossing the town in 25 minutes to get to the brigade. After meeting the US volunteers, Brett asked me to take a family to the phone office to help make a call to the states. There had been a family emergency, so the father, mother, daughter, and son all had to leave immediately. It hurts us so much when this happens, but it does happen. Family members die or get deathly ill while their loved ones are serving overseas. It is an important decision to work through before coming. You would be surprised how often illness in the family back home is a concern for our travelers. Some people choose not to travel because of these concerns and others go ahead and come, never knowing if the decision will be right. Having family members go through emergencies is a tough thing to have happen while you're so far away.

~Pray, then make the best decision you can at the moment and be at peace with your choice.~

My father's sister, my aunt, died of cancer while my parents were spending four months with us here. I will never forget my father's last phone call to her. He assured her that he was still her big brother and would take care of her. My parents had planned to stay with her on their way home. Soon after, we got news that she had passed away. Four years later I was to get the news three days later that my mom had died. We had been out of phone reach serving a visiting team. It can be tough. Brett left the brigade to take the family to the airport in the capital, four hours away. He would return late the next day. Pam asked the boys and me to fill in for the family by helping at the brigade. We were thrilled at the chance to serve.

Cruz took names at the door and sat the patients down. Daron helped in the pharmacy filling bags. Deni, Orlando, Lorenzo, and Nolan helped the people getting their hair washed with medicine for hair lice. My job was to translate for the doctor. It was great fun and the boys were exhilarated to be helping in a brigade. We did well enough that they asked us to come help the next day too. It was an awesome experience for us all.

Many days the boys would spend hours outside picking strawberries and eating them right off the runners. They ate large ones, red ones, sweet ones, sour ones. We were in strawberry heaven on earth. I allowed them to cook inside, mixing the strawberries with sugar. This used up a lot of sugar and gas for cooking but they were happy. We picked many bowls of strawberries to give away to thank people who had done us favors. The strawberry part of the farm was delicious.

This farm grew potatoes too—lots of potatoes. We ate potatoes at least once every day: whole baked potatoes, mashed potatoes, Jo-Jos dipped in hot salsa, French fries, potato soup, and hash browns. It was divine. Some of our trees were apple trees and even had apples—not perfect apples but good sour green, scrunched up apples all the same. Historically, apples were foreign grown, and seasonal apple-giving became an important part of the Christmas tradition. Large, bright red, shiny apples are bought as gifts to eat on Christmas Day. But imported apples are expensive. Now we were beginning to produce our own home grown apples. The apples on our farm never hit the ground though. They were picked and eaten at whim. Maybe they would have made a good pie.

Tall pine trees filled one large corner of the farm; towering overhead they created a shaded park like area below where the chickens clucked and squawked in peace. We collected our own eggs and never killed a chicken to eat. The chore of feeding the chickens was given to Orlando because it was so easy. He didn't like it anyway. We were rich with plants, animals, nature, and outdoor freedom. This was a place where boys could truly be boys. Because modernization was not king, a lot had to be done by hand with sweat on the brow. Even buying food wasn't easy.

Once a week it was necessary to take the bus to the next town for food shopping. It was a ten-minute walk to the bus then a twenty-five minute bus ride. The open-air market was small, dusty, or muddy, depending on the weather, but had everything you would need. There were even a few specialty shops around for the odd things one needed occasionally: a lamp, plastic table, hairdryer, alarm clock, etc.

One day while out shopping, I stopped by to visit the judge, introduce myself and tell him about our home. The judge was not busy and invited me in. He was a short, round man who stuttered.

"Nice to meet you, Judge." I extended my hand to shake his, a custom rarely done by women.

"N-n-nice to m-m-meet you, Kimi."

"I work with the Children's Services and have six boys living with me in Maranila."

"I s-s-see. W-w-what do you need f-f-from m-m-me?"

"I just wanted to introduce myself and let you know we were here."

"Oh, th-th-thank you. You're n-n-not married?"

"No, it's just me and the boys."

"Do you h-h-have a boyf-f-friend?"

I raised my eyebrows and looked him in the eyes. "Yes. He lives in the capital." Trying to look casual as I realized I was thinking of Pablo.

"M-m-maybe I will g-g-give him a reason f-f-for moving c-c-closer to you."

He seemed to be an overly friendly judge.

~Meet the officials in your area; they will hear about you. You are the guest.~

It is vital to respect the authority in the country you're serving. Because we offer a free service or community activities, the authorities do support us, but any transgressions that violate the law or hierarchy of authority will be admonished. You are in their nation, their town, under their authority. They are allowing you to work, don't know you well, and cannot have their jobs threatened or be publically embarrassed by some foreign volunteer who wants to help people. You must be aware of the laws and follow them since ignorance is not an excuse. This is why your community connection leaders are so important. They can be your legal guide and defense. These leaders can also fill you in about any power plays or supposed power plays going on in your area so you may respect both sides while promoting what is right for your works. No project is worth a legal battle. Get Christian legal counseling if you find yourself in a situation you can't get out of. My personal advice would be to shake the dust off your sandals and move on to the next town if the legal atmosphere is not positive in your area. Most missionaries are not sent to help change the nation's legal system.

This judge was excited to have us in his community and offered me more boys—forty, if we had the beds. Honored by his confidence I agreed to take only one eleven-year-old, as we didn't have forty beds. This small boy was an orphan because first his father died of AIDS, then his mother. It is said that AIDS in our nation has been stopped only by the great number of faithful wives—its killing ends with them because they do not pass it on to anyone else. Tragically, the faithful wife still gives up, through no fault of her own, what is most precious to her—life with her loved ones— but we honor their legacy with this statement.

Donaldo was with us a short time before he mentioned that his grandmother lived in the next town, so we went exploring to find her. He led me right to her very small shack located about a mile out where she cared for six of her grandchildren. She was emotional—she thought she had lost him forever. Within minutes little friends from all sides gathered around to greet Donaldo. Her happiness disappeared as we were preparing to leave, quickly she asked him to return to live with her and he agreed. We walked directly to the judge and got his permission for the move.

Taking the bus home we filled up two bags with his new used clothes and gifts. He looked like a miniature Santa Claus weighed down by two huge, heavy bags filled to the brim. I carried two more bags to give to his baby cousins filled with smaller children's clothing that had been donated to us. We hurried to the bus, as daylight was waning and I needed to catch the last bus back home again. Approaching his grandma's house, we were met by small, medium, and large cousins with a few aunts who had come to greet him. I left quickly, glancing back at the sun setting behind the mountains, waving to the active group of children playing in the street and the smiling grandma waving good-bye from her doorstep.

I would never hesitate to help a grandparent who is taking care of grandchildren. To ensure that your gift is properly received, deliver the food, clothes, or school supplies yourself. It is wise not to gift more than they can use in a day or week. If you wish you may return later to gift another small amount. For example, it is wonderful to give a big hundred-pound bag of rice sure to last a large family for two months. But unless you are OK with them passing on a lot to relatives, some of whom might show up to collect a real or invented debt, or selling off some to get the cash to spend on other things it is too hard to monitor the gifting. And who wouldn't want to share a rice blessing with all your beloved ones? Or sell a little to buy what your child needs?

~Please try not to say you will come back with more, just do it if you can. For one reason or another most all of the promises made are broken.~

Be sure to remember you can gift the family something of Jesus too: Christian items, postcards that you've written on, bookmarks, coloring books and colors, stickers, and the like. These small items will be present in their home even after the food is gone. A lasting personal gift could be a beautiful small Christian poster for the wall, putting it up for them before you leave. Women love inviting beauty in their homes to greet their guests. Years from now it will be there where you left it, speaking its message to those who look.

School supplies are always super gifts, yet giving too much could cause small but unwanted problems. Giving ten pencils to one student for school will ensure that he will pass some on to his family or friends, and there will be pressure at school for him to sell a few at a discount, or what he has will be stolen from his desk. This gives credence to the habit of gifting many people with a small gift, the way the short-term missions teams do. This may seem like giving almost nothing, but it is wise and together we do make a real difference. Gifting school supplies in quantity at school is even better. The teacher can help, as she has surely donated regularly from her own pocket. Have the students mark their names on the items with a permanent marker, or give each line of desks the same color, at least limiting the chance of confusion later. Again, wall posters for the teacher will be treasured for years to come. In this country they can even have Jesus or His name on them.

Donaldo had found his home with his grandma again and that left me with six boys. When one boy leaves, another one always comes to take his place. Next came the news about Riki. His aunt said he was getting too mixed up in the gang stuff and asked if he could live with us. It was important to be firm, so I agreed to it as long as he understood that he had to live by the rules and support the Christian way of life in order to be in our home. He really just wanted to be with his brothers.

Riki arrived the next day by bus and got registered at the private high school in the neighboring town, which had an advanced study program. Cruz and Daron had decided to attend the high school in our little town. Nolan, at fourteen, was too big to be in third grade so he stayed home with me to homeschool. Orlando, Lorenzo, and Deni went to the primary school. Lorenzo was the second tallest in the whole school, Deni was the third. Because some of my boys were so tall and white, the townsfolk assumed they must be mine.

This led to many questions as they tried to clarify what kind of family we had.

"Are you the mother of some of those boys?"

"No. But I'm their mom now."

Politely, she received my answer. "Do you have *gringo* (American) boys in your home?"

"No, I don't."

She thought awhile. "Do some of those boys have a mother or father who is *gringo*?"

"No, they are all natives."

"Oh" her eyebrows rose, "Some of them look so tall and white."

"Yes, they do."

The tallest of all my boys was Nolan at five foot six. Tall by our national standards, which is the local way only way of viewing things. It is a great honor to adopt new standards of observation. One grows when one can redefine terms like tall, poor, beautiful, or too heavy, too far to walk and on time.

After completing all the registrations for school, it was time to buy school clothes again. We got up at four a.m. to take the five o'clock little minivan bus to the next town to catch the six o'clock bus out of that town for the four-hour bus ride into our capital so we could get done in time to catch the last bus home that same day. We did all this in order to buy top-quality but cheaper school pants and shoes. The bus ride there and back cost me about $4 per person but I counted it as a mini-vacation day. It would be exciting.

The boys knew their way around the downtown area of our capital, so I gave them money and sent them off shopping in groups with a time limit to meet at the buses. Everyone knew they had better return on time as this was the last and only bus trip back home for the day. Orlando and I went one way, Cruz and Daron another, Riki, Lorenzo, Nolan, and Deni another. At three P.M. the four brothers were already on the bus waiting and showed me the high-quality but somewhat expensive school shoes they each had picked out. I was happy with their purchases because boys need quality shoes. Orlando and I decided to buy some mangos to take home and left them on the bus waiting for Daron and Cruz. Minutes later when we returned, the boys had bad news for us.

Lorenzo and Deni were nervous. "The bus attendant got off the bus and some other guy we don't know got on."

"Yeah, he asked Riki and Nolan if they would help him put some boxes into a truck for fifty pesos each."

"Riki said yes, and when they were gone two other bigger guys got on the bus, gang guys from the hood." The word "hood" is US movie slang which does impact youth all over the world.

"Yeah, they came back to us, blocked the way and said we had to give them our shoe boxes or they would hurt us."

"One held a knife."

Riki added, "It was a setup. The guy took Nolan and me just a short distance from here, then told us the boxes had already been loaded so we weren't needed. By time we got back the others had already robbed Lorenzo and Deni."

"They stole all our shoes."

They had been victimized, possibly with the accomplice of the bus driver and attendants who couldn't say no to the gang guys either. Again, be on guard at all times for theft.

If they hadn't shown me their purchases, I may not have believed their story, but it was true—they had been assaulted. We all knew I would be a target but had assumed they would not. I was relieved to see the boys were safe from harm but we had lost four pairs of very good quality school shoes on our own bus where we felt protected. At least they didn't steal all that they had bought. As male teens they had felt a little invincible to crime, believing they were one of the gang. Now they realized they were targets just like everyone else and felt more vulnerable than before. We returned home by eleven P.M. and bought cheaper shoes from the open-air market the next day.

The primary boys had school from eight to eleven and then again from one p.m. to two-thirty. This meant they had to walk to school and return twice a day. We lived on the outskirts of town, a bit of a walk. Some of the children who lived too far out stayed at the school for lunch. Even though the government requirement for school attendance was a school uniform and shoes, many in our community could not supply all that for their children, so the rules were quietly overlooked. Most children did show up with shoes even if they were only black rubber boots, but some did come barefoot. Some children wore uniforms worn out from years of wear, torn, faded, but sufficiently intact for attending class. Everyone did what they could to help these children attend; after all, no one denies the advantage of education for the future of children.

Because many children did not eat well at home the government had a free lunch program available. The lunch included a multivitamin that the mothers were complaining about. They didn't want their children getting the multivitamin because it made them ferociously hungry afterward and the mothers had no extra food to give their children. The doctor was stumped. She needed to convince these mothers that multivitamins were critical for their children, especially when they had no food. My suggestion was mixing it in with the Kool-Aid and not telling anyone. I asked Sonia, Greg's wife, since she was now a practicing doctor for an idea and she suggested telling the moms that this multivitamin was special, that it made the children feel as if they'd eaten a big serving of meat. The lunch and vitamin program probably helped those children more than we all know, and I am grateful that the government has tried to fill this need for their most at-risk communities.

~To have an effective project or ministry, you must continually be aware of the momentary community attitudes toward your work. Hook up with a reputable leader.~

Orlando was elected secretary and Deni was elected president of their new school. We were excited; it was a good step. Deni worried a little, as he has a stuttering problem. But he learned that if he wrote out his talks and practiced in order to say them from memory, he didn't stutter! Lorenzo and Deni challenged and mostly dominated the best in recess basketball—including every girl. Boy, did they feel awesome.

To begin the year, the parents are invited to meet the teacher and see their child's classroom. This school was very modest and built in the same style as most country schools. The classrooms form a "U" shape around a concrete center and recess area. Behind the school was a garden area attended by the agriculture classes. Tall trees dotted the corners of the yard, providing some shade on sunny days. I sat in Orlando's room with all the other parents. It was a little dark and not too brightly painted. The old chalkboard desperately needed new refinishing. The teacher began roll call, calling out the names of our children so we could be counted as present. I was the only new parent in the room; the others all had known each other for years. Suddenly, I thought he had called my son.

"The mom of Orlando Brock."

I paused, not answering. Orlando's name was Gomez, not Brock. Brock was my maiden name. I laughed, realizing what he had done.

The parents glanced at me nervously. They knew that Orlando Brock was my son even though he looked quite Indian, a beautiful Indian I might add. Yet, I was laughing and not answering.

"Present." I grinned broadly.

Orlando was my son; I had claimed him and he had claimed me. He had even claimed my parents. Adorable. I called my mom and dad to let them know we had another Brock in the family.

Nolan got started on his homeschool program. He chose a children's Bible to begin to learn to read. As we were reading, with him slowly sounding out the words, I noticed he read groups of two letters backward sometimes. He did this so often I began to say, "Reverse it," and he would. Nolan had dyslexia. He was fourteen years old, had gone to school every day for seven years, wasn't passing his grade, and no one had diagnosed him. He continued forward, practicing reading with me every day with the same joy he always had taken to the classroom.

~Identification of special needs is gaining in this country, but most needs do not receive any special assistance.~

He learned to read well enough that I signed him up for a radio school called "Teacher At Home." We would listen to the radio program every day, do the work, and then go in to a school for a test at the end of the course in order to get credit for the grade. It was so perfect I signed up all the boys. After school they would come home with little or no homework so we did "Teacher At Home." With this program I noticed my fourth-grade boys were not capitalizing correctly, spelling correctly, and had trouble forming good paragraphs, so we worked on those things. In the evening from seven to eight we did their public school homework or they drew by candlelight. When it was time for the boys to take their tests, I learned that the scores would not count because they were enrolled in public schools. But that was OK, they all passed their tests and that's what mattered to us.

Nolan was the only one who could receive credit for passing. As Nolan began his test for first grade he carefully wrote in the name box: Nolna. He looked up at me cautiously. This was a test so I could say nothing, but by the look on my face he could see the worry. He asked quickly, "That is backward isn't it?" and changed it. I left to sit down with the other parents during testing accepting that he might fail. But he surprised me. Nolan passed the test on his own. He was pumped. He could read a test and had passed first grade—reading and math. Thank God for "Teacher At Home."

~Find out about programs already active in your neighborhood. Highly dedicated people donate their time and money to help as they can. Join them.~

We continued with the study times. All the boys took "Teacher At Home." Soon my three public school boys were on the honor roll. Our home study had filled in their learning holes and set them ahead. That's when I noticed that Lorenzo had a slighter case of dyslexia, which he strongly denied. He wasn't like Nolan he said, absolutely not. I told his father, Pablo, who wanted to deny it also. The stigma was too great. It was mild and affected him lightly, so I quieted down. Lorenzo continued every year to struggle with his classes and testing but because of his high intelligence his dyslexia got by undetected. If you personally have any learning disability, your testimony would not only educate students and teachers on how to identify the signals but also teach them how to work with it. Your testimony would help take the sting out of the label too. Make sure your message claims you as victorious as you really are.

Short-term mission teams also visit schools, maybe teaching an English lesson or playing a math game. Their testimonies educate the community about personal triumphs that are not discussed in schools here. Wise testimonies educate their listeners to be more informed morally and socially. Don't assume you are the first person to bring up an issue but do speak about it as if some of your listeners aren't yet informed. These moments of sharing add a spark of quality to life. The effect is cumulative, each person doing their part. God gave us different talents and passions—that way whatever he wants done in the world will get done. Nolan was learning to read, and the boys were on the honor roll, but they weren't yet the boys you'd want your daughter to hang out with studying unsupervised. Morally they had a lot of maturing to do.

Unfortunately, the use of gas-generated electricity would become Cruz's downfall. He had noticed the small tank of gas stored in the shed to be used for filling the generator. He started the habit of inhaling fumes. One time as we were talking I noticed he seemed to talk, walk, and look a little drunk. I confronted him and kicked him out immediately, my heart parting in two. He was my son but he had to go. He took the bus money, his belongings and went to the orphanage where his brothers and sisters were living to see if he could work with them. The director put him in charge of twenty-five little boys, one of them his little brother Waldo. Cruz was the house father. He slept in their dorm, was in charge of cleanliness, got them ready for school, lined them up on time for breakfast, and monitored them while playing. His older sister Vilma was in charge of a girl's dorm. This was the orphanage where Freddy had been raised and his younger brothers and sisters still lived. It was a blessing for Cruz and a relief for me. At least he was in a Christian atmosphere and not on his own alone.

No one ever spoke about the abuse of inhaling gas to me. A real national problem is boys who inhale glue; you will see them on the streets sniffing out of small plastic bags or dirty-looking empty Coke bottles. This is why it's best not to give money to kids on the street, many of them buy drugs. A better donation would be to offer to buy food if they eat it in front of you, or donate to a group that serves this population. Plus there is a government run center that takes in street kids, feeds them, has learning activities and gives them a place to sleep. A visit would be great and they also could use your support.

Since Freddy and Cruz had behaved so badly around the girls, Pam and Brett decided it was best not to combine our groups. Proximity leads to influence and affection, and my boys were not strong Christian young men. I had to accept their decision, so we began to limit our activities to attending church together on Sundays. The girls didn't understand the separation and felt I was the one demanding the distance. I decided not to say anything. The boys noticed we were not being invited into the girls' home anymore and when we visited the farm they were asked to stay together outside, away from the homes. This was not fun but necessary. No girl could say at any time that any one of my boys was with them in secret, or had said or touched them inappropriately. Church was the activity we shared.

To get to church the boys and I would walk the hour out to the girls' farm. Most days were cold, and many were rainy and windy too. There we would wait for a ride the rest of the way to church in Pam and Brett's big cars and truck. The church was another ten-minute ride into the hills, into the outback where people could grow up and live out their life rarely visiting a city. The road was good but the round log bridges we had to pass over crossing the riverbeds were scary. Even though we drove out every week, I felt a little unsure on each trip.

~Our roads are not always well maintained; accidents and deaths do happen. Recognize this additional risk that you will be exposed to.~

The one-room tiny wood church was adorable. It sat on a hilltop overlooking miles of tall pine forests almost void of human contact. It was made of adobe mixed with straw and built with two-by-four board beams and wooden benches sitting on a dirt floor. There was one hanging bald electric bulb fueled by a gas generator that allowed the preaching to continue into the night. The pastor was named none other than Jesús. He was a country man who loved Jesus so much he had to preach. His teachings were based on his daily Bible investigations and the answers he found to his questions. It was a perfect church for my boys. He had a great heart and told many stories that brought us all to adore him. His wife and two daughters were sweet as apple pie.

Pastor Jesús asked to be hired to work on our strawberry and potato farm. Carol agreed and hired him before leaving for the US with Peter. Pastor Jesús would walk two hours in the morning to our farm, work all day, and then walk the two hours home at night. I think he got paid about five dollars a day, a little above the going rate. He enjoyed being available for my boys. We were so blessed by his presence. The boys had to help in the fields for one hour every day after school—this gave them time alone with Pastor Jesús.

Pastor Jesús loved to tell his stories and listen to theirs while working. He told them of many great adventures full of moral consequences and learning. He was completing our family by being the male spiritual role model. These moments bonded the boys with their pastor and he with them; they all loved this time together. Riki mentioned that he wanted to raise money to buy Pastor Jesús a bicycle so he would not have to walk so far to work. We began looking for ways to earn the money, Riki put himself into action. He got the boys to sell what we had lots of: strawberries. Little by little they finally raised the $110 to buy a sturdy, well-made bike for the pastor. Riki was elated buying and presenting the bike, a new one; our pastor deserved the best. Pastor Jesús was deeply touched and was able to get to work much more quickly.

~Helping someone get to work is a great blessing. Bikes are happily received.~

The teams that came to Pam and Brett's would always attend church, so we got to meet them. One group was a construction team made up of about ten really big guys. The youngest was the biggest, called Big Boy. When we sang in Spanish they politely listened and clapped with the music. Suddenly, we noticed they were singing with us. This was a song they too sang in their church, and they were joining us in English. Really loud male voices joined ours raising up a praise to the Lord that filled the church. English mixed with Spanish, our voices booming in praise together. It was a wonderful moment. We felt united as true brothers and sisters in Christ at that time; united by the soul. We would never forget them.

Once we were in church during an earthquake. The whole church was made of wood so as the ground began to tremble we looked to the pastor for guidance. He raised his hands to the sky and began to pray. Before I could say, "Should we go?" Nolan had leaped in one jump from the front of the church to the back door, maybe eighty feet. He was out in a flash. Everyone else paused. The church continued to shake, swaying back and forth. Finally the words squeaked out, "Should we go?" just when the quake quit. Fun, I like earthquakes.

Pastor Jesús was a spiritual pillar for us. The day his son was born was no exception.

"Today at 9:20 A.M. my son was born. Today at 11:05 A.M. he went to be with the Lord. I held my son in my arms for a short time, loving him with moments that must now last me a lifetime. But I know where my son is, and I know that he is greatly loved and cared for. So I asked myself, 'What blessing did I receive today from my heavenly Father?' And I thanked my Father God that I got to know my son for two hours."

We cherished our time in this church. The rides home from church were on the back of a flatbed pickup, these were the difficult minutes for me. We would head home around nine P.M. when it was really cold out. The wind whipped by us as we huddled together on the dusty wood slated truck bed trying to keep warm. But the sky was wondrous—so dark, so blue, filled with stars. The boys liked this test of courage in the freezing cold, gazing in silence at the amazing night vastness sprinkled with uncountable stars. We would discuss science and bible. If scientists are so smart ask them what surrounds the universe, or ask them to explain how the soul has come from nothing, exists, but when we die turns back into nothing, or ask them the odds of a car building itself if all the proper parts were floating around in space. Science is a field of study; the Bible is studied. What is agreed upon is that everything is cyclical, eternal, and amazingly organized for life.

~ Overseas one can have a unique opportunity to observe a side of God that can only be seen by living vulnerably in the world with its natural forces in daily life.~

Riding in the back of pickups is technically illegal but commonly permitted. Too many people would have no way of getting around if it was truly outlawed. Once in our little town, a pickup full of people taking off for the mountains jerked quickly throwing a lady of about thirty off the back panel. Hitting the ground headfirst, she got up quite dazed with blood running from her nose and was helped back in. The man next to me mentioned that she wouldn't live the night. Sonia's own sister died falling off the back of a pickup at age sixteen, leaving Sonia as the only surviving child. She hates seeing people crammed into the backs of pickups. I could tolerate it better if they didn't sit on the edges or stand. How would they protect themselves if the pickup braked quickly? Horrible accidents have claimed many innocent lives.

~You can travel like the folks here in the back of a pickup if you must, but sit far down and make sure your driver is sober.~

Nolan decided to get baptized when the pastor offered to sign people up. The whole church, about 20, met at a natural spring creek park. Pastor Jesús explained what being baptized meant, he then invited the three people to be baptized into the icy cold water. Nolan came up grinning. We took pictures and celebrated at home with a chocolate cake. The next day was Nolan's fifteenth birthday, so I allowed him to go by bus to La Paz by himself to spend his birthday money—five dollars. He took the bus and returned home on time, happy with his purchases. He forgot to mention about the pornographic magazines he stole but remembered to show them to all the boys. One day baptized, the next day stealing pornographic magazines. Nolan was one of a kind.

~If this truly is your God-given work, nothing will diminish your passion.~

Once a month I had to take the long bus ride into the capital to report on how the boys were doing. This meant I had to stay all night in the city and leave the boys alone.

Because Luis's dad, a pastor, was on our property, it seemed not too much could happen at the house, yet my worry was that the boys might sneak off and get into trouble or be blamed for things done by others. But it was required of me to report to the government, so I arranged for one boy to be the cook and assured them the pastor would be dropping in on and asking around town to see if they were behaving. Riki was the oldest at sixteen and Orlando the youngest at eleven, so things went quite well, according to them.

These trips were a lot of work. Usually I stayed all night at my cousin's house which was a great catch-up time for us as a family. Then I would leave early the next morning for the government office, give my report, do any needed shopping, and try to be at the bus stop by one p.m. This bus would drop me off at Tesigua, right in the middle of this nation, in time for the last bus at four heading out into our department. Arriving at La Paz by seven P.M., I would sit in a ten-by-ten foot wood shack restaurant by the bus stop until the night students got off school at ten P.M. It would take another twenty-five minutes to get to my stop.

Once there it was pure darkness and impossible to see anything, not even the dirt road. It was usually pitch dark because the clouds and rain were almost always present and no one had electricity out there. So I advanced by shuffling my feet in order to follow the gravel trail and peering deep into the darkness trying to see. By listening to the sounds of the creek I could find the location of the bridge and inch carefully across, then walk past a few more houses to our yard, with the creek gurgling at my left. Sometimes it was so muddy I arrived clomping in with completely hidden mud-caked shoes.

Finally, the boys went with me on one trip to visit their fathers at the new prison and stay with relatives in the capital. It was still necessary to pass the undies inspection, which turned out to be worse than the other prison. The women were filed into a room in groups of five. Together we had to reveal and squat a few times. The female guard absentmindedly speaking to no one in particular said, "The *gringa* is pretty." Quickly pulling up my panties, with my face turning beet red, I tried to pretend I didn't understand Spanish. Geez, comments too.

We took each father a pair of jeans and a shirt. Cruz's father was in the back part with the fifty-and-older men. Pablo was in one of the buildings up front that housed three hundred and fifty men. His boys, he, and I all sat outside at a table and talked. Pablo didn't mention the letter requesting matrimony and neither did I. We just politely sat and talked like parents about his sons. He then let us know that he was the one in charge of his building's prisoners. The prisoners always choose a leader for each building, as the guards don't enter into the prison except for riot control and surprise confiscations. He was in charge of everything: cooking times, bedtimes, cleanliness, loudness of music, shower safety, and TV time. This, of course, could be dangerous if you got someone mad at you. He had to work to keep everyone in balance doing what they should do and stay alive too. He also made himself responsible for taking people to the hospital, encouraging and reassuring them, helping them to call home and get legal counsel. He took care of his three hundred fifty. My good news was that

Nolan had just been baptized and Pablo surprised me by saying that he had too. He had decided it was time and took the offer to be baptized by the visiting preacher at the prison. I called the boys over to hear the good news. In the back of my mind I was thinking, *If he is lying, his sons will never forgive him.* Pablo requested Christian books and music for the small group that met with him in his cell. Before dark we left heading into the capital to visit family, eager to share the good news.

It seemed a great opportunity to have the boys visit the Children's Services workers in the main building with me in person—this was very fun. The ladies remembered them from their original placements and were happy to see how strong and healthy they looked and acted. They promised to visit us soon at our new home, even though it would be a long, hard trip for them. And within the month they did. Then they told me I could visit a new office in Aguasales each month, only three hours from us. No more long overnight monthly trips to the capital.

Lorenzo had been complaining about a toothache. I talked him into taking the bus with me to La Paz to visit a dentist we had met at the brigade. We were standing on the main road waiting for the bus with Riki, who was on his way to classes.

"I decided I won't go to the dentist."

"Lorenzo, you have to go.'

"No, I don't."

"Your tooth has been aching for days; you need to see a dentist."

"Well, I'm not getting on the bus. You can forget it."

Riki tried to talk him into it. "It'll just get worse. The dentist will help you."

"If it hurts now, I can just imagine someone poking around in there. I'm not going."

I butted in. "Lorenzo, she will make the pain stop. Just give her a try."

"If she hurts me I won't be responsible if I react like a man."

Riki and I chuckled. "Everyone goes to the dentist. It'll be all right."

~Many, many people here have never visited a dentist. Dentistry is a luxury.~

The bus pulled up and he reluctantly got on. At the dentist's office a small child was finishing his appointment when we arrived. The child began to cry loudly, both Riki and I laughed and glanced at Lorenzo. He almost got up and walked out but didn't. The dentist was very good with him.

Chapter 14
United by Spirit

My church in the US had written asking if our number two pastor, James, could visit. The church body was interested in helping out because of the enormous damage Brutis had left us with. Pastor James arrived full of energy and smiles. He enjoyed scouting out the little town, walking out to Pam and Brett's mission, and playing basketball in the town court.

"Hey, Kimi, your boys tried to beat me in basketball."

"Did they make it?"

"They're good."

"That's a nice way for our town to meet my pastor."

"Yeah, especially since I took my shirt off. I don't think they've seen that much hair on a person before."

Not only did I imagine he was right, but that no one would believe he was my pastor.

"Hey, you know the guy that played basketball with the hair all over? He's my pastor."

"Funny."

Once alone I told him about Pablo and our growing relationship. He mentioned a friend who was a powerful Christian witness after serving his time in jail.

"He has conquered his past and is a mighty man of God."

"How do you know he won't fall again?" my questioned loomed.

"He is so strong in the Lord that I'm sure he won't. What do you think about Pablo?"

I was not sure about Pablo, but it was evident he had great things to offer Jesus. Plus, he was committing himself and we were bound by my special relationship with his sons. I was talking myself into a romance.

That night we gathered around to pray with Pastor James. He had come for a purpose.

“Well, boys, I’ve come here because our church wants to help the Brutis victims who are homeless.”

Riki raised his hand.

“Yes Riki.”

“We’re homeless.”

Pastor James gulped. “Yes, we are thinking about helping you too. Let’s pray.”

~People who are poor are not ignorant of it. They know life can be different although it probably won’t change for them. They try to accept and enjoy life as it is while hoping for change.~

We were sad to see Pastor James leave, but he left us with some cassettes of the church services, some even had him leading worship and singing with his great booming voice, now a voice we could call our own. And Pastor James was true to his word. He returned home and told people about Kimi and the boys. My church congregation had a membership of eight thousand at the time, so this was a tremendous blessing. Finally, my home church was united with us, even though almost no one there knew who I was. But the Lord took us to heart and decided to bless us with this relationship. The Holy Spirit was truly in control.

Riki was becoming a prayer warrior. Our nightly prayer times would end with his prayers. When each boy had finished, Riki would take a deep breath in anticipation. The other boys would position themselves to get comfortable since it would be long. Then, Riki would begin his prayers, his monotonous voice gently filling in the silence for twenty to maybe thirty minutes every night. He began asking me biblical questions most every day, exploring his new venue of thoughts. I decided to gift him my bilingual Bible, one of my few treasures. He was independently seeking the Lord; this was the gift for my sacrifice. But teens are a mixed bag; our job as parents is to walk through the good and bad times with them.

Riki decided to walk every day to school so he could spend his bus fare on “stuff.” His school was a two-hour walk away, and since he had chosen afternoon high school, his walk home was in the dark. This decision did not please me, but he was old enough to decide for himself. As the months went by, little by little he started to get thinner and thinner, his already-slim inherited build looking gaunt. It seemed he really wasn’t eating with us, always claiming he had already eaten, wasn’t hungry, or would eat later.

Worry set in so I finally confronted Riki. He denied everything and insisted he was eating just fine. Watching him, my new ploy was to make comments at the moment, publically exposing his pattern. He continued to deny there was a problem and still was not eating at home. Having been educated in the US to the truths about bulimia and anorexia, his problem looked to be urgent. Catching moments with him, I identified the diseases, what they did, why they appeared, and how to cure them. He still resisted, denying any problem. After four weeks of this, I finally caught him alone and confronted him with all my influence.

“Riki, you don’t seem to be eating much.”

“I eat enough.”

“You’re looking too thin.”

“I still can lose some weight.”

“No, really you can’t. Why aren’t you eating?”

"I am eating. I'm just not too hungry."

"But you are walking miles every day. You need to eat a little more."

"I will."

"But you don't."

"You just don't see me."

"Well, if you lose any more weight, I'll have to insist you take the bus."

"Don't tell me what I can do."

"Riki, it is important for your body to eat well while you're growing."

"Who needs you? I can take care of myself."

A stronger strategy was needed to win. I spoke in a whisper, "If you stress your body out too much, the sex thing won't get up when it's supposed to. You can really hurt yourself. Check into this; you'll find out it's true."

Done. Riki started eating normally and decided walking home at night in the dark was too dangerous so began taking the bus. I was still curious as to exactly what he had been eating, if anything, all these weeks.

~ Mental illnesses are not commonly addressed in this country and are at best under diagnosed and/or undertreated.~

Because Riki went to the next town for high school every afternoon, it was easy for him to pick up things for me at the market. Agreeing to buy six pounds of beans, he would take the money, and bring home what looked like five pounds of beans—it was hard to tell. To verify the truth I took the bus one day to buy six pounds of beans for myself. Knowing the prices more or less, it did look like Riki was not giving me enough for my buck but with no concrete proof it was difficult to confront him. After a couple hours spent shopping, I was early for the bus home and went into a nearby *pulperia* store to wait. The lady greeted me.

"Good day."

"Hi."

"Are you Riki's mother?"

"Yes, I am." I was surprised, since I didn't know the lady. "How do you know Riki?"

"He comes in every day to buy 2 cup cakes."

Viola. His habit had caught up with him.

Now I knew that he had been eating *something*. His addiction to home baked cup cake's hasn't ever ended as far as I know.

Later that week we discovered someone had stolen many things from the locked shed. There were no signs of breaking and entering, so we were without words. How did they get in? Costly items had been stolen. It would my responsibility to pay the value of the items stolen unless I could find out who got in and make them pay. Looking out over the farm and town it seemed like a very safe place to live to me, but one never knows when a friend may decide to rob you and sell some of your things. Especially because it appeared to some that we get "free" money by way of donations, so this makes a few people feel as if we have too much. It could be difficult to find out who had been in our shed or the guilty one might be standing very close to me.

~You are not as vulnerable to the difficulties in life as others, and they recognize this. They know there's always another dollar with your name on it.~

Things continued to go downhill with Riki. He fell in love with a twenty-three-year-old that was constantly flirting with him. He was sixteen. She worked in La Paz, far away from my watchful eye and community gossip, but she made sure she got to speak to Riki everyday. I still wonder why she was after a sixteen year old. But, in the end, at home gossip got the best of their passion.

Riki's high school planned to go on a field trip to the country's historical Indian ruins. These magnificent ruins are located in the far north of our country. They are well known worldwide and are full of hot archeological findings even today. Every national should visit this important historical cultural center, but many never have. Riki was getting his chance. After agreeing to pay for the trip something happened that made me back down.

The boys told me Riki had said he was not really going to go to the ruins. He was going to leave the group and go to a hotel with the girl for two days. True or not, I couldn't let him go. There was no real way of knowing if he really would be with his high school or not, and I couldn't risk having him stay with a "woman" in a hotel for two days, all paid by me. Even if he was lying just to impress them the boys and I would never fully believe that he had stayed with his class; the harm had been done. The trip was canceled. He was furious and refused my authority in the decision. I offered to go with him to prison to talk to his dad about it but he refused. When Pastor Jesus came to visit, Riki spewed out anger and insults toward me without taking a breath for what seemed at least five minutes.

When he paused, I looked at the pastor and said, "He can't stay here." And the pastor agreed. Riki left for his aunt's house the next day. Once he was gone the boys admitted that Riki had been the one who had broken into the shed. He had taken the screws out of the roof shingles and lowered himself down into the locked shed. Then he lifted up the items to be sold to the other boys waiting on the roof as the shed door was bolted. When he had stolen as much as was wise he swung himself up onto the roof, and screwed the shingle panels on again. He had a future. I just wasn't sure where that would be. Maybe he could to pay me back for the loss once he became employed, wishful thinking.

My next two-day visit to the capital was to report to the government combined with a visit to the fathers in prison. Cruz's father was sick that day so I left money to help him buy some medicine. Pablo seemed to agree with my decision to have Riki move back to aunt's house. The boys and I had picked out some Christian books and music to leave Pablo; he was elated. Since becoming a Christian he had left the protection of the drug group, so he was much more vulnerable than before. In this prison there was one killing a day or around 365 a year inside the gates. The druggies held great power over many of the other groups. Leaving the druggy group was a precarious step—to me it represented his commitment to a new life.

Because Pablo was in charge of his building, he could not leave to go live in the safer Christian block. In his sheeted-off bed area of six bunks stacked three high, four of the men had been killed within the last nine weeks. I had just met the fourth man killed my last trip there. A few days earlier he had gotten someone mad at him by mouthing off during a card game and knew he might be killed at any moment. This man talked quickly about his faith and his previous life in the church, he had been a pastor at one time. The next day he was mobbed and knifed to death on the stairwell. Pablo was shaken after his murder, as he was after each murder. This time I was too.

Because the danger seemed to be closing in some Christians offered to move into the empty beds to surround Pablo. They had Bible study, played spiritual music, and protected one another. Pablo's life was more at risk because of his decision to leave drugs and the protection of the drug gangs, but he was not alone, now he was one of the Christians. Every visit was stressful for us as we never knew if the fathers would be alive when we got there. The shrill siren of the ambulance while arriving or leaving gave us all a chill. We just never knew who would be next.

In our short time together Pablo told me about a vision he had had. His vision was of a model home for boys, for about forty boys. The same number as the judge had given me. The home was located in the country, and he imagined himself helping boys stay away from drugs by giving and living out his testimony as the father figure. Because of his time in prison the boys would probably take his authority seriously. He would be more respected and feared because of his survival over his past. I took his vision to heart, God was uniting us.

Arriving home late in the night exhausted from the two-day trip, I found the boys had had a party. Daron had been in charge of cooking, and decided they could all eat whatever they wanted—after all, what could Kimi do about it, right? There was no food to be found: cake mixes, meat, Jell-O packets, sandwich bread, sugar, cereal, cookies, milk, and chocolate were all gone. I was furious. Their punishment would be to cook and eat outside in the shed for one week, only rice, beans, and tortillas. No negotiations. Their first breakfast outside they decided to eat strawberries, as they were unorganized to prepare anything else. Later in the day, they built a fire in the outside stove and cooked lunch and dinner, huddling around to keep warm. I ate alone inside the big house, content. Little by little, the food was restocked packing it all home on my back. They complained a bit but I did not give in. One week of just rice, beans, and tortillas was more than they could stand. They never pulled that trick again.

My daily jaunt into town, about twenty minutes, was enjoyable. Because it was so beautiful in the mountainous forests, the ¾ mile walks began stretching out to the other end of town. Turning around, and walking back they became forty minutes long. Passing all the small homes functioning without electricity and with the occasional water supply reminded me of the hard reality of country life. Radios blared the news in rapid fire Spanish, children screamed while bathing in the freezing water and outside air, women chopped the firewood to stoke the outdoor stove topped only by a flat iron plate while smoke pushed up from the chimney stacks. Each worn down shack was outlined by picture perfect sprawling country flowers, large leafed overgrown bushes, fruit trees (usually banana or plantain) enveloped by steep hillsides of endless evergreen trees. Picturesque views took my breath away, every corner pleased my senses. The countryside was beautiful. Each swing in the road displayed a view so quaint that my heart would leap thinking maybe it was there we would build our “forever” home—each and every curve.

But country reality also took control. Roads were dusty, rocky, or sometimes filled with puddles that stretched from one side clear to the other, taking up the whole road. After a lot of rain, the roads became incredibly muddy. Sometimes after the ox carts passed, the mud was so thick it caked onto your shoes like bricks. In these moments my desire to have a car seemed unwise, best get an ox.

For much of these walks I would pray, taking advantage of the time to be personal and a listener to Father God. I also regularly whined about the cold to anyone who would listen. Once home it would be time to prepare lunch and then return later to town to get items from the *pulperia* for dinner- all this walking and not one pound lost. Indignant about my lack of weight loss after four faithful months I e-mailed my doctor in the US. Forgetting that I was still overseas, he told me to cut out the fast food restaurants! Once corrected, he told me ladies at this age found that the weight didn't like to come off. Looking on the positive side, he wrote, just imagine what you would've weighed if you hadn't been walking and eating healthier. I tried to rejoice but it didn't work.

~Simple country life includes fresh air, a need to walk, and healthy eating. It is just what the doctor ordered.~

Pam and Brett shared a great blessing with us. The soldiers from the US had sent dried food lunch packets that were expired to be given to needy people. They were selected and shared with us. Since we got home so late on Sunday evenings, we began eating our lunch bags for dinner. There were about five different packs. Each one contained a meat dish, a vegetable dish, fruit, and a desert. The boys were thrilled. We would quickly heat up the meat packets in hot water on the gas stove. The menu was steak in sauce, chili and beans, macaroni and cheese, spaghetti, and chicken in sauce. The fruits were made with sweet sauces or mixed. The deserts were cookies, and chocolate or granola bars. It made you want to become a soldier. During this time, one of our month's donation deposits did not come in, and so these dinners were necessary for us.

~Many thanks to the military donors.~

School gave my boys the time they needed for socializing. Orlando had a light skinned girlfriend and Deni had a dark skinned girlfriend. Orlando always spied good-quality girls, but he rarely acted on it; he just admired them from a distance. No girlfriends were accepted at home, so these school romances were just right for their ages. A few months later I was told at the *pulperia* that a little primary girl, one of our own, had died the day before of a heart attack on the way to the hospital in the capital. They told us this was brought on by the bite of a *chicharra*, which is an insect whose bite can be deadly years later causing the heart to fail. It was sad that it affects country people who live in shacks because the bugs can enter at night to bite. This threat does scare children as well as adults as they settle down to sleep.

Talking this over with the boys, I realized the little girl and her mother had been with me on the bus the day before heading for the hospital. Orlando listened and then followed me around all afternoon and stayed by my side until bedtime. That night he asked if he could sleep with me. I thought about it awhile and said OK. He was just ten years old and I wanted to fill that gap and be his real mom and him to be my real son. He slept on top of my covers, bringing in his own. The next night he asked me again. This time I said no explaining that people in town might not think that it looked right. His almond shaped eyes opened wide, his eyebrows rose in surprise and he paused, thinking about my words, then never asked to sleep with me again.

Years later I was to learn that the girl in town who had died of a heart attack because of the bug bite was Orlando's girlfriend admired from a distance. I fumed inside, no one had told me. My boys had denied me that chance to be there for him, the chance for Orlando to really receive a mother's love and protection in a time when he needed it most, during deep loss. Praise the Holy Spirit I had accepted his request to sleep with me that one night. Through the years, Orlando has held on to the belief that his loved ones die or leave him, and he feels more vulnerable than the average person to loss.

Our life was becoming settled, the daily routine directing most hours, but what we didn't know was that a miracle was about to happen. I got word through e-mail that my church in the US had asked for a donation to build us a "forever" home. We were touched, and I was humbled. My church was so big that there were hundreds of people with great ideas clamoring for a chance to begin their ministries and countless ministries struggling to grow. It was difficult to get even three minutes on the podium to talk about a new ministry. Pastor James asked for and was given permission to seek donations for "Kimi and the boys" one Saturday service and all the Sunday services. That was the first part of the miracle.

The hearts of the congregation responded and a record collection was taken. They had enough money donated to build a house big enough for us all—the second part of the miracle had happened. Yipee! My boys would have their "forever" home. It would take a few months to get the money deposited with the sister church in the capital and then cleared with the bank. Jesus had blessed us greatly with a true miracle. We were united in Spirit with the will of God with my church in the US.

~Use an already legalized US recognized ministry to accept your donations. Any donations sent in your personal name are counted as US income and are not tax deductible.~

Soon we would move back to the tropical part of paradise; it was just too cold for me in Maranila. To get started a new location had to be found.

Dreams of the beach appeared, yes! We could build our home on one of the tropical beaches in the north. Our home could be surrounded by cute little cabañas sitting right on the oceanfront for our guests. They could wake up to a fresh ocean breeze, coffee made by the maid, and swim at any hour. Every week we'd have someone new flying in to volunteer with us. Then my thoughts turned around. It could be so great that our guests might never leave. Young bikini-clad volunteers would titillate the boys to excess while innocently detailing their Christian beliefs. Secret drug-smuggling stories and 365 days a year with happy hour right around the corner would entice the boys in the wrong direction. Then a friend told me to watch out for the sand crabs. The opportunity to live on a tropical beach for the rest of my days was given up for my boys. God would surely reward me later.

Pam and Brett thoroughly loved their icy, tropical, isolated country location in Maranila, but just out of curiosity I asked Brett where he might have chosen to live, now in hindsight. He mentioned that a town called Tesigua was a treasure, located in the center of the country, with a fresh climate, pine-treed mountains, and claimed as the sixth largest city in our nation. Tesigua had many public and private vocational high schools and bilingual schools, which grabbed my attention. My boys would need choices in higher education. This was one gift our home could give them. Daron, Orlando, and I took the two-hour bus ride headed for Tesigua the next day we had free to scout around.

My great plan for house hunting was to get off the bus in the middle of town and ask around for the same denominational church as I had in the US, hoping to maybe get a little help from the church family here. Finding the church was not easy. It had closed and moved months earlier. Asking some neighbors where the church had moved to one kind man travelling on his bike said he would show us. He walked alongside me holding on to his bike as we meandered fourteen blocks, crossing the whole town. He took me to a partially finished unpainted building just big enough to be considered a church where he thought there had been an evangelical church sign.

We were warmly greeted by the family living in a shack home located right smack on the front steps of the building. He had been right; this was the church. The little elderly lady gave me the number of the pastor, who agreed to meet us that same hour. Pastor Ginmer was in the process of finishing the building to live in with his family and had plans to build a bigger church next door. At that time only the kitchen, one bedroom, and the bathroom had concrete floors. The rest of the house had well-swept dirt flooring. But the house had a roof, windows, doors, electricity, and water. None of the rooms were painted, and there was no inside ceiling in the house. He offered to rent us his home for free until we had our own. Because it had always been difficult to find a home big enough and cheap enough for us, we were thrilled. He was a real blessing.

~Overseas homes are smaller than the average US homes and usually contain more family members. Personal space is sacrificed but the price is right.~

Chapter 15
The Chosen Life

We returned to Maranila and announced our plans to move within the month. But Daron had other plans. A few days later he mentioned that we were out of sugar and offered to walk to the *pulperia* store for me. With enough money to pick up a few other things he slipped out back, grabbed a suitcase full of his belongings and snuck out to the bus. Daron had decided to venture out on his own. I was saddened by his choice but knew Daron would have to decide for himself which way his life was to go.

We all began packing and were on the move again. Brett and the boys loaded up the flatbed truck and we were on our way. The boys would be changing schools, but hopefully this would be our permanent city and maybe their last school change. We arrived at dusk and unloaded our things quickly into the house. I got the room with a floor, while the boys shared two very large rooms with dirt floors. They were happy with their large rooms and private space. As the truck drove off, we all stood in the street and waved good-bye to Brett. We were alone and home again.

School was still in session, so the boys had to quickly be registered into their new schools. Walking to the nearest primary school four of the boys got enrolled. Orlando was in sixth grade while Deni and Lorenzo were put together in the same fifth-grade class. Nolan was put into night school for older students who still wanted to pass primary grades. He was in heaven; he had nothing to do all day. Classes started at six P.M. and ended at eight. It was a teenager's dream. In the country there was farm work to be done, but here in the city we had TV, buses, neighbors, and no work. I had to find something for him to do during the day; he couldn't just sit around and watch TV. There was no choice, Nolan helped me with chores—"women's work"—and did it grudgingly.

Because Cruz had graduated from sixth grade, he got to choose his "high school"—seventh through ninth grades. He chose to be enrolled in a private high school where he could graduate in electricity. It was expensive—thirty-five dollars a month—but he would leave with a license to practice.

Life was calm in the city; it was easier for me to get around and shop. The boys enjoyed all that a town of eighty thousand could bring. There was a movie theater with tickets costing a dollar fifty, a park near the house where soccer games were held and gang youths hung out, lots of neighborhood *pulperia* stores, frequently passing city buses for twenty cents, taxis for eighty cents, lots of people, and best of all—cable TV. They spent hours watching cable TV, which was permitted because it kept them inside. But before long they perfected the art of getting lost while visiting the *pulperia* store around the corner sometimes returning hours later. And it was impossible to find them; they could be anywhere, so the rules became stricter, a logical time limit for going to the *pulperia* was set. If they wanted to visit friends or watch a soccer game, they just had to let me know exactly where they would be. Spot checks had to be made just to let them know it was serious.

~Male children have historically been permitted to discover their community, hang out, not report their whereabouts, and stay out all night, imitating accepted male adult life, as opposed to the girls who are not permitted to do any of that and are responsible for a lot of work at home.~

We got the sudden news that Pablo would be set free from prison without ever having been formally accused by a court. They reasoned that even if he had been guilty, he would have already completed the sentence, so he was free to go. The boys were all in school at his dismissal time, so I went to the prison alone to get him. Passing through the large black metal gates into the front courtyard where the guards were I felt very anxious and nervous. Pablo was there with six other prisoners lined up, with a guard facing them. He had two very large packs full of his only possessions. It was customary for a leaving prisoner to gift all that he could to those staying, and Pablo had done that, the least he could do for those left behind. The guard in charge of pronouncing the lineup men free came up to me.

"We are sad to see Pablo go. He has been a great support for the prisoners."

"Thank you for saying that."

"We wish you the best on the outside, Pablo. You deserve a good life."

"*Gracias, mi capitán.*"

He was handed his walking papers, we picked up his bags and left for the buses. I felt as odd as he must have felt. Pablo had not been outside prison for almost four years, and things had changed. Pablo felt unsure and extremely excited. He had made it out alive, but the life he knew had vanished, and he was starting over from scratch. The bus ride was two hours long. We talked, looked out the window at the changes in the countryside, and talked some more. We talked about the past, we talked about the future, and we talked about everything that had happened on the outside during his four years in jail. We were free and together.

Before the bus had reached the center of our new town, he asked me to marry him again, and this time I agreed. Four weeks would give us enough time to get the wedding ready. I was in shock. So much was happening at once, but all felt positive. God had brought me here for a purpose. He was gifting me a family, complete with husband, children and a ministry that would include us all. We approached the high school, which was having a concert, so the streets were full of people. Pablo was overwhelmed as everything seemed new. I had arranged to rent a bed in a neighborhood grandma's house for about $9 a month in advance. We took a taxi for eighty cents and let Pablo stay in the house with the boys.

Soon after arriving we announced our wedding plans, and the boys just smiled. They knew that was coming, how I'll never know. Pablo was home and with his family. His sons, Deni, Lorenzo, and Nolan, were ecstatic. Orlando and Cruz were a little unsure but hoping for the best. I was sure this was God's will for our family. Riki's aunt called and said he wanted to return and be given another chance. We decided he could return to be with his dad, his brothers, and me.

A few days later the government pulled up with three brothers: Ronaldo (four), Gabriel (five), and their big brother Danilo (thirteen). We only accepted boys above the age of nine, so we were a little taken aback, but they were just the cutest little guys. Ronaldo was almost the same height as Gabriel, and they looked like twins. Danilo had a very serious, hard look to him. He was not happy. They came with nothing, no clothes—nothing. Their dad had a problem with alcohol and drug abuse. He had made it unsafe for their mom to stay, so she left after a beating, taking the bigger three of her seven sons with her. Days later a younger son was visiting his grandparents when she showed up, so he went with her too, leaving Danilo to be responsible for his youngest brothers. After a year of neglect and emotional abuse, the neighbors finally called the government to get Danilo and his two little brothers. The Family Services brought them to us because no other families would take a boy Danilo's age. We looked around for extra clothes and put the two little guys in the same bed. They probably slept better that way anyway. We now had nine boys.

The next day we went to the country market to buy shirts, pants, shoes, socks, underwear, belts, and school uniforms. It was fun shopping for new clothes for the boys. The little guys felt spiffy, but Danilo was embarrassed and mad at being in this situation. Mad continued to be his most comfortable feeling for many years. The trip cost us over a hundred twenty dollars; the shoes alone were twenty dollars each. We really didn't have the money for this, but a retired lady from my church sent twenty-five dollars and a couple with a young son in North Dakota sent fifty, so we were able to get by and still eat. And boy, did they look nice in their new clothes.

The home rules had to be adjusted. Each boy had been responsible for washing his own eating utensils, bedding, and clothes. Now we had two little short guys who could barely reach the sinks. We found wooden blocks for them to stand on so they too could wash. When they were done I rewashed their things. It worked well because most of the fun for them was playing in the water. The only difficulty was they later told everyone life with Kimi was hard. "We've been working since we were five years old."

~Young children do manual work here. Little boys use machetes and little girls wash heavy loads of clothes, chop wood, and cook over an open fire.~

Pablo and I filed with a legal assistant for our marriage certificate. We had to present birth documents, nationality papers, an AIDS test, proof of divorce (me) and legal ID. Pablo had to return to his birthplace and request a new birth certificate with an additional note stating that he had never been married and was not now married. We planned the great trip across the country to meet his family and see where he grew up. I figured this document was worth the cost. We left the boys for one night in the care of our neighbors, whose house was smack against the front porch.

~Always let someone know where you are going to be travelling and when you will be back. Unexpected difficulties happen frequently.~

Both Pablo's parents had died, so the family was made up of his two sisters lived in the capital and three younger sisters and a younger brother who still lived in the countryside. We took the bus to the capital and then caught another bus heading south from the open-air market. The whole trip took about six hours and ended at the closest major town to his family, Valle Seco. Before the bus had even parked, Pablo looked out the window and saw one of his sisters. She was walking among the crowd with her son buying groceries. It's a strange thing about families—Pablo recognized her walking in a crowd of people in the wrong town, seeing her only from the back. Incredible. We caught up with them, which was a blessing for us.

Sara took us to the right minivan bus and we all got off at "the big rock." Then we walked through the wilderness, followed a dried creek bed, passed Pablo's one-room schoolhouse, hiked up a mountain, and over into a valley. It was around ninety-five degrees—cool for this part of the south. After we had walked two and a half hours, I was red-faced, sweating, and exhausted.

Carrying all her purchases on her head, Sara had to slow down for me.

The valley was beautiful. There the family had five small adobe homes, cows, and no neighbors for as far as the eye could see. The other family members came out to greet us. His sisters had grown up and lived there on the mountain all their lives. They hauled water up a steep hill by bucket for all their needs. A bit away from the houses was a small running creek where Pablo had bathed when young before heading off for school. There was no electricity. There were no roads; a car or truck could not enter. Together in this small family group they worked, raised their children, and took care of one another. Pablo's elderly aunt lived in the last house; she was so old she told me she would never leave the valley. It was too hard a trip for her now; she would die there.

Sara made us a great dinner of shrimp, rice, and tortillas—a meal fit for royalty. While eating my shrimp dinner, a small chicken quickly crossed my plate but I didn't let it bother me. We talked into the night with candlelight flickering off the ceiling. Outside you could see trillions of stars twinkling over the silent valley. My bed was made of a boxed frame with cord crisscrossed in a woven pattern to provide a netlike mattress. It was covered with a thin sheet. Pablo slept in the hammock. The rest of the family slept near us, doubled up for the night to accommodate two extra sleepers.

Homegrown coffee heated up over a morning fire is the best ever. Pablo was eager to eat the native chicken eggs, much better he says than the big white eggs we buy in the market. Tortillas were hot off the fire. Breakfast in the campo is wonderful. It was an honor to meet Pablo's family before the wedding. He had not visited them there for over fifteen years, and they were thrilled to see us.

We took off the next day for their little town to get the birth certificate with the inscription stating that Pablo was truly single. This trip would be shorter than yesterday's, as we would be crossing "the big river". At the edge of the river, we met up with a neighbor who was waiting to cross. Everyone took off or changed some of their clothing—draping them over their shoulders to remain dry while crossing. The river crossing was wide and higher than waist deep. In order to be safer we all linked hands, making a human chain, and crossed together. As we were venturing forward, deep in middle of the roaring river, the conversation changed to swimming.

The man on my right said, "Never learned to swim."

Pablo's sister said, "Can't swim."

Pablo said, "Me neither."

No response came from me. I could swim, so obviously it would be me risking my life to save whoever had trouble crossing the river—and it could be all three of them. Wonderful.

I prayed for our safety and proceeded with each step a little more carefully.

We were almost all the way across when we saw a young nineteen-year-old man nearing the water to cross in his small underwear while holding his clothes up high over his head.

"Hi, Jacobo."

"Hi there, sis-in-law."

"Kimi, this is Sara's brother-in-law."

"Nice to meet you." I smiled, trying not to focus on the wrong parts.

"Pablo, brother-in-law, where have you been hiding yourself?"

The family reunion was a happy one. Jacobo crossed the river alone and waved to us from the other side. That was the last time we would see Jacobo. Four years later we heard that he had drowned crossing the river at night. Nature still reigns in the countryside. Sadly we lost a good young man.

~Take great caution in the wild. Nature is a powerful force that we're not used to.~

We reached the far shore and then changed our wet clothes for our "town" clothes and continued on the trail. The town was quiet, dusty, and run-down, a little like a ghost town. The south seems to be getting drier every year; the cornstalks stand tall but dried yellow. The heat melts across the countryside. Droughts have made this part of the country desperate. Because of the extreme heat and continuous lack of rainfall, all the youth have gotten out of the south as soon as they could. Mostly the elderly remain, caring for their empty homes and watering their thirsty farms alone.

The older folks came to greet Pablo, asking him why it took him so long to return for a visit. We even saw Pablo's first-grade teacher, who had taught him in the one-room schoolhouse. Pablo remembered this teacher by his white hair. Now Pablo had white hair too, even though he was only thirty-six. We got his birth certificate with the marriage-available note in a one-desk, one-room, one-man office and caught the minivan out of town, stopping to meet his brother and sister-in-law, who lived by "the big orange tree."

Raul and Lana greeted us along with their baby daughter, Wendi. Their tiny, almost one-room house was surrounded by many chickens, pigs, and cows. Raul had inherited the farm animals after their father's death and decided to stay in the south. His animals did well at multiplying—he had animals everywhere. The problem now in the south was that there was little corn to feed them. Before dark we caught the last minivan out to the highway, where we waited alongside the road for the last big bus heading toward the capital. It was an honor and pleasure to visit them all. We prayed for rain.

The next morning we showed up at the courthouse in Tesigua to file for our legal marriage. The actual marriage paper filing didn't cost much. What was to cost me was the eye contact going on between Pablo and the married legal aide. I tried to convince myself that this couldn't be happening while we were filling out our marriage certificate. Ignoring the strong feelings, I buried my doubts concentrating on the thrill that my future with Pablo would bring. We were registered to be married in five weeks. Jesus was restoring what Satan had taken from me.

In order to attend a sister church to mine in the US, we took the bus forty-five minutes down the hill to the next large town on Sundays. The church was very small but the pastors were wonderful. The whole congregation consisted of the pastoral family, one man with his four very young children, two women and their children, us and our boys, and a single twenty-one-year-old girl who was best friends with the pastor's daughter. Neighborhood children filled up the rest of the church, and we all felt blessed to be serving them. I began to notice that the twenty-one-year-old was always eyeing Pablo. If we sat away from her, she would get up and move closer to him. Also during church she would stand backed up against the wall to listen to the preaching instead of sitting. She would look back and give a smile toward Pablo each time the pastor said something cute or surprising.

The boys started noticing her behavior too and began making quiet jokes. Evidently, I was invisible to this girl. My reaction was to stare at her while she grinned from ear to ear at my husband-to-be, but she never seemed to notice. I too changed seats, putting myself between her and Pablo every time she sat close to him. My heart was breaking. It seemed best not say anything to Pablo or I would seem horribly petty, and in church nonetheless. Nor could it be mentioned to the pastors, as she was their daughter's best friend. My suffering was in silence.

Then it ended. One Sunday the pastor's daughter asked everyone in the church to give a Christian kiss to another. Wonder who requested that great idea? The twenty-one-year-old came right down the aisle and kissed my husband-to-be on the cheek. I couldn't stand it anymore. As much as I loved the pastors it was time to look for a new church. We changed churches that week claiming the bus fare and long ride were the problem.

Our new church was in the center of our own town but a forty-five-minute walk from the house. It was a good church, full of really young people. We felt comfortable there. Sunday evenings we made and ate dinner early to get to church on time. The walk home was usually nice but we arrived home around ten P.M. A little late for Gabriel and Ronaldo, yet they never complained, they just walked and walked and walked. After all, they were not attending school yet, but that soon changed.

Danilo entered night school with Nolan because he had only finished up to second grade. Gabriel got the privilege of going to kindergarten. He was happy. Ronaldo got to go for just two hours a day to pre-kinder.

One day Ronaldo left for school and Gabriel came to me crying in great heaves. He showed me the identical two left school shoes he had. We looked all over for the other shoe, and then finally walked to school. I called for Ronaldo and sure enough he came walking quite sprightly with two right shoes.

Gabriel loved to eat and was the chubbier of the two. He was watching TV when one of the older boys walked in and changed the channel. That was it he decided, the last straw.

"I'm outta here."

He picked up a pillowcase, filled it full of his clothes and went walking out the door.

The whole family followed him to the street, some of the boys snickering in the background. Probably the ones that had turned the TV off.

"Gabriel, why are you leaving?" we asked.

He didn't turn around to answer.

"Gabriel, where are you going?"

He didn't flinch. Down the road he marched, all two feet of him, alone.

"Come back! You can't go by yourself!" we implored.

He sauntered slowly, nearing the main road, continuing to ignore our pleadings. We felt he might run if one of us started running behind him, so Danilo decided he'd try to stop him.

"Gabriel, where are you going?" He ran up from behind.

"To live in the hills."

"Better come back."

"Why?"

"What are you going to eat?"

"There's lots to eat there. Grass."

"Well, Kimi has cooked American tacos for dinner. Why don't you come back just for dinner and you can leave tomorrow?"

Gabriel paused.

"OK."

The joy was that we finally had cable. The problem was there were many shows we didn't want the boys watching, especially the X-rated ones. It was tough tracking the shows, but I was a hound. Our home was set up to help these boys become good godly men. No shows about drugs, sex, or violence would be permitted. But even the commercials got to me sometimes. I remember walking into the room and seeing a large, naked, female butt revolving slowly, showing off the results of liposuction—stimulating—I imagine. My reaction was to stand between the boys and the TV when things appeared that embarrassed me.

Don Francisco has a very popular family show called *Sabado Gigante*—Gigantic Saturday. The last time I watched it was when they had the competition of the fanny. Yep, women dressed in thong bathing suits moved to the music, strutting their butts sexually for the close-up camera shots so we could pick a winner. It has been over ten years now and somehow we are always busy Saturday evenings so we don't have to watch an old man promoting unhealthy sex during the family hour. That was not the first time Don Francisco had shown vulgar things on his show, but that was the last time I would sit in my living room surrounded by teenage boys and feel embarrassed by what was being shown on *Sabado Gigante*. The boys still say, "Kimi hates Don Francisco," which is not true. I hate his show.

~TV in your new country may be more vulgar, sexual, violent, and even gorier than you may be used to. Other nations may see TV in the US as more vulgar, sexual or violent.~

Our days were busy, trying to manage eight boys on $425 a month. In a ministry where you receive children, the children always come before the increase in donations, if the donations ever increase. The start-up costs for receiving one boy are great, as the child usually comes with only the clothes on his back. Each time a boy came, we just had to find a way to stretch the money, one person extra, no pesos more. My limit was one pound of meat mixed with vegetables for us all, even when we numbered twenty. When buying hotdogs, we cut them in half and then sliced them down the middle, they looked bigger that way. A can of tuna would make many sandwiches if you just spread a little on the bread as if it were mayonnaise. Eggs, cheese, and avocado helped give us variety. We drank Kool-Aid, still the cheapest choice, and ate a lot of rice, beans, and tortillas to fill us up. Of course, walking instead of driving a car saved us loads of money, and kept me in good shape.

~Buying a car is easy; selling a car is difficult. Car repairs can be expensive and time consuming. Gas costs more than in the US.~

We got a surprise visit from Tim, the husband of the couple who had been sending us three hundred dollars a month so faithfully. He had decided to visit with a friend, Don, and meet the boys. We were thrilled to show them all that had been done with his family's Holy Spirit blessings. He later admitted that he had come with an ulterior motive—to check out Pablo. Tim needed to know if he was truly a worthy guy who would support the essence of the ministry. While he confessed this, we all looked over at Pablo, busily ironing my jean skirt, oblivious to the English words. They said he had passed. That was the last time I would see Tim. His gift to us was Don, who became a blessed supporter for the boys. The wedding was one week away.

Our pastors from our old church down the hill were very excited to be involved in the wedding. We signed the documents with the municipality to be married and selected to have the ceremony in the huge pine-filled park just blocks from our house. In this culture the husband picks the color of the wedding dress. Pablo's favorite color was avocado so I had a wedding dress made just for me in a soft avocado color with lace that he had picked out. The boys were nervous the day of the wedding. As we were leaving the house, a few of them said they had decided not to attend. They finally gave in but the exchange did upset me. I was nervous enough all by myself—what I needed was their support on this special day.

In the large park ground's gazebo we had the pastor pronounce us husband and wife. In attendance were our boys, Greg and Sonia, the pastor, his wife, their daughter, us, and one uninvited guest the pastor's daughter brought,—the twenty-one-year-old girl, dressed in avocado. The wedding started late, as Pablo and the pastor were gone looking for film for the girl's camera. She wanted a memory photo, I'm sure. My heart sank with each passing moment trying to make merry while we all waited. Our wedding had none of the usual ceremony: no music except our singing, no flowers, no bridal shower, no gifts, no honeymoon. Our outdoor wedding provided no chairs, no electricity, no walls and, luckily, no people in the park. We were alone surrounded by beautiful tropical nature celebrating the beginning of a new future. What man had taken from me, God had replaced. I had a loving husband, wonderful boys, and a "forever" home to be built. We were in step with His will by just being together and seeking His love. We finished by all going to a Chinese restaurant to eat. The wedding cost us $350.

Intimacy was a little tricky for Pablo and me. We did have a bedroom somewhat separated from the boys, and it did have a ceiling, but we were sided by the only bathroom in the house. We tried to be quiet, although there were never any moments to grab when *all* the boys were gone, but the heat of passion wins even in the most crowded of homes, leaving some families with ten or more children. The bathroom was not even too private; it was unusually tiny. The door was a sheet curtain and the shower had a showerhead falteringly attached. It seemed someone might get electrocuted because we could gently feel a shock every once in a while. Once I was stepping out of the shower and Nolan swung open the curtain door. He just stood there a foot away from me. Covering as much as possible with my two arms I stammered in English then in Spanish for him to shut the door, or curtain, or whatever it was.

Also my complaints must include hanging clothes out to dry. Hand-washed clothes hung to dry do smell wonderful and feel very good, but everyone in the house and whole neighborhood can see your undergarments hanging in the breeze for hours. At this time *only* white, tan, and black women's under things were sold. All styles were full-covering underwear, like grandmas wear—no cuts or bikini styles. Mine were small and really colored, with all kinds of prints and patterns and styles. My sinful undergarments flew in the wind, attracting unwanted attention. Very likely more than one fellow lady Christian was praying for me.

~You can buy most anything overseas but undergarments are a good thing to bring from home in abundance.~

Washing my new husband's clothes was an honor, or something like that. He inspected the dry clothes, pointing out any areas that were questionable so I could wash them again. Hand washing jeans is not fun, especially if the guy is an outside worker. Wet jeans weigh a lot. Wringing out jeans to hang dry is heavy work too. Hand washing men's underwear, dirty socks, and handkerchiefs is a little gross, just the thought of it. Pablo insisted that all his clothes must be ironed, even the jeans. Many here are big on ironing because the space needed for dressers or hanging clothes is in short supply. Plus, hang-dried clothes dry with more wrinkles than machine-dried clothes, so ironing is necessary.

We then got word that Pastor James would be visiting again with a group. Three men and three women came to help us out with hugs, friendship, and support. Pastor James told us they had come to help locate the land for our "forever" home. We were honored to receive them, and the team really did get to experience life as we lived it in our home. The men were offered to sleep in the other back room with no floor. The women and I took over our gracious neighbor's little home facing the front steps of our house. Their family went to stay at Grandma's. That gave us two tiny bathrooms, one in each house. Even though we were always very short on money, we had bought new mattresses, sheets, pillows, towels, blankets, and one plastic chair for each team member. What we had had was just not adequate for our guests.

~If you ever stay overnight with friends or a family they surely have incurred extra costs for opening up their home to you. Try to gift them some extra cash or a special food item before you leave.~

Life as we live it began: We were on water rationing so the city schedule for our area was no water during the days, just nights. The electricity went off almost regularly during dinner preparation around five o'clock. And the rooster crowed right outside the window keeping our guests awake all night long. One morning our guests awoke with a smile, they noticed the rooster had been perfectly quiet all night. A team member went outside around the back and found, hanging from a rope upside down, the semi-unconscious rooster. One of the boys had tied the rooster to the tree the night before hoping he would quiet down. I guess he forgot he had been tied up and tried to fly off. The rooster did recuperate well.

Spaces were small. Bathing was accomplished mostly by hauling buckets of water into the bathroom and splashing the cool water on oneself. The house was Spartan to say the least. Looking back, I feel this may have been a great experience for them. The romanticism of poverty is a fallacy when with the reality of a difficult daily life appears.

The team's purpose was to help us look for land. Since we had no transportation, this was a great gift. They had brought two vehicles. We prepared to take off into the never ending countryside and explore. The ladies offered to help make the tuna sandwiches needed for the trip. It would be an American lunch. I jumped to assist and gave them the loaves of bread, mayonnaise, and two cans of tuna. They quickly made nine sandwiches. I was shocked. We needed thirty-four. They had piled on the tuna as if we were in the States. Here we just paint the bread with the flavor of tuna. With no more tuna, we quickly opened up all the sandwiches and attempted to steal enough to paint a few more sandwiches. We ended up with only twenty-four.

~Misunderstandings arising from poverty issues are difficult to avoid. Be sure to laugh at yourself, enjoy the moment and eat one painted sandwich less.~

The drive out to the land was a long ride on a dirt road. The countryside was dotted with small farmhouses, animals and perfect green pastures. The land for sale was on a hillside and had no real flat area. It did have a view for miles and miles of the mountain peaks clear into the next nation, they tell me. It was an amazing view. The mountaintops rolled as far as the eye could see, surrounded by clouds lying just low enough for the peaks to protrude. It was breathtaking. But the claim that the land had a natural spring, although true, was exaggerated. The water would supply a household of maybe four people. Plus, there was a bus that passed only once a day two miles up the road, and schools were far away. We weren't ready to be self-sufficient so far away from modernization, and we needed a good water supply. As gorgeous as the view was, we knew we had to pass on this land and returned home.

Drinking water is a more urgent need for us than even washing water. No one drinks water from the tap except a few hard core country people—it must be purified. We had chosen to buy our water already purified. It is sold in ten-gallon plastic jugs that we get from the water truck as it passes once a week. While the team was visiting, we ran out of water, so our water errand boy for the week had to purify the jug with drops of iodine. He forgot. It would be rude to name him here publically—it was Orlando. With the water not purified the team got sick. We, of course, were fine. They were the only team ever to visit us that became sick. Sorry, Pastor James.

~Drink and brush your teeth only with purified water. Take our parasite and worm pills every six months or every plane trip home.~

There were some problems with my older boys visiting inside the little house facing our steps. There were two girls (one teen) and a brother who lived there with a mom and grandma. The mom worked and was not always home. My boys became good friends with the brother. My problem was when it looked like the mom was not home my boys always seemed to be missing.

Time after time I reminded them they must ask permission to go inside the house, and it was not permissible to visit when the mom was not home because of the girls. They kept disappearing. Once I was looking for a couple of our boys and noticed the door of the neighbor's house was open. The two sisters were sitting on a bed talking with someone. I went over and called my boys out. Then it happened again a little later. Returning to call for my boys I entered the doorway to see who was hiding in the bedrooms. My boys were there, *with* the mother. She was ticked.

"Why won't you let your boys visit my house?"

"I will, just not when you're gone."

"What difference does that make?"

"My boys cannot be alone with your girls in your house; it's not OK."

"Why is it not OK?"

"Because there is no adult with them."

"So you think my girls are not proper?"

"I'm not worried about your girls; I'm worried about my boys."

"My girls are Christians and have been raised in a Christian home."

"Well, my boys come from various homes, and I'm not even sure what they might do."

"You don't trust my girls. The church will hear of this."

"I can't allow my boys in your home when there is no adult."

"You are way out of line."

~Cultural impasses with your neighbors may never be resolved, as this one wasn't.~

The boys waited for a few hours until the team was done eating and we were all together, including my pastor, before confronting me. Remember, boys here get to do whatever they want. Riki led the group as they approached me.

"We're not going to follow your silly rules."

Riki crossed his arms across his chest.

"Well, to stay here you have to obey."

"We don't need to ask you to visit friends."

"I need to know where you are."

"You don't need to know this. I can go wherever I want."

"You need to obey me. Unless I ask you to do something illegal or threaten your safety, you need to do what I ask."

"That's ridiculous. We are males. We will decide where we want to go when we want."

Pablo remained silent.

"The rules of our home are for all."

"We won't follow the Bible of Kimi."

House rules could not be negotiated. Feeling highly embarrassed, as they had chosen to confront me in front of my pastor and the group from the States, I still stood my ground.

Pastor James spoke up and gave the boys a teaching; they didn't like the outcome, but they accepted his authority. The Bible says they must obey their mother and father. Pastor James asked which boys were ready to do that. All raised their hands. Pablo looked on, trying to stay out of the discussion. Pastor James had helped out greatly in a tense moment. All forms of help are appreciated in the ministry. We simply can't do it all.

~It would best not to mix ministry children with your own in your home. These boys were all together before our marriage so we remained the same after the wedding.~

Before the team left, they shared with us the amount of the miracle blessing—over $40,000 from my church would be sent dedicated to build a "forever" home for the boys. It was the largest single offering the church had ever received in one weekend and remained so for about ten years. The Holy Spirit had made the connection. The miracle was so huge my thoughts began to wonder what I might have done to encourage Jesus to entrust me with so much!

Then the memories flooded back. During the darkest part of the divorce, when everything was threatened—unjustly losing my marriage, home, work, and health—I decided Satan would not take the only thing left me—a thousand dollars in my checking account. I wrote a check to the church requesting it be dedicated to missions if possible. Satan could take nothing else from me. "He who is faithful in very little will be faithful also in much," (Luke 16:10) and maybe Father God had used this dedication as proof that I could handle more. It is in the worst moments of our lives that we prove our integrity, showing if we are or are not controlled by the world. We prove how faithful, honest, loving, and dedicated we are to Him and His promises. Yet, it is also true that the more God gives you, the more responsible you must be.

Enthusiasm filled the air. We had to pick a name. "Kimi and the boys" was OK but not complete. The boys talked for days, Cruz leading the discussions. Finally, they decided to be called The Chosen Boys. We began the paperwork with the government to become a NGO (Non-governmental Organization). The Chosen Boys was born.

~Follow all laws concerning your ministry. You are responsible to know what they are in your country.~

Pablo joined in the organization of daily chores and discipline, yet he also began making excuses for not joining us in family prayer. During prayer we would talk about daily issues, and then the boys would pray. Pablo did not want to pray aloud so I did not ask him to pray when he did join us—just the boys. Using this time for discussions allowed old thoughts and beliefs to be changed into new ones, opportunity to analyze situations piece by piece and then together we became united in prayer. Pablo soon began coming late, stalling on his way to join us, and then, finally, not coming at all. Quickly the boys began to try to follow suit. Taking the hint, family prayer time was canceled rather than allowing it to become a negative experience. This was a larger loss for us all than I realized at the moment.

Pablo and I began looking for land on our own.

~Land title problems abound. Take extreme precautions when buying, you could lose it all.~

We jumped on the bus every day and got off wherever it took us. Then we'd ask at the neighborhood *pulperia* store if there was any land for sale. This was very time consuming as the church wanted us to find the land fast. We looked and looked but nothing was right. Then we prayed if the Lord didn't find us the land in one week, we'd buy a pickup with part of the money so we could really look for land fast. That next week we wandered onto a jewel in the forest.

Just twenty minutes from town by bus and a twenty-five minute walk led us to a little *aldea* town that had some land for sale. We went looking for the real estate worker who owned a small piece of land nearby. Entering the metal gate between two tall concrete posts, Pablo exclaimed, "Wouldn't it be wonderful to live here amid this forest?" But the land was not for sale—it was land the real estate agent had saved for himself for his retirement days. This spot was twelve acres divided by three small forests and cut off at the back by a cliff that must be half a mile deep, filled with a strong, rushing creek and overlooking miles and miles of forested hillsides, packed in by an overwhelming mountain range. It looked like the "chosen" property to us. The next day the owner, for some odd reason, agreed to sell us the land. The Holy Spirit had moved his heart! His price was $20,000, by far the best and cheapest price we had been offered. Miracles never stop. We would spend the other half on the house. The boys felt happy but apprehensive. Could this really be true? Would we really be building our own home?

Riki took it as a threat since he did not consider himself a Chosen Boy. Riki continued to try to split our family because he knew he could get his father's alliance. Every day he rejected my authority and broke the rules, encouraging his brothers to side with him while his father remained silent. Pablo didn't want to argue with Riki as he had been away so long and Riki had been his support. This left me against Riki fight after fight. Without Pablo's protection I finally had to draw the line

"If you can't follow the rules you can't stay.'

"I'll stay if I want."

"No, you must go. You can go tomorrow."

"Then we're going too," said his brothers.

Pablo stood still and said nothing.

"Fine. You can all go. Your dad too since he's the one that should be taking care of you anyway. You all need to be gone in the morning."

Our home rules would be honored.

Pablo made no progress with me that night so the next day he got all the boys together. He did not say he accepted my rules, he didn't say they were *our* rules, but he did ask the boys to follow *my* rules. This problem of divided authority remained with us. Pablo did not instill the rules as coming from us both. He simply requested obedience for the sake of peace. Riki finally decided to return to his aunt's house to study in the capital and the other boys agreed to follow the rules. We had eight boys now.

Soon after, the government came to the front door with one small nine-year-old named Jorge. His father was a street person and his young mother had been shot to death while working in a tiny cafe. He said people killed her because they thought she had said something she didn't say. We took him to the market for our now-ritual for receiving new boys and bought him all that he needed to get by. He became the leader of the little guys. Gabriel and Ronaldo were his pals. Jorge was entered into second grade. Before the week was out, the teacher said he must behave better or he'd be kicked out of school. He straightened up for a few days but was back in trouble again soon. The law was laid down, if he didn't study, we would send him away, and the government would put him in a center. He improved just well enough to stay.

The neighbor called me over one day. Jorge and this neighbor's son had climbed up on his car and had jumped up and down on the hood, breaking the glass windshield. Because Jorge was older, the neighbor wanted us to pay for it. Jorge tried to blame it on the man's little son, but, quite frankly, none of us bought it. We had to pay. Jorge lied, cheated, and stole often, but being that he was only nine, we were usually able to get to the truth. He was too young to trick us completely. Yet, over time he would improve.

One trip to the capital I stopped to get a copy of each boy's birth certificate. All were found except Orlando's. He couldn't be found in the system anywhere. At home, Orlando began joking that he was really Mexican. Funny, but the truth was we really didn't know. Later, we made a trip to the capital together carrying the papers from the government concerning him. They let us enter behind the main office to look up all kinds of variations of his name. No luck. Orlando did not exist in the system. We returned home a little let down. That's when it was decided we would make a trip to Pedro del Sur to look for Orlando's old house. He was elated, except that he got carsick travelling.

~Many people here get car sick as they haven't travelled much at high speeds during their lifetime. It can be truly horrid on long, windy car or bus rides. ~

In order to avoid disaster, Orlando had not eaten before boarding the bus. I sat by the window next to him with a few plastic bags. A man asked him who I was. Orlando said I was his mom. Then he leaned his head on my shoulder, smiled at the man, and went to sleep. He did not get sick.

Once on the far side of Pedro del Sur, we took a taxi to the neighborhood he thought he remembered living in. It was huge. We walked and walked, looking for clues. He began reminiscing, trying to remember facts. He was picked up by the police waiting for a bus near his home, so we went to the bus stop. Half a block down from the stop, we found the room his family had rented. The people there thought that the previous renters had moved five blocks up and ran a car repair shop from their house. The dad's name was right. We walked and asked around, finally finding the house. The mother came out and said no, her husband was not the same man. Orlando did not recognize her as his stepmother so we knew she was right. Leaving the house, Orlando began to cry. The neighbors were all watching, and the stress had been too much for him. He had really hoped to find his father.

Nearby was the first detention center Orlando had been sent to, so we made a surprise visit. The center looked the same to Orlando but it looked a little run-down to me. Searching through their records they found his date of entry but no date for leaving. Orlando at seven years old had visited the doctor three times for a stomachache. How I wished I could have been there for him, poor little guy. My mother's heart ached. His father and stepmother had visited on his eighth birthday to announce the arrival of their new child and then left. He was so cute and adorable the center employees got the public school to accept him into first grade. Every day Orlando would get dressed in his uniform, walk out of the center to attend public school, and return by himself.

The government regulated his center to receive only gang youths so they transferred him to Sister Rose. His parents never visited him again. We still had no birth certificate for Orlando, but it was important that we had gone to visit what was left in his memories. He also didn't know where his grandmother was and now hoped to look for her. Our trip home was good. Orlando's home was with us.

~Now the law requires that the government give you the child's birth certificate at the moment they enter your ministry or home. Do not accept any child without papers.~

Cruz got word that his two little brothers had escaped from the center where they were living and had gone searching the highways to find him. They were caught the next day, so we all felt better. But by the next week they had escaped again. Honoring my request the orphanage gave permission for me to receive the two little boys. Cruz and I went to the capital and spoke to the judge with a note from the orphanage permitting the change of custody. The judge said she was in favor of this change, but we had to return in five days for the court appointment with all the documents. We should have made it to court but never did because of Cruz.

Cruz went ballistic. He had an emotional meltdown due to the pressure he felt at receiving his little brothers into the home. He was not ready to be responsible for them. Cruz lashed out. He hated me, said I was a witch, said he would tell everyone I stole money. He was out of control and I kicked him out of the house. Not knowing where to go, he stayed around outside the front door until he quieted down. Believing he would not enter the house while Pablo was there, I let him stay outside on the porch for the night.

The next day we rented a room for him close by for $5 a month and moved his stuff. Cruz was out and his little brothers were not legally able to join us, ever. This hurt me deeply. I loved Cruz and wanted to raise his brothers with him, but his outbreak had been too destructive. Soon after, Cruz quit eighth grade with only two months to finish the year. He could not set himself free from the emotional hurts of his past nor embrace the hope of a bright future. Jesus asks us to give our burdens to him and walk free but it has to be our choice. Cruz couldn't let go of the pain. As a mother, I would be there for my son through the difficult times and try to help him choose wisely, but we would not be sharing the same home. Cruz would not be moving with us to the farm.

~You must show with your actions that verbal abuse or violence cannot be accepted in the ministry at any time. Leave any unsafe situation immediately and make sure you have witnesses.~

Chapter 16
Sweat Equity

The Holy Spirit had found our property and now sent us a new support in the way of a volunteer engineer. Mr. Darrel arrived to help us design the boys' home—a gifted talent. He got off the plane sick, very sick. His son had passed onto him an almost incurable cold before leaving. Mr. Darrel forced himself to visit the farm right away. When we got him home his condition became even worse. The second day of his visit he didn't even come out of his room. We tiptoed around wondering if we should call him to eat. The third day he came out for five minutes to eat soup, then went back to bed. The fourth day we listened from outside his door to make sure he was still breathing because he never came out. The fifth day he was able to stand, so we ran him to the airport and put him on the plane. The ghost of Mr. Darrel (since we never really saw him) arrived safely home in the US. I figured that would be his last trip here as being sick overseas is the worst feeling ever.

~Many missionaries return home sick. It is a devastating way to leave your ministry. Plan ahead to cover for any absence you may have to make.~

One great sacrifice to being overseas is the risk of illness or injury. This country does have medical facilities and medical care, but it is much like the States in the fifties. Some things we have, some things we don't. Some hospitals make you bring your own purified water. You must pay the entire hospital bill before you can be checked out—all of it. Although costs are much cheaper than in the US, it is still quite costly. A stay of six days in the hospital without surgery cost me almost five hundred dollars a day. You must have a plan. While here you will eat unprocessed foods, breathe clean air, drink more water, walk more, watch less TV, use the computer less, and work more to keep your house running. This will aid overall health. If you need help for common ailments, the doctor at the pharmacy will attend to you, even giving shots. This means minor health care costs less. So, you win some and lose some.

A wonderful family I knew, looking much like the von Trapp family in *The Sound of Music*, had to leave on a moment's notice because the mother got deadly ill. They closed up their house and went. After two months of absence, their church here found a university student to stay in the house to watch over it. After a few days, the neighbors reported that it looked like she was selling items and hauling off large bags of things from the house. They called me over to look around on the inside with them as a witness. We found many of the household items gone, and the house in total disarray and full of empty boxes. The family sent back word to pack only a few things and donate the rest to the church. Truly, it can be difficult when you become very ill overseas.

A good friend of mine had a short-term missions team visiting, and one spry fifty-something man climbed a tree and fell, dying almost instantly. Everyone was in shock. They tried to call his family, but he had listed only his own phone number for emergencies. It took days for them to contact someone. It is very expensive to send a corpse back to the US. Here, funerals are done within twenty-four hours because they don't use the hard-to-find chemicals needed to keep the body "fresh." Plan and expect the unexpected.

~If you die overseas it may be difficult to get you back to the states in time for burial. Make a list of family names and phone numbers readily available for quick emergency contact.~

People who do get sick overseas commonly go home and never come back. But Mr. Darrel would prove me wrong. He ended up visiting enough times to meet a wonderful Latin lady near his age and marry her and as God would have it, they're still married. He was faithful to his mission and sent five different floor plans for us to choose from for the "chosen" home. We got to work.

Every morning at six a.m., with the floor plans in hand, Pablo rounded up the night school boys and walked to the taxi, squeezing everyone in. The ten-minute taxi drive would leave them a twenty-five minute walk to the farm. There they met up with the neighborhood construction worker and his two older sons. The little guys and I would bring in lunch on occasion: rice, beans, tortillas, cheese, and avocados. Yes, we took the food on the bus, walked twenty-five minutes, ate with the guys, walked twenty-five minutes back, and caught the bus home. After lunch the group of schoolboys showed up to work their two hours in the afternoon. A few Saturdays and finally Sundays too, everyone worked all day.

Pablo felt great. After so much time locked up, he was free to walk and work outside with his sons and Chosen sons. Pablo is a hands-on supervisor. He has to be working with the crew and not just watching them. Building was one of his gifts and building a "forever" home for boys was a vision the Lord had provided for him. Jesus, in his mercy, was allowing Pablo the greatest gift of all—to rebuild his natural place in his sons' lives by adding brick to brick.

The work was excellent for the boys too, especially the night school boys who only attended classes for two hours. Working on the house kept them busy during the days and gave them pride to be laboring like men. Learning the construction trade was a blessed benefit. The after-school boys whined and complained a lot, even though their share of the work was for only two hours and their homework from school brief. Yet, they were proud as arm muscles grew and stomachs rippled, solid as metal. Suddenly, they were all working in sleeveless shirts. It was a great unifying time for the Chosen Boys.

~There are laws for working ministry children; make sure you know what they are.~

The house was taking shape. The foundation was done. The house would be sixteen hundred square feet, large for a home here and good sized for a family of four in the US (we packed in up to seventeen boys and two adults). The front of the house was built on a small slope so we could put in five rows of steps leading to the front door. These could double as seating when groups came. The front patio was small but outlined with four graceful arches. These gave the house a bigger appearance from the road. The kitchen was separated from the dining room by another arch and counter space. Beautiful. We asked for a design that had the dining room open up into the living room so someone could preach or talk from any corner and be seen by everyone seated.

The bedrooms were made small. We wanted only two boys per bedroom to avoid any kind of possible sexual abuse or violence by two against one at night. I had learned this from the detention center. They wanted to feel protected at night and not to be publically exposed when changing clothes. There were no doors on the rooms, just sheet curtains so we could hear everything at all times and no one could be locked in. They put their clothes on shelves instead of inside dressers so we could check for drugs, stolen items, and newly bought things easily at any time. We put brothers together whenever possible. The bathroom was separate from the shower. Outside the back door we built a huge water basin for washing that collected rainwater from the roof and another smaller basin for stored purified water.

Good news soon came—another short-term missions team would be coming with Pastor James to help us finish building. An electrician, a house renovator, a plumber, and three women came to help us to put on professional finishing touches. We were also blessed with a financial advisor, along with his wife, who put us first in their hearts and donated his services to give us legal status in the US. The house got wired for electricity, the plumbing was put in and the kitchen and dining room were adorned with much-needed ceiling fans. The doors and windows were still on order, but not to worry too much in this tropical climate. Because Pablo is a quality-check-type personality, the house is notable quality throughout. So together, in less than six months, these two men and all these boys built our sixteen-hundred-foot brick home with a little help from our friends. Jesus is our Provider.

~Building overseas can be much more of a nightmare than in the US. Choose your workers carefully and supervise well.~

Holy Week is a one-week vacation when we celebrate the risen Christ and cancel classes. On this vacation the boys asked to go swimming in a natural swimming hole in our new *aldea*. We loaded up our gear and headed walking for the natural picnic area. Carrying food and swimming gear for so many boys is not easy, especially because there's no drinking water in the woods—or bathrooms for that matter. We walked at least thirty minutes into the hills before coming upon a huge, deep, rounded dip in the landscape. A small waterfall poured into a perfectly formed water hole complete with small sandy beach areas. The incline was so steep going down we had to sit and scoot part of the way—carrying all our stuff, of course. Two other neighbor boys were already there and greeted my boys graciously. Together they jumped and swam and climbed and ate and yelled and had a great time. The moment was precious. Our miracle had begun.

Many feelings overwhelmed me. As we were celebrating Holy Week my dreams and all that I was as a person had come together, a completion in Christ. Coming to this country I had little to offer but hugs and the simple service of a Christian woman. Jesus had protected and guided me all those years, preparing me to receive a beautiful blessing of family planned by His will. I had been "chosen" for more than I could have ever dreamed. With little talent the Lord has allowed me to do much. But the work had just begun—sweat would be my equity.

Unknown to me, the future would hold losses greater than I would have imagined, they were almost more than one could bear. It was in these moments that I truly felt and understood the words we so innocently sing in church "Lord, I surrender all." So much sacrifice was being required of me for so little gain. Yet, even in the face of huge losses, I remained determined to live for His glory each day of my life no matter what the cost. We are not guaranteed to see the victory, just sent to plant the seeds.

If you too are truly being called to hug overseas, join us in simple service for one week, one month, or one year and complete your life assignment. It would be a shame to miss it.

"God didn't say it would be easy. He said it would be worth it."

Chapter 17
Now You

"For we are God's handiwork, created in Christ Jesus to do good works, which God prepared in advance for us to do." Ephesians 2:10

Personal Preparation

Focus your time beforehand on preparing for that moment when the window of opportunity in your busy schedule opens allowing you your time overseas. Read autobiographies, travel logs, National Geographic, articles on group dynamics and cultural issues, watch the Discovery Channel, learn about governments and their history. Study a language, any language, if you don't know where you'll be going. Any language learning helps. Get a passport. Find out about shots and illnesses, the prices of airfare, weather and climate, current political unrest in various places of the world. You need to learn where you may not want to go. Talk to people, choose a friend from a foreign country, discuss your ideas with your friends and family, join a missions group, or attend functions. Use this time to educate yourself.

I found my hidden information gem was gained by attending a dynamic church. The preaching spoke of a multitude of personal issues: how to handle addictions and illnesses, goal setting for achievement, handling failure and success, risk taking, financial analysis, personal character traits (honesty, forgiveness, respect, honor), culture, family and work relations, time management, life-and-death realities, daily joy and appreciation, marriage and divorce, but especially one's influence in the world through work and family by living a life of value—all these through the eyes of Jesus Christ and the belief that life is eternal, beginning now. I didn't realize how much I had been made complete, ready to accept the challenges of using wisdom while serving others very different from myself. I think I used every ounce of knowledge gained throughout the years with my boys. Praise Jesus for my great church and pastors.

Wait on Him

Use this time to decide, reconsider, and decide again, allowing your decisions to begin to take form, unify, and have staying power. In order to be truly effective for God, you must seek His will for your life. Take the time to pray, and make sure you're on the same page. Follow in His footprints. This part of the trip is very exciting for Him too.

Begin Serving at Home

To become better prepared to use your talent, you might also volunteer with serving groups in your own community. Servers do not use God to complete their assignments—they complete His. They let God use them for His glory, so be open and find out how you may fit. Chose a group and be free to serve in the way they most need you at the moment. The experience, ideas, and information you learn by this hands-on work could be invaluable later. You'll learn a lot about what works and what doesn't, and gain great insights for overseas success while benefitting your own community. Maybe you'll realize you might not want to serve as you first envisioned, or maybe you'll realize how much more you would like to get involved. Service in action will utilize your hidden talents and bring you great joy.

Healthy Habits

Get rid of your bad habits, please. We have enough problems. Protect us from the curse of gaining more bad habits by allowing us to meet you as a model of health and freedom. If you truly are being called to do something overseas you will contain your undesirable habits and promote what works best for your new neighbors. Make sure the legacy you leave is positive.

Talents Needed

Common talents of common people are in great demand. I will admit some professions are easier to envision as having great value overseas: a doctor, nurse, plumber, teacher, pastor/preacher, dentist, orphanage volunteer, or construction worker.

But there are many hidden talents that you may have not recognized that are needed. How can regular folks bless others as an independent missionary?

Look for your talent here:

- A tap, ballet, or jazz dancer teaching one dance and dancing for one performance.
- A golfer taking the pastors or politicians golfing.
- A person who likes to cook cooking with the kids and making something special at the orphanage.
- A financial advisor teaching a class on the effects of interest on loans.
- A tax collector explaining why taxes must be collected.

- A garbage collector planning a recycle program.
- A plumber teaching how to put in a toilet.
- A fireman talking about treating burns and how to put out a fire safely.
- A mom teaching how to provide a loving and safe environment for your child.
- A realtor explaining how to buy and sell wisely (location, location, location).
- A grocery clerk explaining how to promote products, read labels, and read expiration dates.
- A blended family discussing the importance of family relationships.
- A pharmacy clerk explaining the importance of vitamins, differences in headache medicines, and expiration dates of drugs.
- A retail salesclerk teaching customer service and expectations of the employee.
- A dad speaking about loving but correct discipline or how to tell when actions are abusive.
- A boss teaching about anger management, employee relations, and interview techniques.
- A bank clerk showing how to count money, how to record, and about customer service.
- A couple sharing about couples' unity and strengths.

- A crossword puzzle enthusiast sharing and giving tactics and advice on how to compete.
- A divorced person promoting staying together and sharing advice on how to live alone.
- A big sister or brother explaining how to be a good one.
- A card-game master teaching games and strategies on how to play or compete.
- A teenager promoting fidelity, honesty, or the importance of graduation.
- A seamstress sewing something special with others.
- A motorcycle rider teaching care, safety and motorcycle repair.
- A cat lover encouraging people to spay their female cats instead of disposing of them because they keep getting pregnant.
- A plant lover planting plants to improve a public place or needy home.
- A news addict giving a class on why watching and reading the news is important.
- A politician encouraging people to be better represented.
- A musician teaching and performing his craft.
- A swimmer talking about the dedication needed to compete and how to handle winning.
- A novel reader sharing and promoting a passion for reading or book clubs.
- A cartoonist teaching about cartooning.

- A salesman modeling how to make a winning sale.
- A chess player teaching and showing how to play chess.
- A PowerPoint presenter teaching and showing how to make presentations.
- A librarian encouraging us to start libraries.
- A postal clerk modeling how to pack packages, how to send them, and explaining the shipping process.
- A cleaning fanatic telling which bacteria they fight against and why.
- A person with an illness stressing how to be active and live a normal life.
- An elderly person talking about aging.

Should I go on?

- An administrator explaining how to be the person hired.
- An accountant teaching about the importance of business and personal accounting.
- An embroidery expert giving classes for gift making.
- An adopted person talking about the value of every child.

Sorry, I made myself stop. We need you with the talent you already possess. Our churches will be more than happy to offer you what they can; maybe a classroom, help advertising or assist you in the production.

To Go or Not To Go

As you solidify your mission, consider the advice of your family and friends. They may have insights or hunches into your personality that could save you grief or even tragedy. If you really are not meant to be overseas, your family and friends will tell you this—or at least hint at it. Be open and listen to them. To ignore or hide your weakness may cost you more than you're planning on later.

Whatever weakness you have hidden is the habit you must control before you can lead. It may become a bigger issue overseas, and we are not equipped to help you. You cannot escape temptation by changing countries—temptation lives inside you. The battles are fought in the mind, so make yourself a winner wherever you are. Talk to a counselor or missions leader in your church. They are experienced enough to guide you, and will share their educated concerns or maybe put you in contact with someone else. God does not demand perfection, but He does demand honest service.

Get Experience Overseas

Getting overseas experience with a group before setting out on your own would be ideal. When you are ready, you could sign up for a short-term missions trip with a group in order to have a little firsthand taste of what you might be getting yourself into. This is what we remember about one short-term missionary:

He was a thin man in his fifties and dressed like an unemployed blue-collar worker. He had come to this country with a short-term missions group and spoke no Spanish.

He moved down to the far end of the table, away from the English-speaking group and pulled out a witnessing bracelet.

"This bracelet tells the story of faith." He spoke in English, giving his well-rehearsed teaching.

The group of three Spanish speakers nodded in unison as if they could understand.

He touches the black bead. "Black is for our sin." He points down.

"Red is for Jesus, *Jesucristo*, who spilled his blood for us". He makes a cross with his fingers. "Our pure heart is white." He draws a heart with his fingers over his own heart. "*Muy bueno*", he said as all the heads nodded in comprehension. "Water baptism is blue." He imitates sprinkling water over his head.

"That Jeff could win over the whole nation if he stayed," commented my pastor who was observing from afar and spoke little English.

"Look how he can communicate without speaking Spanish; they understand what he's trying to say," said his wife who speaks no English.

The three Spanish speakers listened and grinned in pleasure, they were understanding a little of the English! Jeff had not let language slow him down from sharing with them. He is remembered by this group today—some still wear the bracelets he left them. If Jeff had been able to stay, it would not have taken him long to memorize his complete talk in Spanish. And with his fearless need to share he could touch many.

Financing Your Stay

Money should not stop you from completing your mission in life, nor should you ignore its importance. Each person's financial situation, spending habits, and living levels are varied. Make sure you have enough money to get to your new country, live comfortably, be independent, get involved, and get home. Some people will actually be able to spend less monthly while living overseas than at home, but they will be living very simply, a lot like campers.

Considering getting a paying job here? Not a good plan. Most the people I know make under three hundred dollars a month. There is also great age discrimination here—it's legal. Teaching English seems to be the only sure thing if you're over forty, otherwise you will be used as a great volunteer. Self-employment can work, but again, a successful income here is a very small amount. We have known of many "stupid" gringos who have invested their money in easy, great ideas and lost it all.

We have a neighbor from the US in his late fifties who has a "young" Latina wife. Counting on his retirement checks as income he bought a little piece of property high on a hill. No electricity, no running water, no road to the house, no nearby schools or neighbors, but a million-dollar view. They had two children together. He invested in goats—it failed. He invested in selling refurbished refrigerators—it failed. He invested in growing coffee plants—it failed. She finally took the children and left him. He lives alone in his house on the hill but continues to tell his grown US kids what a perfect life he lives with his "young" wife. It is much harder to be successful here than it appears. Have a good plan for finances before you come.

Staying longer brings on a different set of issues. Airfare is expensive. Here are some questions to consider:

If you decide to stay long term, how often will you be able to visit home? Honestly?

If you are a couple, what will you do if one wants to drop everything and go back?

Or if your spouse dies, what will you do?

Does your health insurance cover you here?

If you have children you want to raise here, what will you do when they choose to return to the States? All of them? Will you retire here with all your children in the US?

Do you have a sufficient retirement already in place? Can you live without a retirement? How? We don't have services here to support retirees.

Financial difficulties can absolutely ruin your life. Be wise and make sure you choose to protect yourself and your family. Never choose to risk all on your ministry. If it is truly from God, He will provide. Be patient and always listening to the Holy Spirit, let Him guide you. Our first mission field is our family, not our ministries.

On the other hand, if you wait until you're very well-funded to go, the moment may never arrive. Don't let lack of large sums of money hinder you in achieving your life's purpose, especially since you are more financially blessed than the vast majority of people who are alive at this moment. Be wise. Use your everyday money more purposefully. Save so you can receive that buying "high" by blessing real people with a small gift of life, like maybe buying them a hen.

Get out of debt. This is not imperative, but it is wise. The less debt you have to worry about, the freer you will be to go and be effective.

Any extreme is probably not healthy, so just adjust your belt accordingly and continue to focus on the goal of meeting your neighbors overseas.

Count on spending double what you estimate when planning and be ready to encounter unseen expenses. That said if you roll with the punches you should be just fine.

Airport Arrival

It is wise for you to have a country contact ready to meet you at the airport. Find out which groups, organizations, or churches work there and get in contact. Ask them if they know someone who could be an in-country contact for you, and be prepared to know what a fair payment would be for their time and state the exact amount before you go, then offer a small tip on top of that. Repeat the conditions of your needs and the payment amount the moment you meet, preferably have it in writing so no misconceptions can appear months or even years later. Your contact could become invaluable or could be very busy and just able to help at the moment.

On one trip to Guatemala, my country contact didn't show up at the airport. After six hours of waiting, it was nearing nine P.M. and the airport was closing for the night. I had no money exchanged and no hotel reserved. A church group was picking up a small girl who had had surgery in the US and I asked if I could hitch a ride with them and sleep on someone's couch. Because I was female they agreed. Just then my ride came running in. Be as prepared as possible, but be ready for anything.

Remember, too, that your new friends must have proof that you are a safe person. When you request a contact, provide e-mails, phone numbers of easily verifiable references, and your workplaces. Include a note from your pastor and the address and phone number of your church. Give as much information as they request.

Some travelers don't have a country contact. My parents traveled while in their early sixties by researching their countries, taking taxis or buses to get around, and staying in hotels until finding a furnished room to rent downtown—all without speaking the language. They met their contacts by accident, some of whom they still write to today. But be careful, very careful. It would be easy to find yourself a victim of crime or even lose your life by choosing the wrong person to trust. Use more common sense while travelling than you would normally.

Investigate your new country beforehand to find out what's available and what is not—each nation is different. Take anything you cannot do without and plenty of it, for the whole trip. Find out if you need medical permission for your drugs or medicine and follow the requirements. Most every other necessity can be bought overseas in one of the major cities. It may not be the same color, size, quality, or brand name, and it may be at a higher price, but you should be able to find what you need.

Skype is a wonderful way to stay in touch with those in the US because it is available at any Internet café and cheap. Be sure to get connected before you leave so you can begin communication once you arrive. It does freeze up in midsentence and sometimes the Internet is down when we do have a chance to call but we count on Skype for communication.

Learn about your overseas country

You are responsible for learning about the nationals and their country but some things are harder to find out before landing. For instance, here we don't smoke cigarettes much as a nation, so be very careful to never smoke inside a building and be sure to ask where you can smoke outside. I don't remember anyone smoking inside or asking to be excused to smoke. It's not a common habit. Sorry, that's the way it is.

Alcohol abuse is common and there is some hidden drug abuse. A shot of moonshine sells for one cent. Please don't come to enjoy yourself on vacation by getting really drunk and thinking no one will see or remember you. We will. Get over your illegal drug use before you come, as they are illegal here too and no one will be able to help you much if you get into trouble. The jails and prisons are horrible. A common bad habit could ruin all your effort at changing our world for the good. You are more of a role model here than you would ever choose to be. You will be emulated, very likely unknown to you, and must be responsible as such. We do not want to encourage our youths to heal from addictions or bad habits you have innocently made more popular without even trying; please leave them at home.

Get ready to miss some of your favorite foods. We do have diet pop, but be sure to have an extra six-pack handy on you or be OK when you are out and can't find any at the moment. Drinks may be served warm if there is no electricity. Please don't complain about our common foods: bananas, rice, beans, and tortillas. We would love to eat the way you do at home, but we can't afford it. We eat more rice, beans, and tortillas than we want to. It is very likely that the food we share with you in our homes won't be replaced easily with our budget—we'll just eat less later. Please accept our offering of food, if possible. We don't want our guests to worry about our poverty. We want to be able to give too. Something to eat or drink is our most humble offering to our out-of-country guests.

As much as we all try to avoid it, intercultural mistakes and unintended wounding happens when peoples of different cultures meet. The advice here is to listen, then ask forgiveness, and forgive—even if it doesn't make much sense to you. Also, conversation misinterpretations do happen, a lot more than we think. "Is Mari in?" The response, "You'll have to wait a while" can mean that person usually doesn't show up to work, she's sick at home and her replacement hasn't been found, she left yesterday for the capital and may be on her way back, she's in the next room typing, or "I'm Mari, but I'm busy."

Divulging private information can be embarrassing too at times. Maybe mentioning your flowered underwear showed through your white pants would seem a great ending to funny story, but only whores here wear colored underwear; that's too much information for us. Or your new country friend mentions to you that she sleeps in a bed with her little brother and boy is he going to be a sexually active guy when he grows up. Each culture has their "tell and don't tell" list. Amazingly, each country's unwritten rules for divulging private information can be quite different.

All these subtleties can't be learned quickly by anyone from an outside culture but still must be taken into account at all times. You do get to be yourself and don't have to change everything for your new country, but please take the new culture into check. Surely they are the ones who truly get to be themselves as you are a guest in their country.

It is great fun to share laughs and tease in a loving way, but it is also very easy to offend. Most jokes just don't translate and it's not always because of the wording, it could be a translation difficulty. "He got fired" was once translated as "He got burnt." Religious jokes would be best left at home, "The rabbi, the priest, and the Mexican…" Also, other cultures' jokes sometimes just aren't funny to us. "She cut off the rat's ears" might make the whole room break out in laughter except you; try to smile just to join in for the moment. Be more careful than you feel you would like to be when winning friends over with humor, most of the time you won't be told how your new friends really took the joke. Be careful of nick names too. A friendly US missionary speaking by microphone greeted the small crowd with "My little Latin friends," which could have been retorted with "My big fat American buddies," but it wasn't. It is best to err on the side of caution concerning humor. Remember, you are in our land, so we will joke and name-call as is accepted for us here. We are the ones at home.

Dress appropriately. Your attire may speak more loudly than you. Again, you don't have to change everything; just be cautious. Jeans and T-shirts are not appropriate all the time even though our weather is fantastic. Female guests should expose the skin where native women do—shoulder and chest exposure is acceptable while showing your stomach, small of your back or wearing shorts that expose the legs is not as acceptable. Realize if you break our rules you will resemble a hooker more than you would like. For men, hairy chests are quite the sight here, so take care when and where you expose yourself. We feel that underwear and bikinis cover the same areas, so swimming in bikinis are like wearing your underwear wet in public. As a nation we mostly wear T-shirts and shorts when swimming. Some pools do have swimsuit rules, but we usually swim in creeks, rivers, lakes, or the ocean.

Please wash and soften your feet often. Wearing sandals takes a toll on the skin, and your feet will look dirtier than you suspect. Don't wear a cap at all times. They are good protection when in the sun but not worn indoors. We do tend to dress more formally: no khaki shorts, no sweatpants or shorts except for PE class at school, no sandals or shorts on men, no tennis shoes on women or long skirts that touch the ground, no thong cracks please, and no socks with your sandals. You can wear these things, and rarely but occasionally we do too, but take care to find out when it's the best time not to wear them. Young people imitate the trends more than those who are thirty and older, and city folks dress more modern than county folks.

Tattoos are gang or jail related here, but we understand they are popular in the US. It is best not to show your tattoo if possible. Because they are negative for us you are sending conflicting messages and what we see counts more than the good works you are doing. I have seen fake tattoos emerge after our teams leave. Not the emulation I was hoping for. That's the reality of it.

Speak with wisdom

It is important to promote the US overseas by good conduct, humbleness, and honest appraisal. People tire of hearing how good it is in the US. They know that. That's why everyone is swimming across the Rio Grande. What they have seen is that the US is not perfect, the US plays to win (even with a push or unfair advantage), and that those in smaller countries usually become the losers in this exchange. You too will learn and notice new views the more time you spend outside the US. Do not say that the US is perfect, yet, at the same time, do not criticize the US. You are too new to understand how your comments might be taken. Your words can be easily twisted, inaccurately repeated, or just plain misunderstood. Your best bet is to say you love your country, the US is not perfect, and you believe your new country is progressing wonderfully and has many things to offer.

Do stand up for Americans serving or working in your new country: military personnel, those in ministry or lay people, government officials, teachers or students, tourists or retired people. Don't share your criticism of these groups; it may encourage random violence. Just look for the positive and admit that everything they do is not perfect but they try.

If you are overseas when the world is criticizing US actions, be cautious—you may be singled out for some negativity. If this does happen, it should be OK to respond with a mild remark such as if you were president you would have done things differently, or that the move was not what you voted for. But it is best not to go into details, just diffuse the situation by being humble and changing the subject to something positive.

They know their country has a million problems so please don't bring them up in conversation. If someone else does, speak lightly about them and be sure not to offer grandiose solutions as if you were a president or something. It's easy to criticize any nation. Please build their nation and culture up in public with honest appraisal. They will recognize the value of your words.

Be patient and polite when requesting better service or repairs, even if the person helping isn't. Many surprises happen as others try to fix your problem, and you may not realize all that's going on behind the scenes. Ask questions in a nice, calm manner assuming the best. Sometimes the person you've asked to help isn't helping or doesn't want to—maybe not because of dislike or meanness but just because they feel inferior or unsure they can really help. Politely find someone else who will help and don't make a big deal out of it.

In our country sometimes there is no water in the hospital, no gas in the gas stations, no phone service at the phone company, no Internet at the cafe, no planes landing at the airport, no bus when there should be, no electricity until tomorrow, no stores open anywhere, no banks open today, no mechanic on duty, no luggage arriving, no notice the streets will be blocked off, and more. Please handle all these surprises as best as you can; yelling in anger and turning a million shades of red looks infantile. Our infrastructure needs help. We live with it, so you can too.

Assume every time you speak in English that someone nearby can hear and understand you. I have had some incredibly embarrassing things said aloud to me that shouldn't have been said by tourists. You can do irreparable harm mouthing off while assuming no one knows what you're saying. This is where a little English and cognates can get you into trouble fast. "She looks like she's wearing pajamas." Not cool. *She* is an easy word to remember, even if you remember nothing from your English class, and *pajamas* is a cognate for *pijamas*. Speak as if you were home. Be polite at all times. You would be shocked to find out how many people had to take a little English in school.

You will notice the salespeople get excited seeing *gringos* arrive to buy. This may be uncomfortable for you because some of them do a hard sell. A good response with the hard sellers is to lower your eyes and don't say anything. You might even have to walk on by, ignoring their pleas. Any communication will be seen as an opening to sell harder, so don't give them any.

When you do decide to buy and the vendor seems very happy and overly gracious, do not assume it's because you bought so much and he's now rich for the month—and certainly please don't say that out loud.

Our prices seem to be about 30 percent lower than in the US. Buying a hundred dollars-worth does not set him up for the month. The items he bought to sell, his store space, and his time all cost money. You are a preferred customer and a tourist. If he gives you a small extra token with your purchases, he may just be responding as a goodwill ambassador for his nation or he wants to be generous. Accept the gift graciously and tell him a thousand thanks.

Offering Help

It's easy to offer help or think you're helping, but it's difficult to give or participate wisely. We need and will enjoy what you have to offer; it just needs to be offered in an appropriate manner. If you hand out money to beggars on the street, you will soon see more beggars, many who will become professional beggars if the work is good. If you buy gum from the teenage boy, you employ him. If you buy gum from a four-year-old, her parents will work her day and night. If you give food to a child beggar you could be accused if he gets sick. Buy him food from a nearby vendor or go into the store with him, or buy packaged food and watch him eat it. If you pay the boys who wash your car window unsolicited at stoplights, they may buy only alcohol or drugs with the earnings. Sometimes beggars or street people earn more than a worker. This makes beggars look and feel quite superior. They will never accept work if they believe there's a chance of earning better money on the street without working at all. All our actions have consequences, so become a wise learner. We want to be a part of the solution, not a perpetrator of the problem.

For emergencies most countries have services available to respond—donate to these groups. Do not try to help a sick person yourself. Even if you are qualified to do so it would be best to let others attend to them. Guide the person to a group or official who can help.

Got a great new idea? Take time to learn and know the country before imposing your vision on us. We all get excited meeting new faces, but many businesses and ministries fail because of avoidable problems. They have lost millions of dollars and many years of hard work because their idea was not right for the time and the people. Listen, learn, and get involved at first by only risking a little.

Until God puts you in charge of much, you are only responsible for a little. Trying to get too big can cause many serious problems for a lot of people. If you feel your ministry is taking off, join up with nationals who are already promoting your vision. If you are involved with medicine or medical services in any way, join an already respected and legal group. Any complaint of death or illness because of your help could land you in jail, maybe forever.

It is difficult to help well. It is easy to help and cause more problems than you solve. The story I heard that clarifies this is the one about a tourist who gave his beautiful watch to a street man out of compassion. That night neighborhood thieves tried to take the watch from the street man but he put up a big fight. They killed him and removed the watch. Pray a lot so your giving protects the people rather than puts them at risk.

Laws

Find out what our laws are and follow them. Just because we are a developing nation does not mean we have no national structure, we are forced to follow the laws and you will be too. That said, we have no police that monitor the speed limit. You will notice this as you drive. Our roadways are human meat grinders. Drive with extreme caution and awareness at all times. The speed limit is posted and somewhat expected to be obeyed.

The police will stop you to check legal car documents along with driver's and rider's documents. In this country you must carry a copy of your passport with you at all times, and the driver must have a valid driver's license or a national or international driver's license after a short time in the country. You will get stopped, so make sure you all have your documents.

~In many countries the police enforce immigration laws along with the federal immigration officers, except in the US where it is being decried as discriminatory and abusive.~

If you park illegally, the police will lock your car wheels. If you are accused of a traffic violation they will take you driver's license and tell you where you can pay the fine and pick it up usually within 3 days. Offering to "buy a coke" for the officer in order to keep your license is expected many times. I always let a native do that part of the bargaining and have never had to leave my license or pay a fine.

A taxi driver might first quickly agree to one amount and then when it's time to pay claim it was really a larger amount. This happens to nationals too. Please do not blow up or things could get a lot worse. Do not threaten anyone with your words or actions or you could be jailed immediately. Do not say "No wonder they kill so many taxi drivers" or any such thing. You must remain calm, negotiate and see how much you can get it lowered. I quit using taxis and now take the bus.

If you are hauled off to jail, have someone bring you a little money in small currency (maybe $5 in *local* currency) for items sold inside the jail, some old clothes, an old blanket, food, and water the first night, or you will have nothing. Don't have them bring you more money or nice things or someone may decide to keep you just for the purpose of demanding payments for as long as they can do it. Any item you take in with you will probably not be returned, leave your watch, belt, rings, or favorite hat with your friends. If you are alone, contact someone before you get to the jail cell. If possible, have them get in contact with some national who can get you an "honest" lawyer. The US Embassy can help a little, but they cannot do miracles. Our system is called the Neapolitan System—we jail first and ask questions later. You will never see a judge face to face, all is written.

~Many innocent people are jailed here every year; try to make sure you are not one of them.~

Most of our foreign homicides are due to guests who get involved in illegal activities. Stay far away from anything that looks illegal. You could easily end up the fall guy or victim.

If you get your name publically smeared it may be best for you to gracefully leave the country for the benefit of the ministry. A fight in court would not be recommended. It could take years and would probably not help at all. If part of your ministry includes a need to fight in the court system to defend your vision, I suggest you do not come.

Take extra care to be in the right place at the right time, rape does occur, violence kills. Mafia types don't take guff. Gang youths want your money and occasionally kill someone just to show others that it's best to hand over what you have immediately.

~You are a prized target for the bad guys, all foreigners are. Blend in as much as possible.~

Choose to miss out on a lot of fun by making safe choices. Keep up extra safe habits no matter how long you have lived here.

Culturally Adapting:

Cultures are a variable thing. Try not to be offended if people greet you with "Hi, fatty" or "Hi, Grandpa" or "Hi, black guy" or "Hi, Chinese girl," and then spend time discussing their disapproval of your appearance. "You look fatter. Too many bananas." These greetings and critiques are not daily but common. They are spoken as honest assessments and not followed by any rejection. I don't like them but I do overlook them—don't let them defeat you. I knew a twenty-three year-old nicknamed Piggy by his family. They told me this name was given to him because of his eyes—which were Asian and exactly the same as all of them! I asked what his real name was and decided to call him by name.

Living alone or mostly alone is a hurdle for many in a new country. People here normally run around within their family group. Foreigners tend to come and go a lot. Most every foreigner you meet overseas you will not know for more than a year. I have only three US friends that count me as family. I've been in this country for over fourteen years; all my other US friends have moved away. Missionary life is like that.

Or the opposite can be true. Circumstances may put you in uncommon communion with others. Many homes are overloaded with people. Family and friends come in and out of our homes as needed. We all just go with the flow. Cousin Harold comes for a visit and stays three years or an oldest son disappears leaving illegally for the US.

You may invite adults you don't really know into your home. They will be in your house using your things, maybe breaking something, or you'll find items may have disappeared (In Spanish we say "It lost itself."). Or the tables may be turned—you may live in their home. So be sure to be a perfect guest if you are in someone else's home and limit the number of people invited to sleep in your home. If you must turn someone down who has requested help from you do so with lots of heart, soft words, a concerned expression and maybe a sandwich or a cool drink. That way they believe you and are not offended by your refusal, don't look at them like "Didn't I just say no?" Living together solidifies cultural understanding and increases moments of cultural misunderstandings. It can be a great adventure.

~Only invite people into your home who are referred to you by a governmental agency, church or another a legal group. It is too dangerous to invite strangers into your home on your own no matter how urgent their emergency is. Pay $3 for them to stay with the neighbors.~

Giving Advice

Try not to. Things are much more intricate than they seem. You know a lot but you don't know it all. The problem in a new country is you don't know when you know it all or when you don't.

"Well, let's cook outside in the adobe stove since there's no electricity now."

Pablo nodded and went for the wood. I carried all three of the ten-gallon pots filled with half-cooked food one by one out toward the back of the house.

Pablo stuffed in five pieces of hard-to-burn wood in the small stove. I grabbed some newspaper, twisted it a little, buried it under the log, and began to light it.

"Why are you burning the paper?"

"Because this wood is too hard to catch fire easily."

"Put this in." He pushed a small piece of wood at me.

"I'm from the north. We know how to build fires. We had to do it every winter to keep our woodstoves going."

He watched. I tried and tried to get the paper burning long enough to catch at least one part of one log on fire.

I shoved in more paper. He watched.

I ran out of paper.

He lit a match and held it to the small piece of wood and it immediately lit on fire—it was covered with sap. Presto.

If asked to give advice, gently add your thoughts, finishing with a way out for your receiver. Be aware of the laws and the general support for them. A couple told me of a maid in Africa who stole from her employers. Fellow missionaries advised them to send her to the police, who cut off her hand and sent her home.

Giving moral advice may seem necessary and needed but best to take great care in what you offer to do or encourage others to do. It may be morally correct for a woman to challenge her husband about his promiscuity but he has the right to leave her if she does. That same moment she could be left to feed herself and all her children, maybe for a lifetime. Helping a woman whose husband is unfaithful or abusive may be right but the consequences may be more vicious than you could imagine. There are almost no protections set up here that can help the wife. So do what Christ has called you to do, but don't assume you are the authority in all fields. It is a delicate balance and great wisdom is needed. Keep yourself close to God in prayer.

~Try to refer people to others unless this is your ministry and you are legally connected to those in this field. Let the system do what it can and the country's people do the rest.~

Romantic Visions

Romantic hidden agendas, such as looking for a mate (younger and better-looking than yourself), seeking a sheltered vacation or unsupervised partying, running from problems, or pretending you're a great hero, or someone famous don't belong here. Most likely these needs you have will not be met and you'll return home to the same set of circumstances you left behind. Focus on the personal impact you wish to have. What you concentrate on will be what you are most successful at.

It is highly unlikely you would meet your spouse but it has happened. Most likely any relationship that is worthy will develop after you have completed the purpose of your trip. It should not develop during your trip if it puts your purpose on the sideline. Clarify your purpose and fulfill it to the best of your abilities, you may have only one chance to bless us here.

Simply a Server

It is said that servers are always ready to step into action, pay attention to the needs of others as well as those of their beloveds, do the best with what they have instead of waiting for funding to begin, and put their all into their life, profession, and ministry. They are faithful, tend to be quiet about their needs, and use authority like a supervisor rather than an owner.

Your ministry should reflect your faith and love, not your goals. Jesus is not concerned about whether others will think you are important or not—your work is to prepare for eternal life with Him. He will give you everything you need to live and serve Him. It is up to you to move forward in faith.

God is more interested in who you are than what you have or show the world. God has not promised to protect us from all life's problems but to help us through them. He knows we develop a stronger character through confronting the difficulties and tests life gives us. Get ready to be tested and win.

Even though it seems you are offering great works to others, it is you who is truly benefitting from the service you give. Your prayers should ask Him for wisdom and strength not just a list of the finances you believe are needed. That's God's plan.

I hope this book will help you to avoid many difficulties or maybe even tragedy overseas but your time may still be summed up as "horrible", or perhaps as "OK, but I'll never do it again", or maybe "magnificent" despite all the obstacles. If you are doing what God has called you to do, your feelings at the moment about your service won't carry great value with Him. He's teaching you for the long run. Since His purpose includes that we be all that we can be, we continue to grow once home. Months later you will realize more of what this purpose may have for your life. Little by little, you will see how this time has changed you.

In church we beg, "God, give us a revival!" "Make me more like you!" "I want to feel your presence every day!" So He responds, guiding us to complete our mission by giving us a chance to experience all that He has created us for. Our leaders are imploring us to be Dorcas servers, to be a part of the love revolution, know our divine connections, fulfill our purpose, be His hands extended, suffer with our brethren, pray in unity and with wisdom, share not just with words, unbury our talent, sow seeds, be the ears that hear, and so much more. Your service is being with Christ in all that you do.

You will take home a vision of life that may challenge your daily life choices. Your new experiences will reform some of your thoughts concerning needs and wants, momentary pleasures versus eternal choices, and your view of time. His ultimate goal, of course, is that you realize you should never quit sharing your purpose and begin to share in your own community until He calls you overseas to share again.

The world is waiting for you. Get into action offering the talents you have. It would be fine to offer these once a month or once a year. You should not invest much more than your time. Continue to use any of the talents you've shared overseas to bless your US neighbors. The US is entering into a new era, very likely of great financial restrain. This is the time of the church, of simple saints offering what they have, thereby becoming a powerfully positive force to the people closest to them. This is the time to reach the last soul globally. God is not limiting you.

This we know is love: Jesus Christ gave His life for us, so also should we give our lives for our brothers. (1 John 3:16).

Whoever wants to be grand should convert himself into a servant (Mark 10:43).

You were made to share your simple talent with others in order to complete your purpose—the one that God has designed you for.

90% of the profits will be donated to ministries and agencies that help children who are homeless or at risk and need help with education, health services, training or employment, housing, legal or family support.

This is your gifting—thank you.

If you wish to donate directly, you may write your tax-deductible check out to:

Lighthouse Missions
%Hug Abroad
PO Box 621
Mandan, North Dakota, 58554

Your gift of:

$25 can buy a pair of school shoes or buy a large three-pound can of powdered milk.

$50 can pay for a pair of jeans and one shirt, or school snacks for four children for one month.

$75 can buy food for a family of four for one week or pay for all of Christmas.

$100 can pay for a tooth to be capped, junior high school studies for three months or for an emergency trip to the hospital for one child.

Thank you for your
hug abroad and
simple service overseas.

The names, places, and events in this book have been compiled and changed to protect the guilty and innocent alike.

Order book at:
www.hugabroad.com

See photos, history, updates, blog and add your comments.

www.ingramcontent.com/pod-product-compliance
Lightning Source LLC
LaVergne TN
LVHW051223080426
835513LV00016B/1383

* 9 7 8 0 6 1 5 9 3 7 9 7 7 *